Papers in ethics and social

D0153919

This is part of a three-volume collection of most of David Lewis's papers in philosophy, except for those which previously appeared in his *Philosophical Papers* (Oxford University Press, 1983 and 1986). They are now offered in a readily accessible form.

This third volume is devoted to Lewis's work in ethics and social philosophy. Topics covered include the logic of obligation and permission; decision theory and its relation to the idea that beliefs might play the motivating role of desires; a subjectivist analysis of value; dilemmas in virtue ethics; the problem of evil; problems about self-prediction; social coordination, linguistic and otherwise; alleged duties to rescue distant strangers; toleration as a tacit treaty; nuclear warfare; and punishment.

The purpose of this collection, and the two preceding volumes, is to disseminate more widely the work of an eminent and influential contemporary philosopher. The volume will serve as a useful work of reference for teachers and students of philosophy.

David Lewis is Professor of Philosophy at Princeton University.

CAMBRIDGE STUDIES IN PHILOSOPHY

General editor   ERNEST SOSA (Brown University)

Advisory editors:

JONATHAN DANCY (University of Reading)
JOHN HALDANE (University of St. Andrews)
GILBERT HARMAN (Princeton University)
FRANK JACKSON (Australian National University)
WILLIAM G. LYCAN (University of North Carolina at Chapel Hill)
SYDNEY SHOEMAKER (Cornell University)
JUDITH J. THOMSON (Massachusetts Institute of Technology)

RECENT TITLES

LYNNE RUDDER BAKER *Explaining attitudes*
ROBERT A. WILSON *Cartesian psychology and physical minds*
BARRY MAUND *Colours*
MICHAEL DEVITT *Coming to our senses*
MICHAEL ZIMMERMAN *The concept of moral obligation*
MICHAEL STOCKER with ELIZABETH HEGEMAN *Valuing emotions*
SYDNEY SHOEMAKER *The first-person persepctive and other essays*
NORTON NELKIN *Consciousness and the origins of thought*
MARK LANCE and JOHN O'LEARY HAWTHORNE *The grammar of meaning*
D. M. ARMSTRONG *A world of states of affairs*
PIERRE JACOB *What minds can do*
ANDRE GALLOIS *The world without the mind within*
FRED FELDMAN *Utilitarianism, hedonism, and desert*
LAURENCE BONJOUR *In defense of pure reason*
DAVID LEWIS *Papers in philosophical logic*
WAYNE DAVIS *Implicature*
DAVID COCKBURN *Other times*
DAVID LEWIS *Papers in metaphysics and epistemology*
RAYMOND MARTIN *Self-concern*
ANNETTE BARNES *Seeing through self-deception*
MICHAEL BRATMAN *Faces of intention*
AMIE THOMASSON *Fiction and metaphysics*

Papers in ethics and social philosophy

DAVID LEWIS

Princeton University

CAMBRIDGE
UNIVERSITY PRESS

PUBLISHED BY THE PRESS SYNDICATE OF THE UNIVERSITY OF CAMBRIDGE
The Pitt Building, Trumpington Street, Cambridge, United Kingdom

CAMBRIDGE UNIVERSITY PRESS
The Edinburgh Building, Cambridge CB2 2RU, UK   http://www.cup.cam.ac.uk
40 West 20th Street, New York, NY 10011-4211, USA   http://www.cup.org
10 Stamford Road, Oakleigh, Melbourne 3166, Australia
Ruiz de Alarcón 13, 28014 Madrid, Spain

© David Lewis 2000

First published 2000

Typeface Bembo 10.5/13 pt   *System* DeskTopPro$_{/UX}$® [BV]

A catalog record for this book is available from the British Library.

Library of Congress Cataloging-in-Publication Data
Lewis, David K., 1941–
Papers in ethics and social philosophy / David Lewis.
p.   cm.
Includes bibliographical references and index.
ISBN 0-521-58249-0. – ISBN 0-521-58786-7 (pbk.)
1. Ethics.   2. Social sciences – Philosophy.   I. Title.
BJ1012.L485   1999
170 – dc21   99-11534
                                                     CIP

ISBN 0 521 58249 0 hardback
ISBN 0 521 58786 7 paperback

Transferred to digital printing 2004

For the philosophers, past and present,
of Melbourne

Contents

Introduction   *page* 1

1	Semantic analyses for dyadic deontic logic	5
2	A problem about permission	20
3	Reply to McMichael	34
4	Why ain'cha rich?	37
5	Desire as belief	42
6	Desire as belief II	55
7	Dispositional theories of value	68
8	The trap's dilemma	95
9	Evil for freedom's sake?	101
10	Do we believe in penal substitution?	128
11	Convention: Reply to Jamieson	136
12	Meaning without use: Reply to Hawthorne	145
13	Illusory innocence?	152
14	Mill and Milquetoast	159
15	Academic appointments: Why ignore the advantage of being right?	187
16	Devil's bargains and the real world	201
17	Buy like a MADman, use like a NUT	219
18	The punishment that leaves something to chance	227
19	Scriven on human unpredictability (with Jane S. Richardson)	244

Index   251

Introduction

This collection reprints all my previously published papers in ethics and social philosophy, except for those that were previously reprinted in another collection, *Philosophical Papers*.[1] I have taken the opportunity to correct typographical errors and editorial alterations. But I have left the philosophical content as it originally was, rather than trying to rewrite the papers as I would write them today.

The first three papers deal with the deontic logic of obligation and permission. Such a system of logic, in which operators of obligation and permission are taken to be dual modal operators analogous to operators of necessity and possibility, can be extended to what is obligatory or permissible given some condition. 'Semantic Analyses for Dyadic Deontic Logic' surveys a number of published treatments of conditional obligation and permission with a view to separating substantive differences – different degrees of generality, as it turns out – from mere differences between equivalent styles of bookkeeping.

The deontic logic of permission (whether conditional or unconditional) ignores the performative character of permission. By saying that something is or isn't permitted (unconditionally or conditionally) we can make it so. But there's a complication. If I say that *some* of the courses of action in which so-and-so happens are permissible, saying so makes it so. But *which* of those courses of action do I thereby

---

1 David Lewis, *Philosophical Papers*, volumes I and II (Oxford University Press, 1983 and 1986).

1

bring into permissibility? 'A Problem about Permission' surveys various possible answers.

In 'Reply to McMichael', I insist that deontic logic, conditional or otherwise, characterizes only the formalities of moral thinking. What substantive conclusions come out will depend on what substantive assumptions went in.

The next three papers concern belief, desire, and decision. In 'Why Ain'cha Rich?' I examine the embarrassing fact that the choices I endorse as rational in Newcomb's problem are the choices that foreseeably lead to bad outcomes. Those who think as I do explain away this embarrassing fact thus: if a powerful predictor sets out to reward predicted irrationality, then it is only to be expected that the rewards will go to the irrational. I ask whether this remark is common ground between both sides of the dispute about what is rational, and I conclude with regret that it is not.

In 'Desire as Belief' and its sequel, I explore the consequence of supplementing standard decision theory with various versions of the assumption that desires are identical to, or are necessarily correlated with, beliefs about what would be good. For some versions, we get a collapse into triviality; for other versions, a collapse into the view that there are some things – what? – that we desire by necessity.

The next paper, 'Dispositional Theories of Value', defends a subjectivist position in meta-ethics: a form of naturalism according to which values are defined as those properties that we are disposed, given a certain degree of empathetic understanding, to desire to desire. The position defended is similar to one that G. E. Moore chose as a target for his 'naturalistic fallacy' argument.

Moral dilemmas in consequentialist and deontological ethics are much discussed; but similar dilemmas can arise also in virtue ethics. In 'The Trap's Dilemma' I discuss Ned Kelly's proof that a policeman cannot be an honest man: because if a policeman has sworn an oath to obtain a conviction if possible, and if the only effective way to do so is to swear a lie, then the policeman is dishonest whether he keeps his oath or whether he breaks it.

'Evil for Freedom's Sake?' explores free-will theodicy as a reply to the problem of evil. It turns out that after we grant several points to

2

the proponent of free-will theodicy for the sake of the argument, we end up bogged down inconclusively in some complicated double counterfactuals. The deadlocked issues bear a striking resemblance to the well-known deadlock we encounter in Newcomb's problem.

'Do We Believe in Penal Substitution?' suggests that we are of two minds on the question of penal substitution. Mostly, we would think it absurd to let an offender go unpunished just because some innocent substitute has volunteered to be punished in his place. So when some Christians explain the Atonement as a case of penal substitution, that seems much at odds with our ordinary thinking. But our ordinary thinking is ambivalent. Though we would think it absurd to allow penal substitution when the punishment is a prison sentence, we think it not amiss if a generous volunteer pays someone else's fine – even if the fine is big enough to be no less onerous than a prison sentence.

In the next two papers, rejoinders respectively to Dale Jamieson and John Hawthorne, I defend and elaborate my account of conventions generally, and conventions of language in particular.[2]

The next paper, 'Illusory Innocence?' seeks to avoid Peter Unger's incredible conclusion that, so long as there is an inexhaustible supply of distant strangers whom we could rescue from urgent need at small cost to ourselves, we are obliged to give almost all we have – and all we can beg, borrow, or steal – to assist them.

'Mill and Milquetoast' argues that liberal customs of toleration may be seen as a tacit treaty to limit warfare between factions: if, for each side, the fear of defeat outweighs the hope of victory, it may be best for all concerned to settle for a stalemate. 'Academic Appointments: Why Ignore The Advantage of Being Right?' asks why we seem to think it wrong to deny academic appointments to candidates simply on the grounds that their views are false. I answer that this custom, again, may be seen as a tacit treaty to limit intellectual warfare. The banned weapon, denial of employment, would make wars more

2 David Lewis, *Convention: A Philosophical Study* (Harvard University Press, 1969); 'Languages and Language' in *Minnesota Studies in the Philosophy of Science*, Volume VII, ed. by Keith Gunderson (University of Minnesota Press, 1975).

costly for all concerned, yet would not give advantage to any one side – hence would not advance the side of truth, whichever side that may be.

'Devil's Bargains and the Real World' and 'Buy Like a MADman, Use Like a NUT' argue against 'paradoxical' nuclear deterrence: the idea that the only effective way – or the most benign way! – to conduct nuclear deterrence is to cultivate an irrational disposition to respond to attack by inflicting vast and useless harm. Although these papers were originally written with reference to the nuclear confrontation between the United States and the former Soviet Union, I fear they are not obsolete. It is all too likely that future history will contain other similar confrontations.

'The Punishment that Leaves Something to Chance' examines a puzzle about punishment. Why do we punish failed attempts at murder more leniently than successful attempts, although it would seem that they are no less wicked? My answer is that the principal punishment is probabilistic: he who subjects his victim to a risk of death is punished by a like risk – the risk that the victim will die, and the perpetrator will thereby earn the full punishment for a successful attempt. Whether probabilistic punishment is just is, however, open to question.

In the final paper, 'Scriven on Human Unpredictability', Jane S. Richardson and I reply to Michael Scriven's argument that, even in a deterministic world, those who so wish have a sure-fire strategy to avoid being predicted: they can replicate the predictions others might make about them, and then do the opposite. We object that Scriven cannot consistently combine all the assumptions he needs in order to argue both that this method of avoiding prediction will work, and that it shows something more interesting than just that prediction will fail if the would-be predictor runs out of time to finish his calculations.

David Lewis
Princeton, May 1998

4

1

Semantic analyses for dyadic deontic logic

1. INTRODUCTION

It ought not to be that you are robbed. *A fortiori*, it ought not to be that you are robbed and then helped. But you ought to be helped, given that you have been robbed. The robbing excludes the best possibilities that might otherwise have been actualized, and the helping is needed in order to actualize the best of those that remain. Among the possible worlds marred by the robbing, the best of a bad lot are some of those where the robbing is followed by helping.

In this paper, I am concerned with semantic analyses for dyadic deontic logic that embody the idea just sketched. Four such are known to me: the treatments in Bengt Hansson [4], Sections 10–15; in Dagfinn Føllesdal and Risto Hilpinen [2], Section 9; in Bas van Fraassen [9]; and in my own [8], Section 5.1.[1] My purpose here is to place these four treatments within a systematic array of alternatives,

First published in Sören Stenlund, ed., *Logical Theory and Semantic Analysis: Essays Dedicated to Stig Kanger on His Fiftieth Birthday* (Dordrecht, Reidel, 1974). Copyright © by D. Reidel Publishing Company, Dordrecht-Holland. Reprinted with kind permission from Kluwer Academic Publishers.

This research was supported by a fellowship from the American Council of Learned Societies.

1 Some other treatments of dyadic deontic logic fall outside the scope of this paper because they seem, on examination, to be based on ideas quite unlike the one I wish to consider. In particular, see the discussion in [4], [2], and [9] of several systems proposed by von Wright and by Rescher.

and thereby to facilitate comparison. There are superficial differences galore; there are also some serious differences.

My results here are mostly implicit in [8], and to some extent also in [7]. But those works are devoted primarily to the study of counterfactual conditionals. The results about dyadic deontic logic that can be extracted thence *via* an imperfect formal analogy between the two subjects are here isolated, consolidated, and restated in more customary terms.

II. LANGUAGE

The language of dyadic deontic logic is built up from the following vocabulary: (1) a fixed set of sentence letters; (2) the usual truth-functional connectives $\top$, $\bot$, $\sim$, &, $\vee$, $\supset$, and $\equiv$ (the first two being zero-adic 'connectives'); and (3) the two dyadic deontic operators $O(\text{-}/\text{-})$ and $P(\text{-}/\text{-})$, which we may read as 'It ought to be that . . . , given that . . . ' and 'It is permissible that . . . , given that . . . ', respectively. They are meant to be interdefinable as follows: either $P(A/B) =^{\text{df}} \sim O(\sim A/B)$ or else $O(A/B) =^{\text{df}} \sim P(\sim A/B)$. Any sentence in which $O(\text{-}/\text{-})$ or $P(\text{-}/\text{-})$ occurs is a *deontic sentence*; a sentence is *iterative* iff it has a subsentence of the form $O(A/B)$ or $P(A/B)$ where A or B is already a deontic sentence. (We regard a sentence as one of its own subsentences.) In metalinguistic discourse, as exemplified above, vocabulary items are used to name themselves; the letters early in the alphabet, perhaps subscripted, are used as variables over sentences; and concatenation is represented by concatenation.

III. INTERPRETATIONS

$[\![\ ]\!]$ is an *interpretation* of this language *over* a set I iff (1) $[\![\ ]\!]$ is a function that assigns to each sentence A a subset $[\![A]\!]$ of I, and (2) $[\![\ ]\!]$ obeys the following conditions of standardness:

(2.1) $[\![\top]\!] = I$,

(2.2) $[\![\bot]\!] = \varnothing$,

(2.3) $[\![\sim A]\!] = I - [\![A]\!]$,

(2.4) $[\![A\ \&\ B]\!] = [\![A]\!] \cap [\![B]\!]$,

6

(2.5)	$[\![A \lor B]\!] = [\![A]\!] \cup [\![B]\!]$,
(2.6)	$[\![A \supset B]\!] = [\![\sim A \lor B]\!]$,
(2.7)	$[\![A \equiv B]\!] = [\![(A \supset B) \,\&\, (B \supset A)]\!]$
(2.8)	$[\![P(A/B)]\!] = [\![\sim O(\sim A/B)]\!]$.

We call $[\![A]\!]$ the *truth* set of a sentence A, and we say that A is *true* or *false* at a member i of I (*under* the interpretation $[\![\ ]\!]$) according as i does or does not belong to the truth set $[\![A]\!]$.

We have foremost in mind the case that I is the set of all possible worlds (and we shall take the liberty of calling the members of I *worlds* whether they are or not). Then we can think of $[\![A]\!]$ also as the proposition expressed by the sentence A (under $[\![\ ]\!]$): an interpretation pairs sentences with propositions, a proposition is identified with the set of worlds where it is true, and a sentence is true or false according as it expresses a true or false proposition.

The sentences of the language are built up from the sentence letters by means of the truth-functional connectives and the deontic operators. Likewise an interpretation is determined stepwise from the truth sets of the sentence letters by means of the truth conditions for those connectives and operators. (2.1–7) impose the standard truth conditions for the former. (2.8) transforms truth conditions for $O(-/-)$ into truth conditions for $P(-/-)$, making the two interdefinable as we intended. The truth conditions for $O(-/-)$ have so far been left entirely unconstrained.

IV. VALUE STRUCTURES

Our intended truth conditions for $O(-/-)$ are to depend on a posited structure of evaluations of possible worlds. We seek generality, wherefore we say nothing in particular about the nature, source, or justifiability of these evaluations. Rather, our concern is with their structure. A mere division of worlds into the ideal and the less-than-ideal will not meet our needs. We must use more complicated value structures that somehow bear information about comparisons or gradations of value.

An interpretation is *based*, at a particular world, *on* a value structure iff the truth or falsity of every sentence of the form $O(A/B)$, at that world and under that interpretation, depends in the proper way on the evaluations represented by the value structure.

Let $[\![\ ]\!]$ be an interpretation over a set I, and let i be some particular world in I. In the case we have foremost in mind, I really is the set of all possible worlds; and i is our actual world, so that truth at i is actual truth, or truth *simpliciter*. We consider value structures of four kinds.

First, a *choice function f over I* is a function that assigns to each subset X of I a subset fX of X, subject to two conditions: (1) if X is a subset of Y and fX is nonempty, then fY also is nonempty; and (2) if X is a subset of Y and X overlaps fY, then $fX = X \cap fY$. $[\![\ ]\!]$ is *based, at i, on* a choice function f over I iff any sentence of the form $O(A/B)$ is true at i under $[\![\ ]\!]$ iff $f[\![B]\!]$ is a nonempty subset of $[\![A]\!]$. Motivation: fX is to be the set of the best worlds in X. Then $O(A/B)$ is true iff, non-vacuously, A holds throughout the B-worlds chosen as best.

Second, a *ranking $\langle K, R \rangle$ over I* is a pair such that (1) K is a subset of I; and (2) R is a weak ordering of K. R is a *weak ordering*, also called a *total preordering*, of a set K iff (1) R is a dyadic relation among members of K; (2) R is transitive; and (3) for any j and k in K, either jRk or kRj – that is, R is *strongly connected* on K. $[\![\ ]\!]$ is *based, at i, on* a ranking $\langle K, R \rangle$ over I iff any sentence of the form $O(A/B)$ is true at i under $[\![\ ]\!]$ iff, for some j in $[\![A \& B]\!] \cap K$, there is no k in $[\![\sim\!A \& B]\!] \cap K$ such that kRj. Motivation: K is to be the set of worlds that can be evaluated – perhaps some cannot be – and kRj is to mean that k is at least as good as j. Then $O(A/B)$ is true iff some B-world where A holds is ranked above all B-worlds where A does not hold.

Third, a *nesting $\mathcal{S}$ over I* is a set of subsets of I such that, whenever S and T both belong to $\mathcal{S}$, either S is a subset of T or T is a subset of S. $[\![\ ]\!]$ is *based, at i, on* a nesting $\mathcal{S}$ over I iff any sentence of the form $O(A/B)$ is true at i under $[\![\ ]\!]$ iff, for some S in $\mathcal{S}$, $S \cap [\![B]\!]$ is a nonempty subset of $[\![A]\!]$. Motivation: each S in $\mathcal{S}$ is to represent one permissible way to divide the worlds into the ideal ones (those in S) and the non-ideal ones. Different members of $\mathcal{S}$ represent more or less stringent ways to draw the line. Then $O(A/B)$ is true iff there is some permissible way to divide the worlds on which, non-vacuously, A holds at all ideal B-worlds.

Fourth, an *indirect ranking $\langle V, R, f \rangle$ over I* is a triple such that (1) V

is a set; (2) R is a weak ordering of V (defined as before); and (3) f is a function that assigns to each j in I a subset $f(j)$ of V. [[ ]] is *based, at i, on* an indirect ranking $\langle V, R, f \rangle$ iff any sentence of the form $O(A/B)$ is true at i under [[ ]] iff, for some v in some $f(j)$ such that j belongs to [[$A \& B$]], there is no w, in any $f(k)$ such that k belongs to [[$\sim A \& B$]], such that wRv. Motivation (first version): V is to be a set of 'values' realizable at worlds; wRv is to mean that w is at least as good as v; and $f(j)$ is to be the set of values realized at the world j. Then $O(A/B)$ is true iff some value realized at some B-world where A holds is ranked higher than any value realized at any B-world where A does not hold. Motivation (second version): we want a ranking of worlds in which a single world can recur at more than one position – much as Grover Cleveland has two positions in the list of American presidents, being the 22nd and also the 24th. Such a 'multipositional' ranking cannot be a genuine ordering in the usual mathematical sense, but we can represent it by taking a genuine ordering R of an arbitrarily chosen set V of 'positions' and providing a function f to assign a set of positions – one, many, or none – to each of the objects being ranked. Then $O(A/B)$ is true iff some B-world where A holds, in some one of its positions, is ranked above all B-worlds where A does not hold, in all of their positions.

The *value structures over I* comprise all four kinds: all choice functions, rankings, nestings, and indirect rankings over I. Note that (unless I is empty) nothing is a value structure of two different kinds over I.

An arbitrary element in our truth conditions must be noted. A value structure may ignore certain *inevaluable* worlds: for a choice function f, the worlds that belong to no fX; for a ranking $\langle K, R \rangle$, the worlds left out of K; for a nesting $\$$, the worlds that belong to no S in $\$$; and for an indirect ranking $\langle V, R, f \rangle$, the worlds j such that $f(j)$ is empty. Suppose now that B is true only at some of these inevaluable worlds, or that B is impossible and true at no worlds at all. Then $O(-/B)$ and $P(-/B)$ are *vacuous*. We have chosen always to make $O(A/B)$ false and $P(A/B)$ true in case of vacuity, but we could just as well have made $O(A/B)$ true and $P(A/B)$ false. Which is right? Given that $0 = 1$, ought nothing or everything to be the case? Is everything or nothing permissible? The mind boggles. As for formal elegance, either choice makes complications that the other avoids. As for precedent, van Fraassen has gone our way but Hansson and Føllesdal and Hilpinen have gone the other way. In any case, the choice is not irrevocable either way. Let $O'(-/-)$ and $P'(-/-)$ be just like our pair $O(-/-)$ and $P(-/-)$ except that they take the opposite truth values in case of vacuity. The pairs are interdefinable: either let $O'(A/B) =^{df} O(\top/B) \supset O(A/B)$ or else let $O(A/B) =^{df} {\sim} O'(\bot/B)$ & $O'(A/B)$.

V. TRIVIAL, NORMAL, AND UNIVERSAL VALUE STRUCTURES

There exist *trivial* value structures, of all four kinds, in which every world is inevaluable. We might wish to ignore these, and use only the remaining non-trivial, or *normal*, value structures. Or we might go further and use only the *universal* value structures with no inevaluable worlds at all. It is easily shown that a value structure is normal iff, under any interpretation based on it at any world i, some sentence of the form $O(\top/B)$ is true at i. (And if so, then in particular $O(\top/\top)$ is true at i.) Likewise, a value structure is universal iff, under any interpretation based on it at any world i, any $O(\top/B)$ is true at i except when B is false at all worlds.

VI. LIMITED AND SEPARATIVE VALUE STRUCTURES

The *limited* value structures are, informally, those with no infinitely ascending sequences of better and better and better worlds. More precisely, they are: (1) all choice functions; (2) all rankings $\langle K, R \rangle$ such that every nonempty subset X of K has at least one R-*maximal element*, that being a world j in X such that jRk for any k in X; (3) all nestings $\pmb{\mathscr{S}}$ such that, for any nonempty subset $\mathbf{S}$ of $\pmb{\mathscr{S}}$, the intersection $\cap\mathbf{S}$ of all sets in $\mathbf{S}$ is itself a member – the smallest one – of $\mathbf{S}$; and (4) all indirect rankings $\langle V, R, \mathfrak{f} \rangle$ such that, if we define the *supersphere* of any v in V as the set of all worlds j such that wRv for some w in $\mathfrak{f}(j)$, then for any nonempty set $\mathbf{S}$ of superspheres, the intersection $\cap\mathbf{S}$ of all sets in $\mathbf{S}$ is itself a member of $\mathbf{S}$. Clearly some but not all rankings, some but not all nestings, and some but not all indirect

10

rankings are limited. Value structures of any kind over finite sets, however, are always limited.

Semantically, a limited value structure is one that guarantees (except in case of vacuity) that the full story of how things ought to be, given some circumstance, is a possible story. That is not always so. For instance, let the value structure be a ranking that provides an infinite sequence $j_1, j_2 \ldots$ of better and better worlds. Let B be true at all these worlds and no others; let A_1 be true at all but j_1, A_2 at all but j_1 and j_2, and so on. Then $O(-/B)$ is not vacuous and all of $O(B/B)$, $O(A_1/B)$, $O(A_2/B)$, . . . are true; yet at no world are all of B, A_1, A_2, . . . true together, so even this much of the story of how things ought to be, given that B, is impossible. A limited ranking would preclude such a case, of course, since the set $\{j_1, \ldots \}$ has no maximal element. In general, a value structure is limited iff, under any interpretation based on it at any world i, whenever $O(-/B)$ is non-vacuous and $\mathbf{A}$ is the set of all sentences A for which $O(A/B)$ is true at i, there is a world where all the sentences in $\mathbf{A}$ are true together.

The *separative* value structures are, informally, those in which any world that surpasses various of its rivals taken separately also surpasses all of them taken together. More precisely, they are: (1) all choice functions; (2) all rankings; (3) all nestings $\mathcal{S}$ such that, for any nonempty subset $\mathbf{S}$ of $\mathcal{S}$, the intersection $\bigcap \mathbf{S}$ is the union $\bigcup \mathbf{T}$ of some subset $\mathbf{T}$ of $\mathcal{S}$; and (4) all indirect rankings such that, for any nonempty set $\mathbf{S}$ of superspheres, the intersection $\bigcap \mathbf{S}$ is the union $\bigcup \mathbf{T}$ of some set $\mathbf{T}$ of superspheres. All limited value structures are separative, but not conversely. Some but not all non-limited nestings are separative, as are some but not all non-limited indirect rankings. Semantically, a value structure is separative iff, under any interpretation based on it at any world i, if (1) A is true at just one world, (2) $O(A/B)$ is true at i for every B in a set $\mathbf{B}$, and (3) C is true at just those worlds where at least one B in $\mathbf{B}$ is true, then $O(A/C)$ is true at i.

VII. CLOSED AND LINEAR VALUE STRUCTURES

A nesting $\mathcal{S}$ is *closed* iff, for any subset $\mathbf{S}$ of $\mathcal{S}$, the union $\bigcup \mathbf{S}$ of all sets in $\mathbf{S}$ belongs to $\mathcal{S}$. Closure has no semantic effect, as we shall see, but

11

we must mention it in order to make contact with my results in [8]. Note that a closed nesting S is separative iff, for any nonempty subset **S** of S, $\cap$**S** belongs to S.

An indirect ranking $\langle V, R, \mathsf{f} \rangle$ is *linear* iff there are no two distinct members v and w of V such that both vRw and wRv. We shall see that linearity also has no semantic effect.

VIII. EQUIVALENCE

We call two value structures *equivalent* iff any interpretation that is based, at a world, on either one is also based, at that world, on the other. Equivalence is rightly so called: it is a reflexive, symmetric, transitive relation among value structures, and consequently it partitions them into equivalence classes. If two value structures are equivalent, they must be value structures over the same set; and if one is trivial, normal, universal, limited, or separative, then so is the other.

If f is any choice function over I, an equivalent ranking $\langle K, R \rangle$ over I may be derived thus: let K be the set of all i in I such that i is in $f\{i\}$, and let iRj (for i and j in K) iff i is in $f\{i, j\}$.

If $\langle K, R \rangle$ is any limited ranking over I, an equivalent choice function f over I may be derived thus: for any subset X of I, let fX be the set of all R-maximal elements of $X \cap K$ (and empty if $X \cap K$ is empty). Note that if the given ranking had not been limited, the derived f would not have been a genuine choice function.

If $\langle K, R \rangle$ is any ranking over I, an equivalent nesting S over I may be derived thus: let S contain just those subsets of K such that for no j in the subset and i outside it does iRj hold.

If S is any separative nesting over I, an equivalent ranking $\langle K, R \rangle$ over I may be derived thus: let K be the union $\cup \mathit{S}$ of all sets in S, and let iRj (for i and j in K) iff there is no set in S that contains j but not i. Note that if the given nesting had not been separative, the derived ranking would not have been equivalent to the nesting.

If S is any nesting over I, an equivalent indirect ranking $\langle V, R, \mathsf{f} \rangle$ over I may be derived thus: let V be S, let vRw (for v and w in V) iff v is included in w, and let $\mathsf{f}(i)$, for any i in I, be the set of all members of V that contain i.

If $\langle V, R, \mathsf{f} \rangle$ is any indirect ranking over I, an equivalent nesting S

12

may be derived thus: let $\mathbf{S}$ be the set of all superspheres of members of V.

If $\mathbf{S}$ is any nesting over I, an equivalent closed nesting $\mathbf{S}'$ may be derived thus: let $\mathbf{S}'$ be the set of all unions $\cup S$ of subsets S of $\mathbf{S}$.

Finally, if $\langle V, R, f \rangle$ is any indirect ranking over I, an equivalent linear indirect ranking $\langle V', R', f' \rangle$ over I, may be derived thus: let V' be a subset of V such that, for any v in V, there is exactly one w in V' such that vRw and wRv; let R' be the restriction of R to V'; and let $f'(i)$, for any i in I, be $f(i) \cap V'$.

We can sum up our equivalence results as follows. Say that one class of value structures is *reducible to* another iff every value structure in the first class is equivalent to one in the second class. Say that two classes are *equivalent* iff they are reducible to each other.

(1) The following classes are equivalent:

> all nestings,
> all indirect rankings.

(2) The following classes are equivalent; and they are reducible to the classes listed under (1), but not conversely:

> all rankings,
> all separative nestings,
> all separative indirect rankings.

(3) The following classes are equivalent; and they are reducible to the classes listed under (2) and (1), but not conversely:

> all choice functions,
> all limited rankings,
> all limited nestings,
> all limited indirect rankings.

(4) Parts (1)–(3) still hold if we put 'closed nesting' throughout in place of 'nesting', or if we put 'linear indirect ranking' throughout in place of 'indirect ranking', or both.

(5) Parts (1)–(4) still hold if we restrict ourselves to the normal value structures of each kind, or to the universal value structures of each kind.

13

So the fundamental decision to be taken is not between our four kinds of value structures *per se*. Rather, it is between three levels of generality: limited, separative, and unrestricted. Once we have decided on the appropriate level of generality, we must use some class of value structures versatile enough to cover the chosen level; but it is a matter of taste which of the equivalent classes we use.

IX. FRAMES

Suppose that an interpretation is to be based, at our actual world, on a given value structure of some kind. Suppose that the truth sets of the sentence letters also are given. To what extent is the interpretation thereby determined? First, we have the truth sets of all non-deontic sentences – that is, of all truth-functional compounds of sentence letters. Second, we have the actual truth values of all non-iterative deontic sentences – that is, of all truth-functional compounds of sentences of the forms $O(A/B)$ and $P(A/B)$, where A and B are non-deontic, together perhaps with non-deontic sentences. But there we stop, for we know nothing about the truth conditions of $O(-/-)$ and $P(-/-)$ at non-actual worlds. Hence we do not have the full truth sets of the non-iterative deontic sentences. Then we do not have even the actual truth values of iterative deontic sentences. (Apart from some easy cases, as when a deontic sentence happens to be a truth-functional tautology.)

To go on, we could stipulate that the interpretation is to be based at *all* worlds on the given value structure. But that would be too rigid. Might not some ways of evaluating worlds depend on matters of fact, so that the value structure changes from one world to another? What we need, in general, is a family of value structures – one for each world. Call this a *frame*. A frame might indeed assign the same value structure to all worlds – then we call it *absolute* – but that is only a special case, suited perhaps to some but not all applications of dyadic deontic logic.

We have four kinds of frames. A *choice function frame* $\langle f_i \rangle_{i \in I}$ over a set I assigns a choice function f_i to each i in I. A *ranking frame* $\langle K_i, R_i \rangle_{i \in I}$ over I assigns a ranking $\langle K_i, R_i \rangle$ to each i in I. A *nesting frame* $\langle \$_i \rangle_{i \in I}$ over I assigns a nesting $\$_i$ to each i in I. An *indirect ranking frame* $\langle V_i, R_i, \mathfrak{f}_i \rangle_{i \in I}$

over I assigns an indirect ranking $\langle V_i, R_i, f_i \rangle$ to each *i* in *I*. (I ignore *mixed frames*, which would assign value structures of more than one kind.) A frame is *trivial, normal, universal, limited, separative, closed,* or *linear* iff every value structure that it assigns is so. An interpretation over *I* is *based on* a frame over *I* iff, for each world *i* in *I*, the interpretation is based at *i* on the value structure assigned to *i* by the frame. Given that an interpretation is to be based on a certain frame, and given the truth sets of the sentence letters, the interpretation is determined in full.

Two frames are *equivalent* iff any interpretation based on either one is based also on the other, and that is so iff both are frames over the same set *I* and assign equivalent value structures to every *i* in *I*. One class of frames is *reducible to* another iff every frame in the first class is equivalent to one in the second. Two classes of frames are *equivalent* iff they are reducible to each other. Then we have reducibility and equivalence results for frames that are just like the parallel results for single value structures.

X. VALIDITY

A sentence is *valid under* a particular interpretation over a set *I* iff it is true at every world in *I; valid in* a frame iff it is valid under every interpretation based on that frame; and *valid in* a class of frames iff it is valid in all frames in that class. Let us consider six sets of sentences, defined semantically in terms of validity in classes of frames. The sentences in each set are just those that we would want as theorems of dyadic deontic logic if we decided to restrict ourselves to the frames in the corresponding class, so we may call each set the *logic determined by* the corresponding class of frames.

CO: the sentences valid in all frames.
CD: the sentences valid in all normal frames.
CU: the sentences valid in all universal frames.
CA: the sentences valid in all absolute frames.
CDA: the sentences valid in all absolute normal frames.
CUA: the sentences valid in all absolute universal frames.

The six logics differ: by restricting ourselves to the normal, universal, or absolute frames we validate sentences that are not valid in broader classes. But the logics do not change if, holding those restrictions fixed, we also restrict ourselves to the separative frames, the limited frames, or the frames over finite sets; or to the indirect ranking frames, linear indirect ranking frames, nesting frames, closed nesting frames, ranking frames, or choice function frames. By these latter restrictions we validate no new sentences.

For instance, take any sentence A that does not belong to the logic **CO**, not being valid in all frames. Then in particular, by our equivalence results, it is invalid under some interpretation $[\![\ ]\!]$ based on a nesting frame $\langle \$_i \rangle_{i \in I}$. Now define $\langle \$_i^* \rangle_{i \in I^*}$ and $[\![\ ]\!]^*$ as follows: (1) for each i in I, let D_i be a conjunction of all the subsentences or negated subsentences of A that are true (under $[\![\ ]\!]$) at i; (2) let I^* be a subset of I that contains exactly one world from each nonempty $[\![D_i]\!]$; (3) for any subset S of I, let $*S$ be the set of all i in I^* such that $[\![D_i]\!]$ overlaps S; (4) for each i in I^*, let $\$_i^*$ be the set of the $*S$'s for all S in $\$_i$; and (5) let $[\![\ ]\!]^*$ be an interpretation based on $\langle \$_i^* \rangle_{i \in I^*}$, which is a nesting frame, such that whenever B is a sentence letter, $[\![B]\!]^*$ is $[\![B]\!] \cap I^*$. It may then be shown (see [8], Section 6.2, for details) that whenever C is a subsentence of A, $[\![C]\!]^*$ is $[\![C]\!] \cap I^*$. Since that is so for A itself, A is invalid under $[\![\ ]\!]^*$. Further, I^* is finite: it contains at most 2^n worlds, where n is the number of subsentences of A. So we do not validate A by restricting ourselves to the class of nesting frames over finite sets, the broader class of limited nesting frames, the still broader class of separative nesting frames, or any other class equivalent to one of these. Exactly the same proof works for the other five logics; we need only note that if $\langle \$_i \rangle_{i \in I}$ is normal, universal, or absolute, then so is $\langle \$_i^* \rangle_{i \in I^*}$.

As a corollary, we find that our six logics are decidable. The question whether a sentence A belongs to one of them reduces, as we have seen, to the question whether A is valid in the appropriately restricted class of nesting frames over sets with at most 2^n worlds, n being the number of subsentences of **A**; and that is certainly a decidable question.

16

We may axiomatize our six logics as follows. For **CO** take the rules
R1–R4 and the axiom schemata A1–A8.[2] For **CD** add axiom A9;
for **CU** add A10 and A11; for **CA** add A12 and A13; for **CDA** add
A9, A12, and A13; and for **CUA** add A10, A12, and A13.

R1. All truth-functional tautologies are theorems.
R2. If A and $A \supset B$ are theorems, so is B.
R3. If $A \equiv B$ is a theorem, so is $O(A/C) \equiv O(B/C)$.
R4. If $B \equiv C$ is a theorem, so is $O(A/B) \equiv O(A/C)$.
A1. $P(A/C) \equiv \sim O(\sim A/C)$.
A2. $O(A \& B/C) \equiv .O(A/C) \& O(B/C)$.
A3. $O(A/C) \supset P(A/C)$.
A4. $O(\top/C) \supset O(C/C)$.
A5. $O(\top/C) \supset O(\top/B \vee C)$.
A6. $O(A/B) \& O(A/C). \supset O(A/B \vee C)$.
A7. $P(\bot/C) \& O(A/B \vee C). \supset O(A/B)$.
A8. $P(B/B \vee C) \& O(A/B \vee C). \supset O(A/B)$.
A9. $O(\top/\top)$.
A10. $A \supset O(\top/A)$.
A11. $O(\top/A) \supset P(\bot/P(\bot/A))$.
A12. $O(A/B) \supset P(\bot/\sim O(A/B))$.
A13. $P(A/B) \supset P(\bot/\sim P(A/B))$.

These axiom systems for **CO, CD, CU, CA, CDA**, and **CUA**
have been designed to use as many as possible of the previously
proposed axioms discussed in [2], [4], and [9]. To establish soundness
and completeness, we need only check that our axiom systems are

---

2 For any fixed C, we can regard $O(-/C)$ and $P(-/C)$ as a pair of monadic deontic
operators. R1–R3 and A1–A3, in which the fixed C figures only as an inert index,
constitute an axiom system for Lemmon's weak deontic logic **D2** (see [5], [6] for
each such pair). **D2** falls short of the more standard deontic logic **D** for the pair by
lacking the theorem $O(\top/C)$; nor should that be a theorem since it is false in case
of vacuity and some instances of $O(-/C)$ are vacuous. Had we used $O'(-/-)$ and
$P'(-/-)$ we would still fall short of **D**: in case of vacuity we would then have
$O'(\top/C)$, but would lose the instances of A3. Rather we would have the logic
K for each pair, as in the basic conditional logic of Chellas [1].

equipollent to those given in [8], Section 6.1, for the 'V-logics' **V**, **VN, VTU, VA, VNA**, and **VTA**, respectively; for those logics, in a definitional extension of our present language, are known to be determined by the appropriately restricted classes of separative closed nesting frames (there called *systems of spheres*). Our **CO** and **CD** are equipollent also to their namesakes in [7] and [9], respectively.

XII. COMPARISONS AND CONTRASTS

It is an easy task now to compare the four previous treatments listed at the beginning. I include also my treatment of **CO** in [7], although **CO** is presented there only as a minimal logic for counterfactuals, without mention of its deontic reinterpretation.

A. *Hansson* [4]. (We take only the final system **DSDL3**.) Language: operators with the truth conditions of our $O'(-/-)$ and $P'(-/-)$; iteration prohibited; truth-functional compounding of deontic and non-deontic sentences also prohibited. Semantic apparatus: universal limited rankings. (The relation of these to choice functions is studied in Hansson [3].)

B. *Føllesdal and Hilpinen* [2]. Language: operators with the truth conditions of our $O'(-/-)$ and $P'(-/-)$; iteration not discussed. Semantic apparatus: semiformal; essentially our universal choice functions. It is suggested that the best worlds where a circumstance holds are those that most resemble perfect worlds. That improves the analogy, otherwise merely formal, with counterfactuals construed as true (as in my [7] and [8]) iff the consequent holds at the antecedent-worlds that most resemble our actual world. But I feel some doubt. Lilies that fester may smell worse than weeds, but are they also less similar to perfect lilies?

C. *Van Fraassen* [9]. Language: $O(-/-)$ and $P(-/-)$; iteration permitted. Semantic apparatus: normal linear indirect ranking frames. These are motivated in the first of our two ways: values realized at worlds are ranked, not whole worlds with all their values lumped together. The idea may be that values are too diverse to be lumped together;

18

but if so, are they not also too diverse to be ranked? (Van Fraassen may agree, for in [10] he has since developed a pluralistic brand of deontic logic meant to cope with clashes of incomparable values.) The need for non-separative indirect rankings does not seem to me to have been convincingly shown.

D. *Lewis* [8]. Language: operators with the truth conditions of all four of ours; iteration permitted. Semantic apparatus: separative closed nesting frames, with normality, universality, and absoluteness considered as options; ranking frames also are mentioned by way of motivation. It is argued that more than limited frames are needed, since infinite sequences of better and better worlds are a serious possibility.

E. *Lewis* [7]. Language: one operator, with the truth conditions of our $O'(-/-)$; iteration permitted. Semantic apparatus (three versions): (α) partial choice function frames; (β) nesting frames; and (γ) ranking frames.

BIBLIOGRAPHY

[1] Brian F. Chellas, 'Basic Conditional Logic', dittographed 1970, University of Pennsylvania.

[2] Dagfinn Føllesdal and Risto Hilpinen, 'Deontic Logic: an Introduction', in Risto Hilpinen (ed.), *Deontic Logic: Introductory and Systematic Readings*, Reidel, 1971.

[3] Bengt Hansson, 'Choice Structures and Preference Relations', *Synthese* **18** (1968), 443–458.

[4] Bengt Hansson, 'An Analysis of Some Deontic Logics', *Noûs* **4** (1970), 373–398; reprinted in Hilpinen (ed.), *Deontic Logic*.

[5] E. J. Lemmon, 'New Foundations for Lewis Modal Systems', *Journal of Symbolic Logic* **22** (1957), 176–218.

[6] E. J. Lemmon, 'Algebraic Semantics for Modal Logic, I & II', *Journal of Symbolic Logic* **31** (1966), 46–65 and 191–218.

[7] David Lewis, 'Completeness and Decidability of Three Logics of Counterfactual Conditionals', *Theoria* **37** (1971), 74–85.

[8] David Lewis, *Counterfactuals*, Blackwell, 1973.

[9] Bas van Fraassen, 'The Logic of Conditional Obligation', *Journal of Philosophical Logic* **1** (1972), 417–438.

[10] Bas van Fraassen, 'Values and the Heart's Command', *Journal of Philosophy* **70** (1973), 5–19.

2

A problem about permission

1. THE GAME

Consider a little language game that is played as follows.

(1) There are three players, called the *Master*, the *Slave*, and the *Kibitzer*. It would change nothing to have more than one slave, or more than one kibitzer, but let us put aside the complications that arise if a slave must serve two masters. (They say it can't be done.)

(2) There is a certain set of strings of symbols, called the set of *sentences*. A player may at any time make the move of *saying* any sentence *to* any other player within earshot.

(3) There is a certain function that assigns to any sentence ϕ, at any pair $\langle t, w \rangle$ of a time t during the game and a suitable possible world w, a value 1 or 0 called the *truth value* of ϕ at t at w. (We leave off the 'at w' when w is the actual world.) ϕ is called *true* or *false* at t at w according as the truth value is 1 or 0.

(4) There is another function that assigns to any such pair $\langle t, w \rangle$ a set of worlds called the *sphere of permissibility* at t at w. Worlds in this set are said to be *permissible* at t at w.

First published in E. Saarinen *et al.*, eds., *Essays in Honour of Jaakko Hintikka* (Dordrecht, Reidel, 1975). Copyright © by D. Reidel Publishing Company, Dordrecht-Holland. Reprinted with kind permission from Kluwer Academic Publishers.

Thanks are due to audiences on several occasions, and especially to Robert Martin and Robert Stalnaker, for comments on previous versions of this paper.

I am told that Thomas Ballmer has developed a theory similar to that presented here. However, I have not seen any details of his work.

(5) There is another function that assigns to any such pair $\langle t, w \rangle$ a set of worlds called the *sphere of accessibility* at t at w. Worlds in this set are said to be *accessible* at t at w. These worlds are the alternatives, including always w itself, that are left open by the past history of w up to t. They share that history, but they continue it in divergent ways. Spheres of accessibility are always contracting (except in trivial cases) and the contraction is irreversible: once a world has become inaccessible, it remains so forevermore. (I am not sure, but perhaps we should impose another condition: if one world is accessible at t at another, then the two worlds have exactly the same sphere of accessibility at t.)

(6) The $\langle t, w \rangle$ pairs on which the functions listed in (3)–(5) are defined include all of those such that t is a time during the game and w is accessible (at the actual world) at the time when the game begins. Let us henceforth tactily omit from consideration all times and worlds but these.

(7) There is a certain symbol ! that may be prefixed to any sentence ϕ to make a new sentence ! ϕ, called an *imperative* sentence, that is true at t at w iff ϕ is true at t at every world that is both accessible and permissible at t at w.

(8) There is a certain symbol ¡ that may be prefixed to any sentence ϕ to make a new sentence ¡ ϕ, called a *permissive* sentence, that is true at t at w iff ϕ is true at t at some world that is both accessible and permissible at t at w.

(9) The sphere of permissibility at any time (at any world) depends as follows on the past history of the world. When the game begins, it is the set of all worlds. Thereafter it remains unchanged except when the Master says to the Slave an imperative or permissive sentence that would be false, when said, if the sphere remained unchanged. Then the sphere adjusts itself, if possible, to make the Master's sentence true. Suppose that at t the Master says to the Slave ! ϕ; and suppose that the sphere of permissibility just before t contains some worlds, accessible at t, where ϕ is false at t. Then the sphere must contract to cut those worlds out: at t, and thereafter at least until the next change, none of those worlds are permissible. If the Master changes the sphere in this way by saying ! ϕ, we say that the Master *commands* that ϕ. Or suppose that at t the Master says to the Slave ¡ ϕ; and suppose that the

21

sphere of permissibility just before t contains no worlds, accessible at t, where ϕ is true at t; and suppose that there do exist some such worlds outside the sphere. Then the sphere must expand to take in some of those worlds: at t, and thereafter at least until the next change, some of those worlds are permissible. If the Master changes the sphere in this way by saying ¡ ϕ, we say that the Master *permits* that ϕ.

(10) The Slave tries to see to it that the actual world is within the sphere of permissibility at all times. If the Slave knows, at a time t, that he acts in a certain way at t throughout the worlds that are permissible and accessible at t – for instance, if he knows that at all such worlds he begins a certain task at t – then he tries to act in that way at the actual world.

(11) Each player tries to see to it that he never says a sentence to another player unless that sentence is true at the time when he says it. The Master, when he commands or permits, is automatically truthful since the sphere adjusts to make him so; other players, and even the Master when he is not commanding or permitting, are truthful by choosing sentences to say that are true at the worlds that conform to their beliefs.

2. COMMENTS

The point of the game, as regards commanding and permitting, is to enable the Master to control the actions of the Slave. What the Slave does depends on the present sphere of permissibility, which depends in turn on the Master's previous commands and permissions. We need not ask why the Slave is willing to play his part. Perhaps he does so by habit; perhaps he is coerced; perhaps he is obligated; or perhaps he hopes that the Master's control over him will be used to his benefit as well as to the Master's. In any case, the game is played. And we may suppose it to be common knowledge that the game is played: each player expects the others to play their parts, expects the others so to expect, and so on.

In this simple example, I have tried to merge two complementary approaches to the study of imperatives. The semantic analysis of ! and ¡ given in (3)–(8) is taken, with slight changes, from Chellas [1] and

22

[2]. The treatment of commanding and permitting as part of a social practice for enabling one person to control another is taken from Stenius [5] and Lewis [4].

If there were only commanding and no permitting, the language game could be described more simply. We could drop (4)–(10) and replace them as follows. If at any time t the imperative sentences said by the Master to the Slave before t are given by the list

(L) $! \phi_1$ at $t_1, \ldots, ! \phi_n$ at t_n,

then the Slave tries at t to see to it that ϕ_1 is true at $t_1, \ldots$, and that ϕ_n is true at t_n. On this account, the only truth value that we need to associate with an imperative sentence $! \phi$ is the truth value of the content sentence ϕ (at the time when it was commanded). We could call *this* the truth value of the imperative $! \phi$, and say that the Slave tries to see to it that the Master's previous imperatives to him are made true. That was my account of imperatives in [4]. But then what do we make of permission? It is easy enough to provide for annulment of commands: the Master may at any time remove an item from the list (L), after which the Slave acts as if that command never had been given. But permissions are not, in general, annulments of particular past commands. A permission may partly undo several past commands, without fully undoing any of them. We need a device for integrating a succession of commands and permissions. A list with additions and deletions is one such device, but it is not flexible enough. The sphere of permissibility is meant to be a better device to serve the same purpose.

Commanding and permitting are not the whole of our language game. As regards all other sentence-saying, the point of the game is to enable the players to impart information to one another. Whenever truthfulness is not automatic, the hearer who expects the speaker to be truthful can infer something about the speaker's beliefs from the sentences that the speaker is willing to say; and often the hearer can go on to infer conclusions about the world, premised on confidence that the speaker's beliefs about certain topics tend to be correct. To the extent that the speaker can anticipate these inferences, he can control the hearer's beliefs by what he says. In particular, one player may wish to inform another about the present state of the sphere of permissibility – that is, about the integrated effect of the Master's commands and permissions up to now. There is nothing to keep him from doing so, given the way we have set up the language game, by using the same imperative and permissive sentences that the Master himself uses to change the sphere. One and the same sentence '! *the Slave carries rocks all day*' may be said by the Master to the Slave to reshape the sphere of permissibility and cause the Slave to carry the rocks; by the Slave to the Kibitzer to elicit sympathy; by the Master to the Kibitzer to explain why the Slave is not working on his usual chores; by the Slave or the Kibitzer to the forgetful Master to remind him what the Slave is supposed to be doing; and so on. It may even be used by the Master to the forgetful Slave as a reminder, with no further adjustment of the sphere of permissibility. Likewise '¡ *the Slave does no work tomorrow*' may be said by the Master to the Slave to grant a holiday; by the Master to the Kibitzer to point out that the Slave's lot is not so very bad after all; and so on.

While I admit to an inclination to play Old Harry with the performative/constative fetish, I insist that I have not erased the distinction between different speech-acts that may be performed by saying an imperative sentence. The sentence may be used to command: the Master says it to the Slave, his purpose is to control the Slave's actions by changing the sphere of permissibility, and truthfulness is automatic because the sphere adjusts so that saying so makes it so. The sentence may be used to inform: either the speaker is not the Master or the hearer is not the Slave, the speaker's purpose is to impart information to one who does not yet possess it, and truthfulness is not automatic. Or the sentence may be used to remind (an intermediate case): again the Master says it to the Slave, but this time his purpose is to impart (or re-impart) information, and although truthfulness would be automatic the Master intends the sentence to be true even without any adjustment of the sphere of permissibility. Likewise for permissive sentences, except that truthfulness is never quite automatic since the Master cannot truly permit what is impossible. These are perfectly good distinctions; my point is only that they need not be part of semantics, insofar as semantics deals with truth conditions. In fact, they must not be. Only if the truth conditions are uniform from one use to another can we use the given formulation of (9).

24

I have no real dispute, however, with anyone who finds it intolerable to say that an imperative sentence, when used to command, has a truth value. In describing the language game I did not really use any semantic terms as primitives. I could have; but the description I actually gave is related to a description using semantic primitives as the Ramsey sentence of a term-introducing scientific theory is related to the theory itself. For instance, 'truth value' serves only as a mnemonic label for the values of the function introduced in (3) by existential quantification. If you dislike that label – or any other – feel free to substitute the euphemism of your choice.

3. PERMISSIBILITY KINEMATICS

I said that the changing sphere of permissibility integrates the effect of the Master's successive commands and permissions, but I did not say exactly how. The requirements in (9) constrain, but do not determine, the evolution of the sphere. When the Master says to the Slave an imperative or permissive sentence that would be false if the sphere remained unchanged, there will ordinarily be infinitely many alternative adjustments that would make his sentence true.

For commanding, at least, it is easy enough to say precisely how the sphere should change. Suppose that at time t (at a given world) the Master says to the Slave ! ϕ, and suppose that a change in the sphere of permissibility is needed to make ! ϕ true at t. Let P be the old sphere just before t, and let $[\![\phi$ at $t]\!]$ be the set of all worlds where ϕ is true at t. Then the new sphere at t, and thereafter until the next change, should be the intersection $P \cap [\![\phi$ at $t]\!]$. All worlds accessible at t where ϕ is false at t must be removed from the sphere, according to (9); but it would be gratuitous to remove any further accessible worlds, since the Master has commanded that ϕ and nothing further, and it would be gratuitous to add any accessible worlds that were not permissible before, since the Master has not permitted anything but only commanded something. As for inaccessible worlds, it makes no difference which are removed or added so I have made the most convenient arbitrary stipulation.

If the sphere's evolution under the impact of commands does go by intersection in the way just proposed, then we have the proper

25

result for the special case that there is only commanding and no permitting. Let the Master's commands before t be: ! ϕ_1 at $t_1, \ldots,$! ϕ_n at t_n. Then by successive intersections the sphere of permissibility at t is $P_0 \cap [\![\phi_1 \text{ at } t_1]\!] \cap \ldots \cap [\![\phi_n \text{ at } t_n]\!]$, where the initial sphere P_0 is the set of all worlds. The Slave, according to (10), tries at t to see to it that the actual world is within the sphere of permissibility at t. That is to say that he tries at t to see to it that the actual world is in all of the sets $[\![\phi_1 \text{ at } t_1]\!], \ldots, [\![\phi_n \text{ at } t_n]\!]$. And that is to say exactly what we said before about this special case: that he tries at t to see to it that ϕ_1 is true at $t_1, \ldots,$ and ϕ_n is true at t_n.

One sort of commanding may seem to require special treatment: commanding the impermissible. Suppose that $[\![\phi \text{ at } t]\!]$ contains no worlds that are both accessible and permissible at t, so that ¡ ϕ is false at t. The Master may nevertheless wish to command at t that ϕ. For instance, he may have changed his mind. Having commanded at dawn that the Slave devote his energies all day to carrying rocks, the Master may decide at noon that it would be better to have the Slave spend the afternoon on some lighter or more urgent task. If the Master simply commands at t that ϕ, and if the sphere evolves by intersection, then *no* world accessible at t remains permissible; the Slave, through no fault of his own, has no way to play his part by trying to see to it that the world remains permissible. We have no idea what the Slave may do to make the best of an impermissible situation. Should we therefore say that in this case the sphere evolves not by intersection but in some more complicated way? I think not. The resources of the language game are not to blame if the Master removes all accessible worlds from the sphere of permissibility by commanding the impermissible. Rather the Master is to blame for misusing those resources. What he should have done was first to permit and then to command that ϕ. He should say to the Slave, in quick succession, first ¡ ϕ and then ! ϕ; that way, he would be commanding not the impermissible but the newly permissible. We could indeed have equipped the language game with a labor-saving device: whenever ¡ ϕ is false, a command that ϕ is deemed to be preceded by a tacit permission that ϕ, and the sphere of permissibility evolves accordingly. But this is a frill that we can well afford to ignore, since it does not enable the Master to do anything more than he can do in the original, simpler language game.

Turning now to the evolution of the sphere under the impact of permissions, we reach the problem announced in my title. The natural parallel to evolution by intersection in the case of commands would be evolution by union, as follows: if at t the Master says to the Slave ¡ ϕ, and if a change in the sphere of permissibility is needed to make ¡ ϕ true at t, and if P and $[\![\phi$ at $t]\!]$ are as before, then the new sphere at t, and thereafter until the next change, is the union $P \cup [\![\phi$ at $t]\!]$. But this sort of evolution by union, unlike evolution by intersection in the case of commands, is far from realistic. There could be a language game that did work that way – the rules are up to the players – but it would lack one salient and problematic feature of permission as we know it.

The problem is this. When the Master permits something, he does not thereby permit that thing to come about in whatever way the Slave pleases – not if the game is to be realistic. Suppose the Slave has been commanded to carry rocks every day of the week, but on Thursday the Master relents and says to the Slave '¡ *the Slave does no work tomorrow*'. That is all he says. He has thereby permitted a holiday, but not just any possible sort of holiday. He has presumably not thereby permitted a holiday that starts on Friday and goes on through Saturday, or a holiday spent guzzling in his wine cellar. *Some* of the accessible worlds where the Slave does no work on Friday have been brought into permissibility, but not all of them. The Master has not said which ones. He did not need to; somehow, that is understood.

Perhaps the incorrect principle of evolution by union in the case of permissions has some correct consequences, as follows. First, the new sphere at t should contain some world in $[\![\phi$ at $t]\!]$ that is accessible at t, if there exists some such world; that much is required by (9). Second, it should be included in $P \cup [\![\phi$ at $t]\!]$; since the Master has permitted that ϕ and nothing further, it would be gratuitous to bring worlds into permissibility where ϕ is false at t. Third, it should include all of P; since the Master has not commanded anything but only permitted something, it would be gratuitous to remove any worlds from permissibility. In short, the new sphere at t is the union of the old sphere P and some subset or other of $[\![\phi \text{ at } t]\!]$, where all we know yet about this subset of $[\![\phi \text{ at } t]\!]$ is that it must, if possible, contain some world that is accessible at t.

Let us return to our example. Hitherto the Slave has been commanded to carry rocks every day of the week, to abstain from the Master's wine, and perhaps other things besides. Now he has been permitted (on Thursday) to do no work on Friday. So the newly permissible worlds are all of the worlds that were permissible hitherto, along with some of the accessible worlds, formerly impermissible, where the Slave does no work on Friday. (If such there be; but in this case there are.) But only some, not all. The worlds brought newly into permissibility include none of those where the Slave does no work on Friday or on Saturday either; nor any of those where he does no work on Friday and drinks the Master's wine.

Why not? Various answers might be given. But though they seem sensible in this case, I do not think any of them lead to any simple and definite general principle of evolution.

Answer 1. To enlarge the sphere of permissibility so that it includes worlds where the Slave does no work on Saturday, or worlds where he drinks the Master's wine, would be a gratuitous enlargement. It would be more of an enlargement than is needed to make it permissible not to work on Friday.

I reply that the same is true of any reasonable enlargement. If the game is to be at all true to life, there will be more than one permissible way for the Slave to spend his holiday. (Even if he is required to spend the day at prayer, still he is no doubt free to choose the points in his prayers at which to take a breath.) Then more than the least possible number of worlds – more than one – must have been brought into permissibility.

Answer 2. To include worlds in the enlarged sphere of permissibility where the Slave does no work on Saturday, or where he drinks the Master's wine, would be gratuitous change, not in a quantitative but in a qualitative way. The newly permissible worlds should be selected to resemble (as closely as possible) the worlds that were permissible before.

I reply that according to my offhand judgments of similarity, that principle instructs us to select worlds where the Slave spends Friday in the gymnasium lifting weights. Among worlds where the Slave does not work on Friday, are not these the worlds most similar to the previously permissible worlds – worlds where he spends Friday carrying rocks? But surely a weight-lifting holiday is not the only sort of holiday that has been made permissible.

To be sure, the outcome depends on the relation of comparative similarity that guides the selection. Offhand judgments are no safe guide. Not every similarity relation worthy of the name gives significant weight to the obvious similarity between rock-carrying and weight-lifting. So perhaps it is true, *under the right similarity relation*, that the worlds that become permissible are those of the worlds where the Slave does no work on Friday that most resemble the previously permissible worlds. But which similarity relation is the right one for our present purpose? This is just a restatement of our original problem, and seems to me unhelpful.

Answer 3. Before the Master's permission, all worlds where the Slave did no work on Friday were impermissible; but they were not equally impermissible. Those where he also failed to work on Saturday, or where he drank the Master's wine, were more impermissible – or more remote from permissibility – than some of the others. (Whether or not they were also more dissimilar from the permissible worlds in other respects, at least they were more dissimilar in respect of their degree of permissibility.) If the Slave cannot (or will not) see to it that the actual world is within the sphere of permissibility, he may at least try for second best and keep the world as nearly permissible as he can. The relation of comparative near-permissibility determines what is second best. Perhaps it is this same relation that selects the newly permissible worlds when the Master enlarges the sphere of permissibility: the worlds that become permissible are those of the worlds where the Slave does no work on Friday that were most nearly permissible before.

I reply that this may be; and that it seems right to connect the problem of evolution under permissions with the problem of second-best courses of action for the Slave. (I am grateful to Robert Stalnaker for pointing out this connection.) Still it seems to me that again the problem has been restated rather than solved. Given the relation of comparative near-permissibility at every stage of the game, we may have a complete principle governing the evolution of the sphere of permissibility; but how does the comparative relation evolve from stage to stage? Is it so that the spheres of permissibility and accessibility at any stage suffice somehow to determine the comparative near-permissibility of worlds at that stage? If so, how?

Answer 4. Perhaps we should look outside the game to the goals it serves. It is to serve some purposes that the Master controls the Slave by commanding and permitting. The Slave either shares these purposes or at least acquiesces enough that he continues to play his part in the game. When the Slave is permitted to do no work on Friday, some worlds remain impermissible because if they were to become permissible and the Slave were to actualize one of them, that would not serve the purposes for which the game is played. It is understood that these purposes require the Slave to work hard and to keep away from the Master's wine. Therefore worlds where the Slave does no work on Saturday, or where he drinks the Master's wine, are not readily brought into permissibility when the Master permits a holiday on Friday.

I reply that either the Slave does know what would serve the purposes in question, or he does not. If he does, then what is the point of a game of commanding and permitting? The Slave might as well simply ignore what the Master says and do whatever he judges to serve the purposes. The game is played exactly because the Slave needs guidance in serving those purposes. But if the Slave does not know what would serve the purposes, and if the evolution of the sphere of permissibility depends on what would serve the purposes, then the Slave is not in a good position to figure out how the sphere had evolved, and hence is not in a good position to figure out what is permissible. For the Slave to suffer this difficulty will itself interfere with the success of the game of commanding and permitting in serving those purposes for the sake of which it is played.

The best that might be done along these lines, I suppose, is as follows. It might be that the Slave knows just enough, and not too much, about what would serve the purposes. Since he knows enough, he is in a position to figure out how the sphere of permissibility evolves when the Master enlarges it, as by permitting a holiday on Friday. Since he does not know too much he remains in need of guidance if the purposes are to be served, and the game does not become pointless. This might be so. But I find it hard to believe that only when a delicate balance has been struck does the game I have described both retain its point and become playable.

Answer 5. At any stage, the sphere of permissibility may be specified by a list of requirements. (The list may or may not match the list of commands by which the sphere was shaped.) Each requirement on the list is satisfied at every permissible world; the worlds that are permissible are exactly those that satisfy every requirement on the list. The list might be as follows:

The Slave carries rocks all day on Sunday.

.

.

.

The Slave carries rocks all day on Friday.
The Slave carries rocks all day on Saturday.
The Slave never drinks the Master's wine.

.

.

.

Find those entries on the list that conflict with the Master's permission that the Slave do no work on Friday. There is one and only one; strike it out. The new sphere of permissibility consists of exactly those worlds that satisfy the remaining requirements.

I reply that it all depends on how you encode the sphere of permissibility by a list of requirements. If you do it the right way, as above, the technique of striking out requirements that conflict with the Master's permission will give the right answer. Unfortunately, there are also wrong ways. The same sphere could have been encoded by another list:

The Slave carries rocks every morning of the week.
The Slave carries rocks every afternoon of the week.
The Slave never drinks the Master's wine.

.
.
.

Now we cannot strike out the one and only requirement that conflicts with the Master's permission; the first two both conflict. We
could strike out both of them; but that will make it permissible to do
no work on Saturday. Or take this list, another that encodes the
sphere:

The Slave carries rocks all day on Sunday or drinks the Master's
wine.

.
.

The Slave carries rocks all day on Friday or drinks the Master's
wine.
The Slave carries rocks all day on Saturday or drinks the Master's wine.
The Slave never drinks the Master's wine.

.
.
.

Now there is no one requirement which conflicts, all by itself, with
the Master's permission; but there are two that jointly conflict with
it. Strike out the right one of the two, and all is well. Strike out the
wrong one (or strike out both) and the results are not at all as we
would wish. Strike out the requirement that the Slave never drinks
the Master's wine and take the new sphere of permissibility to consist
of those worlds that satisfy the remaining requirements on the list.
This enlargement brings into permissibility worlds where the Slave
does no work on Friday, does no work on Saturday either, and spends
both days drinking the Master's wine. (It would also bring in worlds

where the Slave does no work earlier in the week, except that by Thursday these worlds are inaccessible.)

So the method of listing and striking out will not work unless we choose the right one of the lists of requirements that encode the original sphere of permissibility. Which one is that? Again we have a restatement of our original problem, not a solution.

How much of a solution is it reasonable to expect? There are cases where it is really unclear which worlds have been brought into permissibility. That means that no principle can be both as definite as we might hope and clearly correct. One such case is given by Thomas Cornides in a discussion of our problem [3]. (He defends a version of Answer 5, but is well aware of the reasons why the procedure of listing and striking out will not always give a determinate answer, even if the correct list is somehow given us.) His example is as follows. First comes the command '! you play only if you do your homework.' Second comes the command '! you watch television only if you play.' And third comes the permission '¡ you watch television and you do not do your homework.' Is it now permissible to watch television, not do the homework, and not play? That is unclear; and I think it might be left unclear even if we knew all that was relevant about the players and about their reasons for playing a game of commanding and permitting. So a principle governing the evolution of permissibility cannot settle this case in a way that is clearly correct.

BIBLIOGRAPHY

[1] Chellas, Brian F., *The Logical Form of Imperatives*, Perry Lane Press, Stanford, 1969.
[2] Chellas, Brian F., 'Imperatives', *Theoria* **37** (1971), 114–129.
[3] Cornides, Thomas, 'Der Widerruf von Befehlen', *Studium Generale* **22** (1969), 1215–1263.
[4] Lewis, David, *Convention: A Philosophical Study*, Harvard University Press, 1969.
[5] Stenius, Erik, 'Mood and Language-Game', *Synthese* **17** (1967), 254–274.

3

Reply to McMichael[1]

Deontic conditionals, whether those of ordinary discourse or the simplified versions invented by intensional logicians, are ethically neutral. You can apply them to state any ethical doctrine you please. The results will be only as acceptable as the doctrines that went into them.

Radical utilitarianism, stark and unqualified, is not a commonsensical view. Agreement with our ordinary ethical thought is not its strong point. It is no easy thing to accept the strange doctrine that nothing at all matters to what ought to be the case except the total balance of good and evil[2] – that any sort or amount of evil can be neutralized, as if it had never been, by enough countervailing good – and that the balancing evil and good may be entirely unrelated, as when the harm I do to you is cancelled out by the kindness of one Martian to another.

Accept this strange doctrine, and what should follow? Exactly the strange consequences that McMichael complains of! Never mind the semantics of deontic conditionals. If you really think that only the total matters, then surely you ought also to think that little is obliga-

First published in *Analysis* 38 (1978), 85–86.

1 Alan McMichael, 'Too Much of a Good Thing: A Problem in Deontic Logic', *Analysis*, 38 (1978), 83–84. McMichael there criticizes Section 5.1 of my *Counterfactuals* (Blackwell, Oxford, 1973).
2 Since we are discussing my treatment in *Counterfactuals*, our topic is what ought to be, not what someone in particular ought to do. See my footnote on page 100. But parallel questions would arise for the deontic logic of personal obligations.

tory (there are always alternative ways to reach a high total) and that much is permissible (no evil is so bad that it cannot be neutralized). It is not in the radical utilitarian spirit to believe in outright ethical requirements or prohibitions.

Order the worlds on radically utilitarian principles; then apply the semantics for deontic conditionals that I gave[3] in *Counterfactuals*; and the results are as McMichael says they are. Most of us would indeed find these results strange and unacceptable, but the radical utilitarian should find them much to his liking. The semantic analysis tells us what is true (at a world) under an ordering. It modestly declines to choose the proper ordering.[4] That is work for a moralist, not a semanticist. If what turns out to be true under a utilitarian ordering is what is true according to radical utilitarianism, not what is true according to our ordinary opinions, that is just as it should be.

Other orderings, other results. For instance, a simplistic non-utilitarian might fancy an ordering on which the better of any two worlds is the one with fewer sins. (It is up to him to tell us how he divides the totality of sin into distinct units.) Under this ordering and my semantics, much is obligatory and little is permissible. Perhaps some of the worlds where Jesse robs the bank have sixteen sins, none have fewer, and some have more. Then what is obligatory, given that Jesse robs the bank, is that there be no seventeenth sin. No course of

3 I did give the semantic analysis under discussion – but I did *not* give it as an exact analysis of any 'items of ordinary discourse'. Rather I meant it as a stipulation of truth conditions for deontic conditionals similar to those already studied by some deontic logicians. These have their interest partly because of their resemblance to the deontic conditionals of ordinary discourse. But I fully agree with McMichael (though for different reasons) that the resemblance is far from perfect. Section 5.1 of *Counterfactuals* is not an essay in ordinary language philosophy. As I stated at the outset (page 96), it is a study of the formal analogy between counterfactuals and variably strict conditionals in deontic logic. I did say that those conditionals 'may be read as' certain constructions of ordinary English. (One might likewise say that the standard existential quantifier 'may be read as' some English construction, though aware of differences between the two.) Surely to say that is to claim nothing more than an approximate likeness of meaning. Since the differences I believe in between my deontic conditionals and those of ordinary language are irrelevant to the difference that McMichael believes in and I do not, I have here ignored them.

4 See page 96.

action with any extra sin is (even conditionally) permissible, no matter how much counterbalancing good there may be. McMichael's argument cannot be made in this case. The only relevant good, sinlessness, is not 'a good which may exist in amounts of any size'.[5]

What is true under a utilitarian ordering or a sin-counting ordering (according to my semantics) ought not to be expected to agree with our ordinary opinions. Ordinary moralists are neither radical utilitarians nor sin-counters. It would be better to ask: is there *any* ordering (more complicated than those yet considered, no doubt) such that what is true under that ordering agrees with our ordinary moral opinions?

But even that better question is not good. Is there really any definite body of 'ordinary moral opinions' to agree with? I think not. We disagree, we waver, we are confused. Few of us singly, still less all of us together, have achieved a stable equilibrium between our utilitarian and our sin-counting inclinations.

---

5 We might also consider an ordering in which the world with fewer sins is better, but in which ties between worlds with equally many sins are broken on utilitarian considerations. Even though we now have a relevant good which may exist in amounts of any size, it remains true that much is obligatory and little is permissible. Avoidance of extra sin is obligatory, given that Jesse has robbed the bank, because no amount of good can outweigh an extra sin.

4

Why ain'cha rich?

Some think that in (a suitable version of) Newcomb's problem, it is rational to take only one box. These one-boxers think of the situation as a choice between a million and a thousand. They are convinced by indicative conditionals: if I take one box I will be a millionaire, but if I take both boxes I will not. Their conception of rationality may be called *V-rationality*; they deem it rational to maximize *V*, that being a kind of expected utility defined in entirely non-causal terms. Their decision theory is that of Jeffrey [2].

Others, and I for one, think it rational to take both boxes. We two-boxers think that whether the million already awaits us or not, we have no choice between taking it and leaving it. We are convinced by counterfactual conditionals: If I took only one box, I would be poorer by a thousand than I will be after taking both. (We distinguish normal from back-tracking counterfactuals, perhaps as in [4], and are persuaded only by the former.) Our conception of rationality is *U-rationality*; we favor maximizing *U*, a kind of expected utility defined in terms of causal dependence as well as credence and value. Our decision theory is that of Gibbard and Harper [1], or something similar.

First published in *Noûs* **15** (1981), 377–380. Reprinted with kind permission from Blackwell Publishers.

This paper is based on a talk given at a conference on Conditional Expected Utility given at the University of Pittsburgh in November 1978. I thank Paul Benacerraf, Jane Heal, Calvin Normore, and Robert Stalnaker for valuable discussion.

37

The one-boxers sometimes taunt us: if you're so smart, why ain'cha rich? They have their millions and we have our thousands, and they think this goes to show the error of our ways. They think we are not rich because we have irrationally chosen not to have our millions.

We reply that we never were given any choice about whether to have a million. When we made our choices, there were no millions to be had. The reason why we are not rich is that the riches were reserved for the irrational. In the words of Gibbard and Harper [1],

we take the moral . . . to be something else: if someone is very good at predicting behavior and rewards predicted irrationality richly, then irrationality will be richly rewarded.

Rationality will not.

(Let us say that irrationality will be richly *pre*-rewarded. That cancels the suggestion, which of course we do not intend, that the irrationality causes the "reward".)

What is the status of this moral? Is it

(1) one more piece of two-boxist doctrine that one-boxers may consistently deny?

Or is it

(2) common ground, something that ought to be uncontroversial?

Can all agree that no matter whether true rationality is V-rationality or U-rationality – indeed, even if it is some undreamt-of third sort of rationality – still the predictor can see to it, if he is so inclined and good enough at predicting, that irrationality is richly pre-rewarded and the smart ain't rich?

I regret to say that alternative (1) appears to be correct. At any rate, the obvious way to argue for alternative (2) is a failure. So it's a standoff. We may consistently go on thinking that it proves nothing that the one-boxers are richly pre-rewarded and we are not. But they may consistently go on thinking otherwise. For it is impossible, on their conception of rationality, to be sure at the time of choice that the irrational choice will, and the rational choice will not, be richly pre-rewarded. V-irrationality cannot be richly pre-rewarded, unless by surprise. (And we did not plead surprise. We knew what to expect.) The expectation that only one choice will be richly pre-rewarded – richly enough to outweigh other considerations – is enough to make that choice V-rational.

Try to imagine that the predictor in Newcomb's problem changes sides. Hitherto, his announced policy has been to pre-reward U-irrationality. He has left a million just when he predicted that the subject was going to make the U-irrational choice of taking only one box. But from now on he will create a new kind of problem. His announced policy henceforth will be to pre-reward V-irrationality. He will leave a million just when he predicts that the subject is going to make the V-irrational choice, whichever that is. (If neither choice in the new problem is V-irrational, he will never leave a million.) He is just as good at predicting as he was before; and he sees to it that the subject is convinced (or close to convinced) that a correct prediction has been made. Now that someone is very good at predicting behavior and rewards predicted V-irrationality richly, it seems that V-irrationality will be richly rewarded (and not by surprise). Why not?

Answer: because the story just told is self-contradictory. The new problem, unlike the Newcomb problem, is impossible. The predictor announces, convincingly, that he will pre-reward a certain choice. Thereby he makes the choice V-rational. But the choice to be thus made V-rational is the V-irrational one, whichever that is. That is, it is whichever one is V-irrational given, *inter alia*, his announcement. So the story says that the predictor makes it the case that one and the same choice is V-rational and V-irrational. Whatever he may do, he cannot do that.

To reach a *reductio* against the supposition that the new problem is possible, let us ask which choice (if either) is V-irrational in the new problem. Let C be the subject's credence function at the time of deliberation; let M be the proposition that the predictor has left a million; let A_1 be the proposition that the subject takes only one box, declining his thousand; and let A_2 be the proposition that he takes both boxes. Let the utility of the payoffs be measured by money. Then we have three cases.

Case 1: $C(M/A_1) < C(M/A_2) + .001$. Then taking only one box is V-irrational, and taking both boxes is not. But if so, $C(M/A_1) \approx 1$ and $C(M/A_2) \approx 0$. Contradiction.

Case 2: $C(M/A_1) = C(M/A_2) + .001$. Then the choices are tied, so neither is V-irrational. But if so, $C(M/A_1) \approx 0$ and $C(M/A_2) \approx 0$. Contradiction.

Case 3: $C(M/A_1) > C(MA_2) + .001$. Then taking both boxes is V-irrational, and taking one box is not. But if so, $C(M/A_1) \approx 0$ and $C(M/A_2) \approx 1$. Contradiction.

All three cases are impossible. Yet if the new problem is possible, one of the three must hold. The new problem is impossible, *quod erat demonstrandum*.

In discussion it has been suggested that the new problem *is* possible; that in the new problem it is V-rational to take both boxes and V-irrational to take only one (so that in this problem V-rationality and U-rationality agree); that the one-boxer must concede that on his view also, predicted irrationality may be richly rewarded, and not by surprise; and that my *reductio* fails because in Case 1, the correct case on this proposal, $C(A_1) = 0$ and $C(M/A_1)$ is undefined. The V-rational subject is imagined to deliberate as follows:

> I'm going to do the V-rational thing. That makes it almost certain that there's no million for me. Then the V-rational thing is to take both boxes and get my thousand, and that is what I'll do.

I object that if the subject is still deliberating, then he is not yet sure (even implicitly) what he will do. If he is, for instance if $C(A_1) = 0$ and $C(A_2) = 1$, then his decision problem collapses as described in Jeffrey [3]; in which case the distinction between V-rational and V-irrational actions in his situation is undefined. But if he is not sure (even implicitly) what he will do, he must be lacking in self-knowledge. He must be uncertain either about his credences, about his utilities, or about the standards of rationality (or irrationality) to which he is going to conform. In this case the third sort of lack of self-knowledge is most plausible. It is therefore inadmissible to suppose him to be deliberating, and yet suppose him already to be certain that he will do the V-rational thing.

REFERENCES

[1] Allan Gibbard and William Harper, "Counterfactuals and Two Kinds of Expected Utility", in C. A. Hooker, J. J. Leach, and E. F. McClennen, eds., *Foundations and Applications of Decision Theory*, Volume 1 (Dordrecht, Holland: D. Reidel, 1978), pp. 125–62.

[2] Richard C. Jeffrey, *The Logic of Decision* (New York: McGraw-Hill, 1965).

[3] ———, "A Note on the Kinematics of Preference", *Erkenntnis* 11 (1977), pp. 135–41.

[4] David Lewis, "Counterfactual Dependence and Time's Arrow", *Noûs* 13 (1979), 455–76.

5

Desire as belief

1. THE ANTI-HUMEAN CHALLENGE

A Humean thesis about motivation says that we are moved entirely
by desire: we are disposed to do what will serve our desires according
to our beliefs. If there were no desires to serve, we would never be
moved more to do one thing than another. Whatever might happen
then would be entirely unmotivated. Here I shall uphold Humeanism
against one sort of opponent.

Our anti-Humean challenges us with this case. The Department
must choose between two candidates for a job, Meane and Neiss.
Neiss is your old friend, affable, sensible, fair-minded, co-operative,
moderate, ... Meane is quite the opposite. But it is clear that Meane
is just a little bit better at philosophy. Gritting your teeth and defying
all desire, you vote for Meane, because you believe that Meane
getting the job instead of Neiss would, all things considered, be good.
Your belief about what's good has moved you to go against your
desire to have Neiss for a colleague and to have nothing to do with
Meane.

We Humeans reply that there are desires and there are desires.

First published in *Mind* **97** (1988), 323–332. Reprinted by permission of Oxford
University Press.

I am indebted to several people for helpful discussion or correspondence; especially
Simon Blackburn, John P. Burgess, John Collins, Frank Jackson, D. H. Mellor, Philip
Pettit, and Michael Smith.

Some desires, for instance your desire to have Neiss for a colleague, are warm – you feel enthusiasm, you take pleasure in the prospect of fulfilment. Other desires, for instance your desire to hire the best available candidate, are cold. Nobody ever said that only the *warm* desires can move us. It is not so that you defied *all* desire when you voted for Meane. You were moved entirely by your desires, however the cold desire outweighed the warm one. We are within our rights to construe 'desire' inclusively, to cover the entire range of states that move us, including for instance the state that moved you to vote for Meane. Humeanism understood in this inclusive way is surely true – maybe a trivial truth, but a trivial truth is still a truth.

Let our anti-Humean grant that the state that moved you was after all, inclusively speaking, a desire. He may insist, however, that it was *also* a belief: the belief (as he said before) that Meane getting the job would be good. Although it may be true – trivially, he sneers – that all motivation is by desire, it is *also* true that some motivation is by belief. Sometimes, what happens is that we do what will serve the good according to our beliefs about what would be good together with our other beliefs – no desire, other than desires which are identical with beliefs, need enter into it.

More cautiously, he might say that some beliefs are, at least, necessarily conjoined with corresponding desires. If you believe that Meane getting the job would be good, then necessarily you desire that Meane get the job. This need not be your only relevant desire (as the story shows). It need not be your strongest desire (though in the story it was). But it must be there. It is just impossible to have a belief about what would be good and lack the corresponding desire.

If the belief and the desire are identical, a fortiori they are necessarily conjoined. Or the necessary connection might arise in some other way, even if the desire is in some way different from the belief. To cover both cases at once, let us take the necessary connection to be our anti-Humean's main thesis, leaving identity as an optional extra.[1]

1 For criticism and defence of several anti-Humean views at least close to the Desire-as-Belief Thesis, see Michael Smith, 'The Humean Theory of Motivation', *Mind*,

Let us suppose that what our anti-Humean proposes is a necessary connection not with 'basic' desire for what is considered good 'in itself', but rather with desire that may be instrumental. For in the example, you did not desire Meane's appointment for its own sake; you were interested in the excellence he would add to the Department. And let us suppose that what our anti-Humean proposes is a connection with an averaged desire that takes account of a range of cases, some better than others and some more likely than others. For in the example, it may be that you considered the case that Meane joined the Department but stopped doing good work, and also the case that he came and surpassed all that he had done before, and you decided what you thought about a probability-weighted average of these and other cases. Only on the basis of that average did you believe that Meane getting the job would be good. Only on the basis of that average did you desire that Meane get the job.

Our anti-Humean has not yet offered any informative analysis of the content of beliefs about what would be good. Maybe he thinks this can be done, maybe not. But he says that we have one handle, at any rate, on the distinctive content of such beliefs: the proposition that Meane getting the job would be good is that proposition X, whatever it may be, such that believing X is somehow necessarily connected with desiring that Meane get the job.

Our Anti-Humean may say how intuitive it seems that a belief about what is good should be necessarily connected with desire, and how right it seems to explain your vote by saying that you believed that Meane getting the job would be good. We can counter in one of two ways. Maybe (1) a so-called 'belief about what would be good' is called a belief by courtesy, but rightly speaking it is not a belief at all but rather it is the corresponding desire; or maybe it consists of the desire plus something more. Then in any systematic

1987, pp. 36–61; Philip Pettit, 'Humeans, Anti-Humeans, and Motivation', *Mind*, 1987, pp. 530–3; and Michael Smith, 'On Humeans, Anti-Humeans and Motivation: a Reply to Pettit', *Mind*, 1988, pp. 589–95. For critical discussion of an explicit desire-belief identity thesis, see J. E. J. Altham on 'besires': 'The Legacy of Emotivism' in *Fact, Science and Morality: Essays on A. J. Ayer's Language, Truth and Logic*, ed. Graham Macdonald and Crispin Wright, Oxford, Blackwell, 1986, pp. 284–5.

treatment of belief and desire, we should not expect these beliefs-by-courtesy to function in the same way as beliefs rightly so-called. Or maybe (2) it is a genuine belief, and not *necessarily* connected with desire; but maybe it is contingently connected with desire and we can explain why it is that, quite often, beliefs about what would be good go hand in hand with the corresponding desires. Our anti-Humean may reply that these explanations of what we say are strained compared with his own. We may reply that we find it hard to see how his could possibly be true. All this skirmishing is inconclusive.

2. THE COLLISION

Decision Theory is an intuitively convincing and well worked-out formal theory of belief, desire, and what it means to serve our desires according to our beliefs. It is of course idealized, but surely it is fundamentally right. If an anti-Humean Desire-as-Belief Thesis collides with Decision Theory, it is the Desire-as-Belief Thesis that must go.[2] So now I shall display the collision.

It is fair to take a simple case; because if our anti-Humean's thesis collides with Decision Theory only in simple cases, that is bad enough. (1) The Desire-as-Belief Thesis only applies to some desires – not including, for instance, your overpowered desire to have Neiss for a colleague. But if the thesis is right, surely it would be possible for some agent – say Frederic, that famous slave of duty – to have only the desires to which the thesis does apply. Let us suppose, for now, that Frederic is moved entirely by beliefs about what would be good; in other words, by desires necessarily connected to such beliefs. (2) Let us suppose, for now, that Frederic does not discriminate degrees of goodness. His desire that A is connected simply to his belief that A would be good – not to beliefs about just how good A would be. (3) Let us suppose that Newcomb-like problems do not

---

2 Decision Theory treats belief and desire as matters of degree. Surely they admit of degree to a considerable extent, but we must of course grant that a thoroughly quantitative treatment is an idealization. The opposite idealization also is of interest, since the truth lies in between. How does the Desire-as-Belief Thesis fare under a thoroughly *non*-quantitative treatment? John Collins has investigated that question. See his article: 'Belief, Desire, and Revision', *Mind*, 1988, pp. 333–42.

arise, so that the 'causal' way of calculating expected value does not differ from the easier 'evidential' way. (4) Let us suppose that Frederic's system of beliefs and desires evolves in accordance with Richard Jeffrey's probability kinematics; and that the Desire-as-Belief Thesis continues to hold – as befits a necessary connection – after any such evolution.

Then the Desire-as-Belief Thesis says that Frederic desires things just when he believes they would be good. Or better, since we must acknowledge that desire and belief admit of degree, he desires things just to the extent that he believes they would be good. To any ordinary proposition A, there corresponds another proposition: Å, the proposition that it would be good that A. Frederic's expected value for A, which represents the degree to which he desires that A, equals the degree to which he believes that Å. And this is so not only for Frederic as he is at present, but also for Frederic after he evolves by probability kinematics. Now, what does Decision Theory say about Frederic's case?[3]

At any moment, Frederic has a *credence* function C. It measures the degree to which he believes various propositions. A conditional credence $C(A/E)$ is defined as a quotient of unconditional credences $C(AE)/C(E)$; and whenever I write a conditional credence, I am imposing a tacit restriction to cases in which the denominator is positive. Credence obeys a principle of additivity: for any proposition A and any partition $E_1, \ldots, E_n$ (a partition being a set of mutually exclusive and jointly exhaustive propositions),

$$(1) \qquad C(A) = \Sigma_i C(AE_i) = \Sigma_i \, C(A/E_i)C(E_i).$$

At any moment, Frederic also has an (evidential) expected *value* function V. It measures the degree to which he desires that various

---

3 I follow the exposition of Decision Theory and probability kinematics in Richard C. Jeffrey, *The Logic of Decision*, 2nd edn., London, University of Chicago Press, 1983, except that, unlike Jeffrey, I split the increments that specify an exogenous change into 'distribution' and 'amount'. I speak of the bearers of credence and expected value as 'propositions'; for present purposes, it does not matter that they might be egocentric propositions, or that they might be taken as sentences.

propositions be true. Value obeys its own principle of additivity: for any proposition A and any partition $E_1, \ldots, E_n$,

$$(2) \quad V(A) = \Sigma_i V(AE_i)C(E_i/A) = \sum_i \frac{V(AE_i)C(A/E_i)C(E_i)}{C(A)}$$

Thus the value of a proposition that might come true in several alternative ways is an average of the values of those several alternatives, weighted by their conditional credences.

Now suppose that Frederic's state changes by probability kinematics, starting from an initial state given by the credence and value functions C and V. The change is given by three things. First, we have an *originating partition* $E_1, \ldots, E_n$; these are the propositions subject to exogenous change. Next, we have numbers $d_1, \ldots, d_n$ which measure the *distribution* of change over the members of this partition. Some of the d_i's are positive; these sum to 1; and when d_i is positive, the credence of E_i is raised proportionally to d_i. Other d_i's are negative; these sum to -1; and when d_i is negative, the credence of E_i is lowered proportionally to d_i. Still other d_i's may be zero, in which case the credence of the corresponding E_i's is unchanged. Finally, we have a positive number x which measures the *amount* of exogenous change. The credence of each E_i changes, up or down as the case may be, by the amount $d_i x$. All other changes in credence are driven by this exogenous change: the credence of any other proposition conditional on any one of the E_i's remains unchanged. So if C_x is the new credence function, we have $C_x(E_i) = C(E_i) + d_i x$ for each E_i; and we have $C_x(A/E_i) = C(A/E_i)$ for any A and E_i. It follows, using additivity for credences, that

$$(3) \quad C_x(A) = C(A)[1 + px], \qquad \text{where } p = \sum_i \frac{C(A/E_i)d_i}{C(A)}.$$

Likewise for Å, the proposition that it would be good that A:

$$(4) \quad C_x(\text{Å}) = C(\text{Å})[1 + qx], \qquad \text{where } q = \sum_i \frac{C(\text{Å}/E_i)d_i}{C(\text{Å})}.$$

When credences change by probability kinematics, expected values may change also, but only in response to the exogenous redistribution of credence over the E_i's. If a proposition A is compatible with several different E_i's, then the redistribution may change the conditional credences that A will come true in good or bad ways, and thereby affect the expected value of A. But this cannot happen if A is compatible with only one of the E_i's. In that case, its value remains unchanged. (Call this the *Invariance Assumption*.) In particular, the value of any conjunction AE_i remains unchanged: if V_x is the new value function, $V_x(AE_i) = V(AE_i)$. It follows, using additivity for values, that

$$(5) \quad V_x(A) = V(A)\frac{[1 + rx]}{[1 + px]}, \quad \text{where } r = \sum_i \frac{V(AE_i)C(A/E_i)d_i}{V(A)C(A)}.$$

Now take any originating partition and any distribution. Hold them fixed and let x vary. We assume that x can indeed vary, at least within some limited range: the partition and distribution never determine the exact amount of change. The Desire-as-Belief Thesis, applied to Frederic's old and new states, says that

$$(6) \qquad\qquad C(Å) = V(A),$$

$$(7) \qquad\qquad C_x(Å) = V_x(A).$$

From (4), (6), and (7) we have

$$(8) \qquad\qquad V_x(A) = V(A) [1 + qx].$$

Now we see the problem: according to (8) the expected value of A goes by a linear function of x, whereas according to (5) it goes by a quotient of linear functions. So the linear function and the quotient must somehow stay equal throughout some range of values of x. How is that possible? Here is one way: $p = 0$ and $q = r$. But then the credence of A must be constant. Here is another way: $q = 0$ and $p = r$. But then the value of A must be constant. These are the only possibilities: because from (5) and (8) we have

$$(9) \qquad\qquad pqx^2 + [p + q - r]x = 0,$$

which cannot hold for more than a single value of x unless both coefficients are zero. So a change by probability kinematics, no matter what the partition and distribution and amount, cannot change both the credence and also the expected value of any proposition A. That is to say that Frederic cannot simultaneously change both his opinion about whether A and his desire about whether A.

This is quite wrong. By imposing the Desire-as-Belief Thesis as a new constraint on Decision Theory, we have *over*constrained it, and made it exclude what can perfectly well happen. Example. Frederic knows that Stanley has often escaped the anger of the pirates by claiming to be an orphan. He now learns that Stanley is in fact no orphan. This discovery has two effects. Frederic reckons that what he can find out, the pirates also will soon find out (perhaps because he will be duty-bound to tell them himself); and so he thinks that the pirates will soon be very angry with Stanley for deceiving them. In addition, he thinks that Stanley will deserve their anger; he believes at least somewhat more than he did before that it would be good for the pirates to be angry with Stanley; and so (in his moralistic way) he desires at least somewhat more than he did before that the pirates be angry with Stanley. Where A is the proposition that the pirates will soon be angry with Stanley, the discovery that Stanley is no orphan brings both a change in the credence of A and also a change in the credence of Å and the expected value of A.

I conclude that our Anti-Humean's Desire-as-Belief Thesis is in bad trouble.

3. DOES THE ARGUMENT PROVE TOO MUCH?

You may think (as I did) that my argument against the Desire-as-Belief Thesis has to be wrong, because it proves too much. For it does not just refute the anti-Humean's grand Desire-as-Belief Thesis; it refutes also the supposition that some modest, contingent equation of desire with belief might hold in some special case. But consider this special case. Suppose Frederic single-mindedly pursues one goal: that the proposition G be true. (For instance, G might be the proposition that he never ever fails in his duty. The example requires that his goal is perfection – a miss is as good as a mile.) Then, scaling V to the unit interval, we have that for any A, $V(AG) = 1$ and $V(A\bar{G}) = 0$, so

49

(10) $V(A) = V(AG)C(G/A) + V(A\bar{G})C(\bar{G}/A) = C(G/A)$.

Likewise for any later state of Frederic given by C_x and V_x,

(11) $$V_x(A) = C_x(G/A).$$

For this special case, we have managed at least to equate desire with *conditional* credence. It may seem that we can do better. For any proposition A, let Å be the proposition that A conduces to G: $A \rightarrow G$, in some appropriate sense of the conditional arrow. It seems that Frederic's desire that A should always equal his degree of belief that A conduces to achieving his goal G. And not just in his present state given by C and V, but also in any new state given by some C_x and V_x. So we get back the supposedly refuted Anti-Humean equations,

(12) $$V(A) = C(A \rightarrow G) = C(Å),$$

(13) $$V_x(A) = C_x(A \rightarrow G) = C_x(Å),$$

this time not from some grand Desire-as-Belief Thesis but just from plausible-sounding assumptions about the case of the single-minded Frederic. Why not?

Answer: because, *pace* intuition, an 'appropriate sense of the arrow' just does not exist. Taking (10) and (12) together, or (11) and (13), we find ourselves dealing with the dreaded 'probability conditional', a supposed connective which makes probabilities of conditionals equal the corresponding conditional probabilities:

(14) $$C(A \rightarrow G) = C(G/A),$$

(15) $$C_x(A \rightarrow G) = C_x(G/A).$$

If we had a probability conditional, we could uphold a modest equation of desire with belief, at least in this special case; we have seen why even this modest equation collides with Decision Theory; therefore we do not have a probability conditional. That was known already: certain trivial cases aside, we cannot give a sense to the arrow such that (14) will hold for all C, A, and G. Even if we fix C, and fix an originating partition and distribution, we still cannot give a sense to the arrow such that (15) holds for all x, A, and G.

You might protest that we need nothing so ambitious. For present purposes, the only conditionals that matter are those that have the one fixed consequent G that specifies Frederic's single goal. It is enough if we can fix C, fix the partition and distribution, and also fix G, and then make (14) and (15) hold for all x and A. But what our present argument shows, when applied to the case of the single-minded Frederic, is that we cannot even do that well. In view of earlier negative results against the probability conditional, that should come as no big surprise.[4]

4. TWO SIMPLIFICATIONS REMOVED

I said that if our anti-Humean's thesis collides with Decision Theory only in simple cases, that would be bad enough. Then I went on to simplify by supposing that Frederic was moved entirely by desires to which the thesis applies, and that he did not discriminate degrees of goodness. You might doubt that trouble in this very special case really is bad enough to matter, if it does not arise in less peculiar cases as well. I disagree; but rather than dispute the question, we can do the calculation over with the two simplifications removed.

Suppose, then, that in addition to the component V of expected value that obeys the Desire-as-Belief Thesis, there is also an 'ordinary' component V_o that does not. The total value of a proposition A is

---

4 For these negative results, see my 'Probabilities of Conditionals and Conditional Probabilities', *The Philosophical Review*, 1976, pp. 297–315; and 'Probabilities of Conditionals and Conditional Probabilities II', *The Philosophical Review*, 1986, pp. 581–9 (with errata noted in the following two issues).

The present argument is very similar to a direct proof that we cannot make (14) hold for fixed C, fixed partition and distribution, and all x, A, and G. That proof, restricted to the case of two-membered originating partitions, appears in the second of the papers just cited.

For the direct proof, we look only at a single conditional – generality over consequents is not much used. But it is used in this way: since we are free to choose G, we may choose it as the disjunction of those members E_i of the originating partition for which d_i is positive. That choice affords a subsidiary argument to eliminate the case that q = 0 and p = r. With G fixed in advance, on the other hand, we can assume nothing about how G is related to the originating partition.

$V(A) + V_o(A)$. Assume still that total value obeys additivity, and also obeys the rule that when a change originates in $E_1, \ldots, E_n$ the value of any conjunction AE_i is unchanged. Let us make the same assumptions for V_o: they would hold if V_o were the whole of total value, and why should the behaviour of V_o change just because we add another component to it? Then V, regardless of whether it is the whole or merely a component of total value, also obeys the two assumptions. Therefore (5) still holds.

Now suppose that Frederic thinks of goodness as something that admits of degree. Let $g_1, \ldots, g_m$ be the degrees of goodness that he discriminates. (If you do not want to assume that there are only finitely many, let our sums be infinite and our probabilities infinitesimal, or switch to integrals and probability densities.) Let $\overset{\circ}{A}_j$ be the proposition that it would be good to degree g_j that A. Instead of (4) we have for each of the degrees

$$(16) \quad C_x(\overset{\circ}{A}_j) = C(\overset{\circ}{A}_j) [1 + q_j x], \qquad \text{where } q_j = \sum_i \frac{C(\overset{\circ}{A}_j/E_i)d_i}{C(\overset{\circ}{A}_j)}.$$

The Desire-as-Belief Thesis now takes the form

$$(17) \qquad\qquad \sum_j C(\overset{\circ}{A}_j)g_j = V(A),$$

$$(18) \qquad\qquad \sum_j C_x(\overset{\circ}{A}_j)g_j = V_x(A).$$

Instead of (8), (16)–(18) give us

$$(19) \quad V_x(A) = V(A)[1 + qx], \qquad \text{where now } q = \sum_j \frac{C(\overset{\circ}{A}_j)q_j g_j}{V(A)},$$

and from (5) and (19) we have (9) as before, except for the redefinition of q just noted. So again there are two alternatives. Either $p = 0$ and $q = r$, in which case the credence of A must be constant; or else $q = 0$ and $p = r$, in which case the component of the value of A that obeys the Desire-as-Belief Thesis must be constant. That is to say that Frederic cannot simultaneously change both his opinion about whether A and the component of desire that derives from his opinions about how good it would be that A. Again this is wrong; and for an example of what it wrongly excludes, we need only modify the story of Frederic. Let Frederic now have an ordinary desire that the pirates not be angry with Stanley; and let him discriminate at least two degrees of goodness, one for no anger and one for deserved anger.

5. INVARIANCE DEFENDED

When he sees how his Desire-as-Belief Thesis collides with standard Decision Theory, our anti-Humean might well hope to avert the collision by some not-too-radical amendment to Decision Theory. One assumption in particular is the main candidate for discarding. Recall how we derived (5), which specified how expected values change in response to an exogenous redistribution of credence over a partition $E_1, \ldots, E_n$. First we assumed Invariance: no change in the value of any proposition that is compatible with just one of the E_i's, and therefore no change in the value of any conjunction AE_i. Then we used additivity for expected values to calculate the new value of a proposition A.

Let our anti-Humean propose to discard Invariance. This blocks our derivation of (5), and thereby blocks the collision between the Desire-as-Belief Thesis and Decision Theory. What is more, this is not just blind tinkering. It seems to make sense by the anti-Humean's lights. There are *two* ways, so he says, that redistribution of credence may change the value of a proposition A. One way is that it may change the conditional credences of the various AE_i's, some of which may be better than others. The other way is that it may change the values of the AE_i's themselves. For each AE_i, he says, we have the proposition that it would be good that AE_i; and why should not the redistribution change the credences of these propositions? Invariance says that only the first kind of change happens, never the second. Why should he accept that?

So far, so good; but discarding Invariance turns out to lead to an unintelligible consequence. It is therefore not an acceptable way to rescue the Desire-as-Belief Thesis.

We note first that it is impossible to discard Invariance only as applied to the AE_i's themselves. For each AE_i may be further partitioned into subcases $AE_iF_1, \ldots, AE_iF_k$, in such a way that each of these subcases is maximally specific in all respects relevant to its value. Since the ratios of probability between the subcases of any single AE_i do not change, the value of AE_i is determined by the values of its subcases. So in order to discard Invariance for AE_i as a whole, we have to discard Invariance also for at least some of the subcases. This means that a change in credence will affect the value of some proposition AE_iF_h that is maximally specific in all respects relevant to its value. How is that possible?

If AE_iF_h were maximally specific merely in all 'factual' respects relevant to its value, and if the Desire-as-Belief Thesis were true, then it would be no surprise if a change in belief changed our minds about how good it would be that AE_iF_h, and thereby affected the value of AE_iF_h. But the subcase was supposed to be maximally specific in *all* relevant respects – and that includes all relevant propositions about what would and would not be good. The subcase has a maximally specific hypothesis about what would be good built right into it. So in assigning it a value, we do not need to consult our opinions about what is good. We just follow the built-in hypothesis.

(Example. How good would it be if, first, pain were the sole good, and second, we were all about to be in excruciating and everlasting pain? – I have to say that this would be good, and so I value the case highly. My opinion that in fact pain is no good does not affect my valuing of the hypothetical case in which, *ex hypothesi*, pain is good. My opinion does cause me to give the case negligible credence, of course, but that is different from affecting the value.)

It is unintelligible how a shift in opinions about what is good could affect the value of any of the maximally specific AE_iF_h's, since these have hypotheses about what's good already built into them. But if not, then the AE_iF_h's should obey Invariance: there is no way left for a change of credence (originating in $E_1, \ldots, E_n$) to affect their value. It follows that the AE_i's also obey Invariance.

6

Desire as belief II

1. REASON AND PASSION

Hume wrote that "we speak not strictly and philosophically when we talk of the combat of passion and of reason. Reason is, and ought only to be, the slave of the passions, and can never pretend to any other office than to serve and obey them" (*Treatise*, Bk. II, Pt. III, Sect. III). What did he mean?

In the first place, Hume's "passions" are sometimes none too passionate. He speaks of some passions as "calm". We would do best to speak of all "passion", calm and otherwise, as "desire".

In the second place, we call someone "reasonable" in part because his desires are moderate and fair-minded. But when we do, I suppose we speak not strictly and philosophically. Strictly speaking, I take it that reason is the faculty in charge of regulating belief. And so I read Hume as if he had said that belief is the slave of desire. Our actions do, or they ought to, serve our desires according to our beliefs. More precisely, taking account of the fact that both belief and desire admit of degree, and not begrudging the usual idealizations that make the topic tractable, our actions serve our subjective expected values according to our subjective degrees of belief. For short: they serve our values according to our credences.

Values and credences belong to propositions: classes of maximally specific possibilities (perhaps egocentric and tensed). The value of a

First published in *Mind* **105** (1996), 303–313. Reprinted by permission of Oxford University Press.

proposition A, written V(A), is a real number; the credence of A, C(A), is a non-negative real number; and the credence of the necessary proposition, C(I), is 1. (We would do well to let these values and credences be nonstandard real numbers so that, for instance, the propositions corresponding to the maximally specific possibilities – call these point-propositions – might all get infinitesimal credence. For there well might be infinitely many point-propositions.) We assume the usual rules of finite (or *-finite) additivity for value and credence: when $A_1 \ldots$ are a partition of A,

$$V(A) = \Sigma_i V(A_i) C(A_i/A)$$
$$C(A) = \Sigma_i C(A_i)$$

where $C(X/Y)$ abbreviates the quotient $C(XY)/C(Y)$. The additivity rule for value shows how belief serves desire: it generates an expected value for the less specific proposition A out of the values for the more specific cases $A_1, \ldots$. Nobody doubts that belief and desire are entangled to this extent, whatever further entanglements there may or may not be.

(A famous difficulty need not concern us here. Suppose a certain action would serve as an effective means to your ends. Yet at the same time it would constitute evidence – evidence available to you in no other way – that you are predestined inescapably to some dreadful misfortune. Should you perform that action? – Yes; your destiny is not a consideration, since that is outside your control. Do you desire to perform it? – No; you want good news, not bad. Since our topic here is not choiceworthiness but desire, and since the two diverge, we adopt an "evidential" conception of expected value, on which the value of the useful action that brings bad news is low. Choiceworthiness is governed by a different, "causal", conception of expected value.[1])

As an empiricist, Hume thinks that passions are where you find them. Desires are contingent. It is not contrary to reason – still less is it downright impossible! – to have peculiar and unusual desires, or to lack commonplace ones. It may be contrary to the laws of human

1 See, *inter alia*, Lewis (1981).

nature, but those laws themselves are contingent regularities. Likewise there are no necessary connections between desire and belief. Any values can go with any credences. Or at any rate – remembering the entanglement of credences in the rule of additivity for values – any values for the point-propositions can go with any credences.

Neither is the rule of additivity for credences unHumean, even though it connects credences necessarily with other credences. By way of professing innocence, we could say roughly this: the credences of point-propositions, at any rate, are not necessarily connected. Any point-credences can go with any pattern of other point-credences. As for other propositions, their credences are mere patterns – namely, sums – of point-credences; and the necessary connection between a pattern and its elements is surely not a necessary connection between distinct existences.

(This is still not quite right. We chose to scale the credences in such a way that all the point-credences sum to 1. Likewise values are somehow scaled, though I had no need to say how. Either we must tolerate the necessities that arise from arbitrary choices of scale, or we must represent credences and values in a way that somehow abstracts from arbitrary choices of scaling. This need not concern us further.)

Thus Humeanism takes point-values and point-credences to be "loose and separate", unconstrained by necessary connections. If there are universally shared desires, that is a contingent matter. If there are universal correlations between certain beliefs and desires, that too is a contingent matter. Someone might have no desire at all for joy, knowledge, or love. Someone might believe just what you and I believe, and still have no desire at all for joy, knowledge, or love. Indeed, someone might believe just what G. E. Moore believed about the simple, non-natural properties of these things and still have no desire for them.

2. HOW HUMEANISM MIGHT BE FALSE

You might fear that anti-Humean moral science would have to rest on anti-Humean metaphysics of modality. The necessity whereby we cannot lack certain desires, or whereby our desires cannot fail to be suitably aligned with our beliefs, would then be necessity *de re*. It would be like the necessity that theorists of "strong laws" discern in the laws of nature, or in the alignment between the laws of nature and certain remarkable relations of universals.[2]

But there is an alternative. The necessity that supposedly governs desire might be a merely verbal, or conceptual, necessity. So those of us who follow Hume unswervingly in rejecting *de re* necessary connections in nature – "strong laws" or whatnot – still can afford to be open-minded about anti-Humean moral science.

It is a familiar idea that theoretical terms introduced in scientific theories denote the occupants of roles set forth in the term-introducing theory. Mass is that which occupies – perfectly, or near enough – the mass-role set forth in classical mechanics. Phlogiston would have been that which occupied the phlogiston-role set forth in obsolete chemistry. Now that we think there is nothing that does what phlogiston was said to do, or even comes close, we conclude that there is no such thing as phlogiston.

It is also a familiar idea that tacitly known folk theories may introduce terms in much the same way that scientific theories do; and, in particular, that our ordinary mental vocabulary consists of the theoretical terms of commonsensical "folk psychology".[3] Belief and desire, among others, are the states that occupy certain folk-psychological roles. And again, when it comes to occupying a role and thereby deserving a name, near enough is good enough. Folk psychology needn't be flawless!

A less familiar, but promising, idea is that the "theory theory" applies also to our ethical vocabulary (Railton 1992; Jackson and Pettit 1995). Schisms within folk ethics are of course an obstacle. But perhaps there is more common ground than meets the eye of us professional controversialists. Or perhaps there is a trajectory toward greater consensus, and we can take the term-introducing theory to be the not-yet-seen (and perhaps never-to-be-seen) limit of that trajectory. Or if all else fails we can go relativist: there are as many

2 See Armstrong (1983) for a defence of one such theory and discussion of others.
3 See, *inter alia*, Lewis (1972).

58

disambiguations of our ethical terms as there are irreconcilably conflicting versions of folk ethics.

Now suppose that folk moral science is an inseparable mish-mash of psychology and ethics. Its theoretical vocabulary is in part psychological, in part ethical. Its tacitly known postulates include some that say what is universally desired, or that say how our desires are aligned with our beliefs. Both psychological and ethical vocabulary appear in these postulates. Further, these postulates specify an important part of the theoretical roles that define theoretical terms. Conforming to them plays a big part in determining whether states occupy the roles, and deserve the names, of belief and desire.

The upshot might be that if someone disdained joy, knowledge, and love; or if he did so despite believing just what you and I believe; or if he did so despite believing just what Moore believed about the simple, non-natural properties; or if . . . ; then his states would not after all occupy the roles and deserve the names of belief and desire (and disdain). The description of the case is subtly contradictory. That is how Humean moral science might be false, and how some anti-Humean theory of Desire by Necessity or Desire as Belief might be true; and without benefit of any *de re* necessity in nature.

I understand the hypothesis that Humeanism might be false in the way just explained. But I do not believe it. For when I consider stories in which supposedly necessary desires go missing, or in which supposedly necessary alignments of desire with belief go haywire, I find I am not at all inclined to doubt that the so-called "beliefs" and "desires" in the story are rightly so called.

(It may be otherwise with still weirder psychological fantasies. When Anscombe tells of the man who desires a saucer of mud, though he has no idea what would be good about having it, the story does seem not altogether intelligible; likewise when Goodman tells the story of the man who expects the future to resemble the past only in respect of gruesome disjunctive properties (Anscombe 1958; Goodman 1955). But what sort of unintelligibility am I detecting? Is it semantic anomaly, the incorrect applying of names to things that could not deserve those names, as when ideas are said to be green? Or is it rather the frustration of my best efforts at empathetic understanding? I do not know. I do not know how to find out.)

So I am doubtful about all versions of anti-Humeanism. But my doubts rest on intuitions that might be easy to controvert. And besides, these theories offer a rich reward: objective ethics. If there are some things we desire by necessity, we surely would want to say that these things were objectively desirable. Or if there were some propositions, belief or disbelief in which was necessarily connected with desire, some of them presumably would be true; then we surely would want to say that the true ones were the objective truth about ethical reality.

Why care about objective value or ethical reality? The sanction is that if you do not, your inner states will fail to deserve folk-theoretical names. Not a threat that will strike terror into the hearts of the wicked! But who ever thought that philosophy could replace the hangman?

3. DESIRE BY NECESSITY

We can go no further talking about anti-Humeanism in general. It is time to examine various versions. A systematic survey of all possible versions, including versions not yet invented, would be nice. But we shall have to settle for less.

Desire by Necessity is a comparatively simple and unproblematic version. In its simplest form, it says that necessarily and regardless of one's credence distribution, certain point-values must be high and the rest low. Scale these as 1 and 0. Let G be the union of point-propositions with necessarily high value: the objectively desirable point-propositions − for short, the *good* ones. Then for any proposition A and any credence distribution C (provided that C(A) is positive, a restriction we shall henceforth leave tacit),

$$V(A) = C(G/A).$$

Refinements are obvious, but we need not consider them in detail. (1) We could have more than just two degrees of objective value for point-propositions. (2) We could distinguish different components of the value of a point-proposition, pertaining to different objective values. (3) We could allow contingent, Humean desires alongside the necessary, unHumean ones − a half-Humean mixed theory.

4. DESIRE AS BELIEF REVISITED

We turn next to versions of anti-Humeanism on which desires are said to be contingent, but necessarily aligned with suitable beliefs.[4] These form a more varied family of theories. One of them, at least, is definitely untenable. Others are not what they seem to be. Maybe some tenable version of anti-Humeanism falls unproblematically into this class. But if so, I do not know what it is.

In the paper to which this one is a sequel, I examined and refuted one especially simple theory in this family (Lewis 1988). (Would-be anti-Humeans hastened to inform me that the refuted theory was but one possible version of anti-Humeanism – something I myself had said at the outset!) I shall call this simple theory "Desire as Belief" – for short, DAB – without any qualifying adjective. DAB says that there is a certain function (call it the *"halo" function*) that assigns to any proposition A a proposition Å ("A-halo") such that, necessarily, for any credence distribution C,

(DAB) $V(A) = C(Å)$.

We might want to say that Å is the proposition that A is, or would be, objectively desirable – that is, good. Necessarily, and regardless of one's credence distribution, one must desire A exactly to the extent that one believes it to be good.

This version of anti-Humeanism is untenable. Except in trivial cases, it collapses into contradiction. Credences and expected values respond differently to redistribution of credence with point-values held constant. Suppose the DAB equation holds under a given credence distribution; it will cease to hold under almost all redistributions of credence.

The refutation by redistribution of credence given in my previous paper was needlessly complicated.[5] To make it simple, and at the

---

4 Instead of speaking as I do of desires necessarily connected to beliefs, you might prefer to speak of beliefs that function as if they were desires; or of states that occupy a double role, being at once beliefs and desires. I take these descriptions to be equivalent.

5 See Arló Costa, Collins, and Levi (1995) for a refutation simpler than my previous one, but somewhat different from the one given below.

same time to make it obvious where the blame falls for the collapse, we note that DAB can be equivalently restated as a pair of equations: necessarily, for any A and C,

$$(DACB) \qquad V(A) = C(Å/A)$$
$$(IND) \qquad C(Å/A) = C(Å).$$

To derive DACB, we recall that DAB is supposed to continue to hold under redistributions of credence, and we redistribute by conditionalizing on A.[6] (That is, we put all the credence on point-propositions within A, but we do not alter point-values or ratios of point-credences within A.) IND follows immediately from DAB and DACB. Conversely, DAB follows from DACB and IND.

Whereas DAB equated values to unconditional credences, DACB equates them to conditional credences. But according to IND this difference does not matter, because the unconditional and conditional credences are always equal. Å and A are probabilistically independent with respect to C, and they remain independent under any redistribution of credence (provided that the credence of A remains positive so that the conditional credence does not go undefined).

Now it is IND, unabetted by DACB, that leads to contradiction. Take any A and C such that C(A) and C(Å/A) are positive, and such that C(A) and C(Å/A) are less than 1. If there are no such A and C, the case is trivial. (We shall take a closer look at the trivial cases in §5 below.)

6 I assume here that *one* way to revise credences is by conditionalizing, and that DAB will continue to hold after any such revision; I do not assume that credences may never be revised in any other way. Nor, *pace* Graham Oddie, was it "a fundamental assumption" (1994, p. 466) of my previous refutation that revisions of credence must invariably go by conditionalizing; or even that they must invariably go by the sort of generalized conditionalizing that Richard Jeffrey has described under the name of "probability kinematics". Maybe Oddie is right that there are other ways for credences to be revised, at least when they are the credences of tensed propositions. (Before I turned out the light, I saw that it was just minutes before midnight. In the course of a long and sleepless night, I undergo a redistribution of credence from the proposition that it is now before midnight to the proposition that it is now after midnight. It is far from obvious that this revision goes by probability kinematics, let alone by conditionalizing.) But that fact, if fact it be, does nothing to rescue DAB from either my present or my previous refutation.

It follows from IND and our stipulations on A and C that all four of the propositions (A∧Å), (A∧¬Å), (¬A∧Å), and (¬A∧¬Å) have positive credence. Then there are various redistributions of credence, by conditionalizing and otherwise, that will make IND go from true to false. (For instance, if we redistribute credence from the shaded into the unshaded region while leaving ratios of point-credences in the unshaded region unchanged – at the extreme, if we conditionalize on (A∨Å) – then C(Å) increases while C(Å/A) stays the same.) This contradicts the claim that IND is preserved under redistributions. DAB can hold only in trivial cases. This completes our refutation.

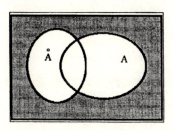

5. DESIRE AS CONDITIONAL BELIEF

It was IND that did the dirty work. DACB had no hand in it. So the obvious line of retreat, after the downfall of DAB, is to keep DACB and junk IND. Exactly this theory of Desire as Conditional Belief has been defended by Huw Price (1989). But not in quite the way that I have presented it: Price presents DACB not as a consequence or fragment of DAB, but as a superior rival to it.

Superior in two ways. In the first place, DACB is immune to refutation by redistribution of credence. With my previous complicated refutation, this took some proving; as for the present simpler refutation, we need only recall that the contradiction was derived not from DACB but from IND.

In the second place, Price argues that "whenever it makes a difference, we should assess a possible outcome under the hypothesis that it is the actual outcome" (1989, p. 122). Well, not always. Not, for instance, when thinking how pleased we should be that a certain undesired outcome has turned out not to be actual. So I question

Price's second reason for preferring DACB to DAB. No matter – his first reason is reason enough.

To understand DACB better, we must learn what it is trying to tell us about the "halo" function: the mapping from A to Å.

> *Initial Lemma.* Whenever C(AB) is positive, C(Å/AB) = V(AB) = C(B̊/AB). *Proof.* DACB continues to hold under redistributions of credence, and in particular under redistributions by conditionalizing on A or on B. Conditionalizing on B turns C(Å/A) into C(Å/AB) and V(A) into V(AB). Conditionalizing on A turns V(B) into V(AB) and C(B̊/B) into C(B̊/AB). So both our new equations come from instances of DACB by conditionalizing.

> *Upward Lemma.* When A is nonempty, and I is the necessary proposition, (Å∧A) = (I̊∧A). *Proof.* If not, we could distribute credence in such a way as to make C(A) positive, and also make C(Å∧A) and C(I̊∧A) unequal. That would make C(Å/AI) and C(I̊/AI) unequal, thereby falsifying an instance of the Initial Lemma.

> *Downward Lemma.* When W is a point-proposition, V(W) = 1 if W is included in I̊, V(W) = 0 otherwise. *Proof.* Let C be any distribution that gives W positive credence. Taking A as W and B as I, and dropping I whenever it appears as a conjunct, the right-hand equation of our Initial Lemma gives us that V(W) = C(I̊/W). If W is included in I̊, C(I̊/W) = 1. If not, then since W is a point-proposition, W is included in ¬I̊; in which case C(I̊/W) = 0.

Desire as Conditional Belief is now unmasked. It is not, despite superficial appearances, a theory of contingent desire necessarily aligned with belief. Rather, it is the very same theory of Desire by Necessity that we have already examined – except that the union of necessarily desired point-propositions, formerly called G, is now renamed I̊. Point-propositions have value 1 if they fall within I̊, value 0 otherwise. So for any A and C, if C(A) is positive, we have V(A) = C(I̊/A).

(When A is a proposition other than I, we did not settle, cannot

64

settle, and need not settle exactly what proposition Å is. All that matters to the value of A is the part of Å that lies within A; and within A, Å and Ĭ coincide. Å might contain all, some, or none of the point-propositions that lie outside A. On that question, DACB plays it safe by giving us no information − unlike DAB, which gave us more information than consistency would allow!)

(We noted that if there are no A and C such that C(A) and C(Å/A) are positive, and such that C(A) and C(Å/A) are less than 1, then the case is trivial. We can now characterize the trivial cases. They are those in which, no matter how we choose A and C, we cannot give positive credence to all three of ¬A, (A∧Å), and (A∧¬Å). There are three ways that could happen. (1) The space might be too small: we might not have three different point-propositions, but only one or two. (2) Ĭ might be empty, giving all propositions a value of 0. (3) Ĭ might be I, giving all propositions a value of 1.)

6. DESIRE AS BELIEF RESTRICTED

We could keep the original DAB equation, but allow it to apply only to point-propositions: for all C and W

(DABR)   If W is a point-proposition and C(W) is positive,
$$V(W) = C(\mathring{W})$$

Conditionalizing on W we have

(DACBR) $V(W) = C(\mathring{W}/W) = \begin{cases} 1 \text{ if W is included in } \mathring{W} \\ 0 \text{ otherwise} \end{cases}$

From DABR and DACBR we have

(INDR) $C(\mathring{W}) = C(\mathring{W}/W) = \begin{cases} 1 \text{ if W is included in } \mathring{W} \\ 0 \text{ otherwise} \end{cases}$

INDR, unlike IND, does not collapse into contradiction. Instead, since it holds for all credence distributions, we have

$$\mathring{W} = \begin{cases} I \text{ if } V(W) = 1 \\ \varnothing \text{ if } V(W) = 0. \end{cases}$$

65

So we're back once more to a disguised version of Desire by Necessity, with a new way to characterize the values of point-propositions in terms of the restricted halo function.

7. INCONSTANCY

Hitherto we have hoped for one fixed halo function that would continue to satisfy the conditions we imposed on it under all redistributions of credence. We have not supposed that each agent might have his own personal halo function in the same way that he has his own personal credence and value functions. But if instead we only require that for any given credence and value functions C and V, there exists a halo function chosen ad hoc to satisfy the desired conditions with respect to that particular pair of C and V, then our task is almost trivial.[7] We need only require that C and V have the right ranges of values: for any A there exists some B such that $V(A) = C(B)$. (This means that values must be bounded above and below, and must be suitably scaled.) Then, appealing to the Axiom of Choice, there is indeed a halo function such that for all A, $V(A) = C(\mathring{A})$.

It's too easy, and no anti-Humean should celebrate such an easy victory. The DAB equation holds not in virtue of any interesting relationship between a desired and a believed proposition, but only in virtue of what it takes for a proposition to deserve the name "Å" – and what it takes is nothing more or less than the right credence, one that equals $V(A)$. There is nothing at all anti-Humean about this little trick. Further, there is nothing that should make us want to say that Å is the proposition that A is objectively good.

8. CONCLUSION

We have examined four theories that sought to implement the anti-Humean idea that desires and beliefs are necessarily aligned. One

---

7 John Collins has noted that if we let the inconstant halo function depend only on V and not also on C, our task may not be so trivial. I have no results to offer about this version of Inconstancy; except only that even if it succeeded it would not deliver objective ethics.

collapses into either triviality or contradiction. Two more collapse into Desire by Necessity – a form of anti-Humeanism, sure enough, but not the right form of anti-Humeanism. Another is not really anti-Humean at all. We could keep trying, but the prospects of success have begun to look dim.

REFERENCES

Anscombe. G. E. M. 1958: *Intention*. Oxford: Blackwell.

Arló Costa, H., Collins, J. and Levi, I. 1995: "Desire-as-Belief Implies Opinionation or Indifference." *Analysis* 55, pp. 2–5.

Armstrong, D. M. 1983: *What is a Law of Nature?* Cambridge: Cambridge University Press.

Goodman, N. 1995: "The New Riddle of Induction", in Goodman: *Fact, Fiction, and Forecast*. Cambridge, MA: Harvard University Press, 1955.

Hume, D. 1739/40: *A Treatise on Human Nature*. L. A. Selby-Bigge (ed.), Oxford: Oxford University Press (1888).

Jackson, F. and Pettit, P. 1995: "Moral Functionalism and Moral Motivation". *The Philosophical Quarterly* 45, pp. 451–72.

Lewis, D. 1972: "Psychophysical and Theoretical Identifications". *Australasian Journal of Philosophy* 50, pp. 249–58.

———1981: "Causal Decision Theory". *Australasian Journal of Philosophy* 59, pp. 5–30.

———1988: "Desire as Belief". *Mind* 97, pp. 323–32 (reprinted in this volume as Chapter 5).

Oddie, G. 1994: "Harmony, Purity, Truth". *Mind* 103, pp. 451–72.

Price, H. 1989: "Defending Desire-as-Belief". *Mind* 98, pp. 119–27.

Railton, P. 1992: "Nonfactualism About Normative Discourse". *Philosophy and Phenomenological Research* 53, pp. 961–8.

7

Dispositional theories of value

Roughly, values are what we are disposed to value. Less roughly, we have this schematic definition: *Something of the appropriate category is a value if and only if we would be disposed, under ideal conditions, to value it.* It raises five questions. (1) What is the favourable attitude of 'valuing'? (2) What is the 'appropriate category' of things? (3) What conditions are 'ideal' for valuing? (4) Who are 'we'? (5) What is the modal status of the equivalence?

By answering these questions, I shall advance a version of the dispositional theory of value. I begin by classifying the theory that is going to emerge. First, it is naturalistic: it advances an analytic definition of value. It is naturalistic in another sense too: it fits into a naturalistic metaphysics. It invokes only such entities and distinctions as we need to believe in anyway, and needs nothing extra before it can deliver the values. It reduces facts about value to facts about our psychology.

The theory is subjective: it analyses value in terms of our attitudes. But it is not subjective in the narrower sense of implying that value is a topic on which whatever we may think is automatically true, or on which there is no truth at all. Nor does it imply that if we had been differently disposed, different things would have been values. Not quite – but it comes too close for comfort.

First published in *The Proceedings of the Aristotelian Society*, Supplementary Volume 63 (1989), 113–137. Reprinted by courtesy of the Editor of the Aristotelian Society: © 1989.

The theory is internalist: it makes a conceptual connection between value and motivation. But it offers no guarantee that everyone must be motivated to pursue whatever is of value; still less, whatever he judges to be of value. The connection is defeasible, in more ways than one.

The theory is cognitive: it allows us to seek and to gain knowledge about what is valuable. This knowledge is *a posteriori* knowledge of contingent matters of fact. It could in principle be gained by psychological experimentation. But it is more likely to be gained by difficult exercises of imagination, carried out perhaps in a philosopher's or a novelist's armchair.

The theory is conditionally relativist: it does not exclude the possibility that there may be no such thing as value *simpliciter*, just value for this or that population. But it does not imply relativity, not even when taken together with what we know about the diversity of what people actually value. It leaves the question open.

Is it a form of realism about value? – That question is hard. I leave it for the end.

What is 'valuing'? It is some sort of mental state, directed toward that which is valued. It might be a feeling, or a belief, or a desire. (Or a combination of these; or something that is two or three of them at once; or some fourth thing. But let us set these hypotheses aside, and hope to get by with something simpler.[1])

1 The most interesting of the hypotheses here set aside is that an attitude of valuing might be a 'besire': a special kind of attitude that is both a belief and a desire and that motivates us, without benefit of other desires, in just the way that ordinary desires do. (Or it might be an attitude that is not identical with, but rather is necessarily connected with, a belief and a desire; or an attitude that is not strictly speaking either a belief or a desire, but is just like each apart from also being like the other.) Valuing X might be the besire that is at once a belief that X is good and a desire for X; where *goodness* just means that property, whatever it may be, such that a belief that X has it may double as a desire for X.

But we should hesitate to believe in besires, because integrating them into the folk psychology of belief and desire turns out to be no easy thing. On the difficulty with instrumental besires, see my 'Desire as Belief' (reprinted in this volume as Chapter 5) and John Collins, 'Belief, Desire and Revision', *Mind* 97 (1988), pp. 323–342: when a system of attitudes changes under the impact of new

A feeling? – Evidently not, because the feelings we have when we value things are too diverse.

A belief? What belief? You might say that one values something just by believing it to be a value. That is circular. We might hide the circularity by maneuvering between near-synonyms, but it is better to face it at once. If so, we have that being a value is some property such that something has it iff we are disposed, under ideal conditions, to believe that the thing has it. In other words, such that we are disposed, under ideal conditions, to be right about whether something has it. That is not empty; but it tells us little, since doubtless there are many properties about which we are disposed to be right.

Further, if valuing something just meant having a certain belief about it, then it seems that there would be no conceptual reason why valuing is a *favourable* attitude. We might not have favoured the things we value. We might have opposed them, or been entirely indifferent.

So we turn to desires. But we'd better not say that valuing something is just the same as desiring it.[2] That may do for some of us: those who manage, by strength of will or by good luck, to desire exactly as they desire to desire. But not all of us are so fortunate. The thoughtful addict may desire his euphoric daze, but not value it. Even apart from all the costs and risks, he may hate himself for desiring something he values not at all. It is a desire he wants very much to be rid of.[3] He desires his high, but he does not desire to desire it, and in fact he desires not to desire it. He does not desire an unaltered,

information, beliefs evolve in one way and (instrumental) desires in another. A besire, trying to go both ways at once, would be torn apart. Intrinsic besires – a better candidate for the attitude of valuing – face a different difficulty. At least in miniature examples, they turn out to be altogether impervious to change under the impact of experience. Not bad, you might think – why *should* experience change our mind about what's intrinsically good? The trouble is that the result applies not only to perceptual experience but also to experience of moral reflection, 'intuiting', and the like.

2 Often in decision theory and economics, 'value' does just mean a measure of desiredness, and all desires count equally. But it's not the sense we want here.

3 On desires to desire, see Harry Frankfurt, 'Freedom of the Will and the Concept of a Person', *Journal of Philosophy* 68 (1971), pp. 5–20; and Richard C. Jeffrey, 'Preference Among Preferences', *Journal of Philosophy* 71 (1974), pp. 377–391.

mundane state of consciousness, but he does desire to desire it. We conclude that he does not value what he desires, but rather he values what he desires to desire.

Can we do better by climbing the ladder to desires of ever-higher order? What someone desires to desire to desire might conceivably differ from what he does desire to desire. Or. . . . Should we perhaps say that what a person really values is given by his highest order of desire, whatever order that is? – It is hard to tell whether this would really be better, because it is hard to imagine proper test cases.[4] Further, if we go for the highest order, we automatically rule out the case of someone who desires to *value* differently than he does, yet this case is not obviously impossible. I hesitantly conclude we do better to stop on the second rung: valuing is just desiring to desire.

Recall G. E. Moore: 'To take, for instance, one of the more plausible, because one of the more complicated, of such proposed definitions, it may easily be thought, at first sight, that to be good may mean to be that which we desire to desire'.[5] Of course he does not endorse the definition, but at least he does it the honour of choosing it for his target to display the open question argument. I don't say that everything we value is good; but I do echo Moore to this extent. I say that to be *valued* by us means to be that which we desire to desire. Then to be a value – to be good, near enough – means to be that which we are disposed, under ideal conditions, to desire to desire. Still more complicated, still more plausible. It allows, as it should, that under less-than-ideal conditions we may wrongly value what is not really good. As for Moore's open question, we shall face that later.

We have this much of an 'internalist' conceptual connection

---

4 It is comparatively easy to imagine *instrumental* third-order desires. Maybe our addict wishes he could like himself better than he does; and not by doing away with his addiction, which he takes to be impossible, but by becoming reconciled to it and accepting himself as he is. Or maybe he just fears that his second-order desire not to be addicted will someday lead him to suffer the pains of withdrawal. Either way, he wants to be rid of his second-order desire not to be addicted, but he wants it not for itself but as a means to some end. This is irrelevant: presumably it is intrinsic, not instrumental, desiring that is relevant to what someone values.

5 *Principia Ethica* (Cambridge University Press, 1903) Section 13.

between value and motivation. If something is a value, and if someone is one of the appropriate 'we', and if he is in ideal conditions, then it follows that he will value it. And if he values it, and if he desires as he desires to desire, then he will desire it. And if he desires it, and if this desire is not outweighed by other conflicting desires, and if he has the instrumental rationality to do what serves his desires according to his beliefs, then he will pursue it. And if the relevant beliefs are near enough true, then he will pursue it as effectively as possible. A conceptual connection between value and motivation, sure enough – but a multifariously iffy connection. Nothing less iffy would be credible. But still less is it credible that there is no connection at all.

In general, to find out whether something is disposed to give response R under conditions C, you can put it in C and find out whether you get R. That is a canonical way to learn whether the disposition is present, though surely not the only possible way.[6] If a dispositional theory of value is true, then we have a canonical way to find out whether something is a value. To find out whether we would be disposed, under ideal conditions, to value it, put yourself in

6 It is a fallible way; for it may be that you cannot put the thing in C without making the disposition disappear. Imagine that a surface now has just the molecular structure that disposes things to reflect light; but that exposing it to light would catalyze a swift chemical change and turn it into something unreflective. So long as it's kept in the dark, is it reflective? – I think so; but its reflectivity is what Ian Hunt once called a 'finkish' disposition, one that would vanish if put to the test. (So a simple counterfactual analysis of dispositions fails.) Could a disposition to value, or to disvalue, be finkish? Yes; here is an example due to Michael Tooley. Suppose, as I shall claim, that 'ideal conditions' include imaginative acquaintance; suppose there is no way to imagine direct electrical stimulation of the pleasure centre of the brain except by trying it out; and suppose that one brief trial would enslave you to the electrode and erase all other desires. Then I think you might well have a finkish disposition to disvalue the experience. If, *per impossibile*, you could manage to imagine it without at the same time having your present system of desires erased by the current, you would desire not to desire it.

[Added 1998] The notion of a finkish disposition was due, originally, to C. B. Martin. See Martin, 'Dispositions and Conditionals', *The Philosophical Quarterly* 44 (1994), pp. 1–8; and my 'Finkish Dispositions', *The Philosophical Quarterly* 47 (1997), pp. 143–158.

ideal conditions, if you can, making sure you can tell when you have succeeded in doing so. Then find out whether you value the thing in question, i.e. whether you desire to desire it. If you do, that confirms that it is a value. (I assume you are one of the appropriate 'we' and you know it.) Now we have this much of an 'internalist' conceptual connection between value judgements and motivation. It is even iffier than the connection between value itself and motivation; and again I say that if it were less iffy, it would be less credible. If someone believes that something is a value, and if he has come to this belief by the canonical method, and if he has remained in ideal conditions afterward or else retained the desire to desire that he had when in ideal conditions, then it follows that he values that thing. And if he desires as he desires to desire, then he desires that thing; and so on as before.

The connection is not with the judgement of value *per se*, but with the canonical way of coming to it. If someone reached the same judgement in some non-canonical way – as he might – that would imply nothing about his valuing or desiring or pursuing.

What is the 'appropriate category'? If values are what we are disposed to desire to desire, then the things that can be values must be among the things that can be desired. Those fall into two classes.

Sometimes, what one desires is that the world should be a certain way: that it should realise one of a certain class of (maximally specific, qualitatively delineated) possibilities for the whole world. This class – a 'proposition', in one sense of that word – gives the content of the desire. To desire that the world realise some possibility within the class is to desire that the proposition be true. Call this 'desire *de dicto*'.

But sometimes, what one desires concerns not just the world but oneself: one simply desires to *be* a certain way. For instance, Fred might want to be healthy, or wealthy, or wise. Then what he wants is that he himself should realise one of a certain class of (maximally specific, qualitatively delineated) possibilities for an individual – or better, for an individual-in-a-world-at-a-time. This class – a 'property' in one sense of that word, or an 'egocentric proposition' – gives the content of the desire. To desire to realise some possibility in the class is to desire to have the property, or to desire that the egocentric

73

proposition be true of one. Call this 'desire *de se*', or 'egocentric' or 'essentially indexical' desire.[7]

You might think to reduce desire *de se* to desire *de dicto*, saying that if Arthur desires to be happy, what he desires is that the world be such that Arthur is happy. (You might doubt that such worlds comprise a qualitatively delineated class, so you might consider dropping that requirement.) But no. That is not exactly the same thing, though the difference shows up only when we imagine someone who is wrong or unsure about who in the world he is. Suppose Arthur thinks he is Martha. If Arthur is self-centred he may desire to be happy, desire that the world be one wherein Martha is happy, but not desire that the world is one wherein Arthur is happy. If instead Arthur is selflessly benevolent he may not desire to be happy, yet he may desire that the world be such that Arthur is happy. If Arthur is so befuddled as not to know whether he is Arthur or Martha, but hopes he is Arthur, he does not just desire that the world be such that Arthur is self-identical! In all these cases, Arthur's desire is, at least in part, irreducibly *de se*.[8, 9]

When we acknowledge desires *de se*, we must distinguish two

7 See Peter Geach, 'On Beliefs about Oneself', *Analysis* 18 (1957), pp. 23–24; Hector-Neri Castañeda, 'On the Logic of Attributions of Self-Knowledge to Others', *Journal of Philosophy* 65 (1968), pp. 439–456; John Perry, 'Frege on Demonstratives', *Philosophical Review* 86 (1977), pp. 474–497, and 'The Problem of the Essential Indexical', *Noûs* 14 (1979), pp. 3–21; my 'Attitudes *De Dicto* and *De Se*', *Philosophical Review* 88 (1979), pp. 513–543; Roderick Chisholm, *The First Person: An Essay on Reference and Intentionality* (Harvester Press, 1981).

8 What we can do is to go the other way, subsuming desire *de dicto* under desire *de se*. To desire that the world be a certain way is to desire that one have the property of living in a world that is that way – a property that belongs to all or none of the inhabitants of the world, depending on the way the world is. This subsumption, artificial though it be, is legitimate given a suitably broad notion of property. But for present purposes we need distinction, not unification. So let us henceforth ignore those desires *de se* that are equivalent to desires *de dicto*, and reserve the term '*de se*' for those that are not.

9 If you like, you can put the egocentricity not in the content of desire itself but in an egocentric mode of presentation of that content. The choice matters little, save to simplicity. See Jeremy Butterfield, 'Content and Context' in Butterfield, ed., *Language Mind and Logic* (Cambridge University Press, 1986).

senses of 'desiring the same thing'. If Jack Sprat and his wife both prefer fat meat, they *desire alike*. They are psychological duplicates, on this matter at least. But they do not *agree* in their desires, because no possible arrangement could satisfy them both. Whereas if Jack prefers the lean and his wife prefers the fat, then they differ psychologically, they do not desire alike. But they do agree, because if he eats no fat and she eats no lean, that would satisfy them both. In general, they desire alike iff they desire *de se* to have exactly the same properties and they desire *de dicto* that exactly the same propositions hold. They agree in desires iff exactly the same world would satisfy the desires of both; and a world that satisfies someone's desires is one wherein he has all the properties that he desires *de se* and wherein all the propositions hold that he desires *de dicto*. Agreement in desire makes for harmony; desiring alike may well make for strife.

As we can desire *de dicto* or *de se*, so we can desire to desire *de dicto* or *de se*. If desiring to desire is valuing, and if values are what we are disposed to value, then we must distinguish values *de dicto* and *de se*. A value *de dicto* is a proposition such that we are disposed to desire to desire *de dicto* that it hold. A value *de se* is a property such that we are disposed to desire to desire *de se* to have it.

It is essential to distinguish. Consider egoism: roughly, the thesis that one's own happiness is the only value. Egoism is meant to be general. It is not the thesis that the happiness of a certain special person, say Thrasymachus, is the only value. Egoism *de dicto* says that for each person X, the proposition that X is happy is the only value. That is inconsistent, as Moore observed.[10] It says that there are as many different values as there are people, and each of them is the only value. Egoism *de se* says that the property of happiness – in other words, the egocentric proposition that one is happy – is the only value. Moore did not confute that. He ignored it. False and ugly though it be, egoism *de se* is at least a consistent doctrine. What it alleges to be the only value would indeed be just *one* value *de se*, not a multitude of values *de dicto*.[11]

10 *Principia Ethica*, Section 59.
11 Someone who said that happiness was the only value might mean something else, which is not a form of egoism at all. He might mean that the proposition that

Insofar as values are *de se*, the wholehearted pursuit by everyone of the same genuine value will not necessarily result in harmony. All might value alike, valuing *de se* the same properties and valuing *de dicto* the same propositions. Insofar as they succeed in desiring as they desire to desire, they will desire alike. But that does not ensure that they will agree in desire. If egoism *de se* were true, and if happiness could best be pursued by doing others down and winning extra shares, then the pursuit by all of the very same single value would be the war of all against all.

Because egoism is false and ugly, we might be glad of a theoretical framework that allowed us to confute it *a priori*. And some of us might welcome a framework that promises us harmony, if only we can all manage to pursue the same genuine values. Was it right, then, to make a place for values *de se*? Should we have stipulated, instead, that something we are disposed to desire to desire shall count as a value only when it is a proposition that we are disposed to desire to desire *de dicto*?

No. Probably it is already wrong to reject egoism *a priori* but, be that as it may, there are other doctrines of value *de se*, more plausible and more attractive. Self-improvement and self-sacrifice are no less egocentric than self-aggrandizement and self-indulgence. Surely we should make a place for putative values *de se* of altruism, of honour, and of loyalty to family, friends, and country.[12] We may entertain the substantive thesis that none of these putative values *de se* is genuine, and that all genuine values are *de dicto*. But even if we believed this – myself, I think it wildly unlikely – we should not beg the question in its favour by building it into our theoretical framework.

---

happiness is maximized is the only value – a single value *de dicto*. Or he might mean that for each person X, the proposition that X is happy is a value *de dicto*, and that these many values of parallel form are the only values. Mean what you please – I take these to be legitimate, but derivative, senses in which a property may be called a value. I only say they should not be confused with, or drive out, the sense in which a property may be a value *de se*.

12 See Andrew Oldenquist, 'Loyalties', *Journal of Philosophy* 79 (1982), pp. 173–193; Michael Slote, 'Morality and Self-Other Asymmetry', *Journal of Philosophy* 81 (1984), pp. 179–192.

What conditions are 'ideal'? If someone has little notion what it would be like to live as a free spirit unbound by law, custom, loyalty, or love; or what a world of complete harmony and constant agreement would be like; then whether or not he blindly values these things must have little to do with whether or not they are truly values. What he lacks is imaginative acquaintance. If only he would think harder, and imagine vividly and thoroughly how it would be if these putative values were realised (and perhaps also how it would be if they were not) that would make his valuing a more reliable indicator of genuine value. And if he could gain the fullest possible imaginative acquaintance that is humanly possible,[13] then, I suggest, his valuing would be an infallible indicator. Something is a value iff we are disposed, under conditions of the fullest possible imaginative acquaintance, to value it.

Compare a version of Intuitionism: by hard thought, one becomes imaginatively well acquainted with X; in consequence, but not as the conclusion of any sort of inference, one intuits that X has a certain unanalysable, non-natural property; and in consequence of that, one comes to value X. My story begins and ends the same. Only the middle is missing. Again, an exercise of imaginative reason plays a crucial role. Again, its relation to what follows is causal, and in no way inferential. But in my story, the consequent valuing is caused more directly, not via the detection of a peculiar property of X.

Can we say that the valuing ensued because X was a value? – Maybe so, but if we do, we are not saying much: it ensues because there is something about imaginative acquaintance with X that causes valuing.[14]

---

13 Without in the process having his dispositions to value altered – see Footnote 6.

14 How does imaginative acquaintance cause valuing, when it does? How does imagination render values attractive? Does it happen the same way for all values? – For our purposes, it is enough to say that it happens. We needn't know how. But we may guess. Maybe imaginative acquaintance shows us how new desires would be seamless extensions of desires we have already. Or maybe we gravitate toward what we understand, lest we baffle ourselves – see J. David Velleman, *Practical Reflection* (Princeton University Press, 1989). But that cannot be the whole story,

The canonical way to find out whether something is a value requires a difficult imaginative exercise. And if you are to be sure of your answer, you need to be sure that you have gained the fullest imaginative acquaintance that is humanly possible. A tall order! You had better settle for less. Approximate the canonical test. Try hard to imagine how it would be if the putative value were (or were not) realised. Hope that your acquaintance comes close enough to the fullest possible that getting closer would not change your response. Then you may take your valuing as fallible evidence that you were acquainted with a genuine value, or your indifference as fallible evidence that you were not. You cannot be perfectly certain of your answer, but you can take it as sure enough to be going on with, subject to reconsideration in the light of new evidence. How sure is that? – Well, as always when we acknowledge fallibility, some of us will be bolder than others.

New evidence might be a more adequate imaginative exercise of your own. It might be the testimony of others. It might in principle be a result of scientific psychology – though it is far from likely that any such results will come to hand soon!

A trajectory toward fuller imaginative acquaintance with putative value X is not just a sequence of changes in your imaginative state. It has a direction to it. And that is so independently of my claim that it leads, after a point, to ever-surer knowledge about whether X is a value. For in learning how to imagine X, you gain abilities; later you have all the relevant imaginative abilities you had before, and more besides. And you notice, *a priori*, relationships of coherence or incoherence between attitudes that might figure in the realisation of X; later you are aware of all that you had noticed before, and more besides. And you think of new questions to explore in your imagining – what might the life of the free spirit become, long years after its novelty had worn off? – and later you have in mind all the questions you had thought of before, and more besides. For-

because some easily understood lives – say a life of lethargy, ruled by a principle of least action – remain repellent.

getting is possible, of course. But by and large, the process resists reversal.[15]

Our theory makes a place for truth, and in principle for certain knowledge, and in practice for less-than-certain knowledge, about value. But also it makes a place for ignorance and error, for hesitant opinion and modesty, for trying to learn more and hoping to succeed. That is all to the good. One fault of some subjective and prescriptive theories is that they leave no room for modesty: just decide where you stand, then you may judge of value with the utmost confidence!

There is a long history of theories that analyse value in terms of hypothetical response under ideal conditions, with various suggestions about what conditions are ideal. Imaginative acquaintance often gets a mention. But much else does too. I think imaginative acquaintance is all we need – the rest should be in part subsumed, in part rejected.

First, the responder is often called an ideal *spectator*. That is tantamount to saying that conditions are ideal only when he is observing a sample of the putative value in question (or of its absence). If the putative value is *de se*, a property, then a sample can just be an instance. If it is *de dicto*, a proposition, it is hard to say in general what an observable sample could be. But if it is the proposition that a certain property is instantiated sometimes, or often, or as often as possible, or in all cases of a certain kind, then again a sample can just be an instance of the property. Anyone happy may serve as a sample of the proposition that total happiness is maximised.

Observable samples can sometimes prompt the imagination and thereby help us to advance imaginative acquaintance. But they are of limited use. For one thing, observation does not include mind-reading. Also, it does best with short, dramatic episodes. A lifelong pattern of stagnation, exemplifying the absence of various values, goes on too long to be easily observed. Samples are dispensable as aids to imagination, and sometimes they are comparatively ineffective. A novel might be better.

---

15 For a discussion of unidirectionality in aesthetic valuing, see Michael Slote, 'The Rationality of Aesthetic Value Judgements', *Journal of Philosophy* 68 (1971), pp. 821–839.

The notion of an ideal spectator is part of a longstanding attempt to make dispositional theories of value and of colour run in parallel. But the analogy is none too good, and I doubt that it improves our understanding either of colour or of value. Drop it, and I think we have no further reason to say that a disposition to value is a disposition to respond to observed samples.[16]

Second, the ideal responder is often supposed to be well informed. If any item of empirical knowledge would affect his response, he knows it. – But some sorts of knowledge would not help to make your valuing a more reliable indicator of genuine value. Instead they would distract. If you knew too well how costly or how difficult it was to pursue some value, you might reject the grapes as sour, even when imaginative acquaintance with the value itself would have caused you to value it. Genuine values might be unattainable, or unattainable without undue sacrifice of other values. An ideal *balancer* of values needs thorough knowledge of the terms of trade. An ideal valuer may be better off without it. Our present business is not with the balancing, but with the prior question of what values there are to balance.[17]

Another unhelpful sort of knowledge is a vivid awareness that we

16 If we had demanded samples, we would have had a choice about where to locate the disposition. Is it within us or without? Is it a disposition in the samples to evoke a response from spectators? – that is what best fits the supposed parallel with a dispositional theory of colour. See Robert Pargetter and John Campbell, 'Goodness and Fragility', *American Philosophical Quarterly* 23 (1986), pp. 155–166, for an analysis of this kind. Or is it a disposition in the spectators to respond to samples? Or is it a disposition of the sample-cum-spectator system to respond to having its parts brought together? For us there is no choice. The propositions and properties that are the values cannot harbour any causal bases for dispositions. Samples could, but there needn't be any samples. Imaginative experiences could, but those are within us, and are not themselves samples of values. So the disposition must reside in us, the responders. Being a value comes out as a dispositionally analysed property, but not as a disposition of the things that have it. Values themselves are not disposed to do anything.

17 Previous theories of hypothetical response may indeed have been concerned as much with the analysis of right balancing as with value itself. If so, they cannot be faulted for trying to characterise an ideal balancer. However my present analysandum is different.

are small and the cosmos is large; or a vivid awareness of the mortality of mankind, and of the cosmos itself. If such knowledge tends to extinguish all desire, and therefore all valuing, it will not help us to value just what is valuable. Likewise it will be unhelpful to dwell too much on the lowly causal origins of things. If some feature of our lives originated by kin selection, or Pavlovian conditioning, or sublimation of infantile sexuality, that is irrelevant to what it is like in itself. Unless he can overcome the illusion of relevance, a valuer will be more reliable if he remains ignorant of such matters.

However, I grant one case – a common one – in which one does need empirical knowledge in order to gain imaginative acquaintance with a given putative value. It may be 'given' in a way that underspecifies it, with the rest of the specification left to be filled in by reference to the actual ways of the world. For instance when I mentioned the life of a free spirit as a putative value, what I meant – and what you surely took me to mean – was the life of a free spirit in a world like ours. In such cases, a valuer must complete the specification by drawing on his knowledge of the world, else he will not know what he is supposed to imagine. To that extent – and only to that extent, I think – being well-informed is indeed a qualification for his job.[18]

Third, it may be said that the ideal responder should not only imagine having (or lacking) a putative value, but also imagine the effect on other people of someone's having (or lacking) it. Thinking what it would be like to live as a free spirit is not enough. You must also think what it would be like to encounter the free spirit and be ill-used. – But again, I think the requirement is misplaced. It is appropriate not to an ideal valuer, but to an ideal balancer who must think through the cost to some values of the realisation of others. In addressing the prior question of what values there are, counting the cost is a distraction to be resisted.

18 Imaginative acquaintance is sometimes thought to consist in the possession of a special kind of 'phenomenal' information. If that is so, of course my own candidate for 'ideal conditions' comes down to a special case of being well-informed. But it is not so – not even in the most favourable case, that of imaginative acquaintance with a kind of sense-experience. See my 'What Experience Teaches' in William Lycan, ed., *Mind and Cognition: A Reader* (Blackwell, 1989).

Often, however, realising a putative value *de se* would itself involve imagining the impact of one's conduct on other people. When that is so, imagining realising the value involves imagining imagining the impact; and that cannot be done without simply imagining the impact. In such cases, imagining the impact does fit in; for it is already subsumed as part of imaginative acquaintance with the value itself.

Fourth, the ideal responder is often said to be dispassionate and impartial, like a good judge. – Once more, the requirement is appropriate not to an ideal valuer but to an ideal balancer. The valuer is not a judge. He is more like an advocate under the adversarial system. He is a specialist, passionate and partial perhaps, in some one of all the values there are. On the present theory, when I say that X is a value iff we are disposed to value X under ideal conditions, I do not mean conditions that are ideal *simpliciter*, but rather conditions that are ideal *for* X. We should not assume that there is any such thing as a condition of imaginative acquaintance with all values at once. (Still less, all putative values.) Imagination involves simulation – getting into the skin of the part. How many skins can you get into all at once? Tranquillity and vigorous activity might both be values; but a full imaginative acquaintance with one might preclude a full imaginative acquaintance with the other. (The incompatibility might even be conceptual, not just psychological.) Then if we value both, as surely many of us do, it is not because of acquaintance with both at once. It might be a lasting effect of past imaginative acquaintance at some times with one and at other times with the other.

A further speculation: it might happen that there were values that could not even be valued all at once. If so, then conflict of values would go deeper than is ever seen in hard choices; because what makes a choice hard is that conflicting values *are* valued together by the unfortunate chooser. An alarming prospect! – or exhilarating, to those of us who delight in the rich variety of life.

Who are 'we'? An *absolute* version of the dispositional theory says that the 'we' refers to all mankind. To call something a value is to call it a value *simpliciter*, which means that everyone, always and everywhere, is disposed under ideal conditions to value it. Then there are values only insofar as all mankind are alike in their dispositions.

Maybe all mankind *are* alike. The manifest diversity of valuing between different cultures – or for that matter within a culture, say between colleagues in the same philosophy department – is no counterevidence. In the first place, people may not be valuing as they would be disposed to value under ideal conditions. In the second place, remember that conditions of imaginative acquaintance are ideal for particular values, not *simpliciter*. So even if all are disposed alike, and all value as they would under ideal conditions, that may mean that some people value X as they would under conditions ideal for X, while others, who are no differently disposed, value Y as they would under conditions ideal for Y. If no conditions are ideal at once for X and for Y (still more if X and Y cannot both be valued at once), there could be diversity of valuing even in a population of psychological clones, if different ones had been led into different imaginative exercises.

We saw that it would be no easy job to find out for sure whether a particular person would be disposed to value something under ideal conditions of imaginative acquaintance with it. It would be harder still to find out all about one person's dispositions. And not just because one hard job would have to be done many times over. It might happen that imaginative acquaintance with X would leave traces, in one's valuing or otherwise, that got in the way of afterward imagining Y. To the extent that there was such interference, each new imaginative experiment would be harder than the ones before.

The fallback, if we are wary of presupposing that all mankind are alike in their dispositions to value, is tacit relativity. A *relative* version says that the 'we' in the analysis is indexical, and refers to a population consisting of the speaker and those somehow like him. If the analysis is indexical, so is the analysandum. Then for speaker S to call something a value is to call it a value for the population of S and those like him; which means that S and those like him are all disposed, under ideal conditions, to value it.

The relative version is not just one version, but a spectrum. What analysis you get depends on how stringent a standard of similarity you apply to the phrase 'the speaker and those somehow like him'. At one end of the spectrum stands the absolute version: common humanity is likeness enough, so whoever speaks, all mankind are 'we'.

At the other end, 'we' means: 'you and I, and I'm none too sure about you'. (Or it might be 'I, and those who think as I do', which reduces to 'I'.) In between, 'we' means: 'I, and all those who are of a common culture with me'. Since mankind even at one moment is not made up of isolated and homogeneous tribes, and since we should not limit ourselves to the part of mankind located at one moment, we may haggle endlessly over how much cultural affiliation is meant.

(We have a piece of unfinished business: if someone is to find out about values by the canonical method, he must somehow know that he is one of the appropriate 'we'. All our versions, absolute or relative, make this knowledge automatic. Not so for *elitist* versions, on which 'we' means 'the best-qualified of us' or maybe 'the most normal of us'. But elitist versions are pointless. We're already considering dispositions under extravagantly ideal conditions; we needn't idealise all over again by being selective about who counts as one of the 'we'.)

If some relative version were the correct analysis, wouldn't that be manifest whenever people talk about value? Wouldn't you hear them saying 'value for me and my mates' or 'value for the likes of you'? Wouldn't you think they'd stop arguing after one speaker says X is a value and the other says it isn't? – Not necessarily. They might always presuppose, with more or less confidence (well-founded or otherwise), that whatever relativity there is won't matter in *this* conversation. Even if they accept in principle that people sometimes just differ in their dispositions to value, they may be very reluctant to think the present deadlocked conversation is a case of such difference. However intractable the disagreement may be, they may go on thinking it really *is* a disagreement: a case in which two people are disposed alike, but one of them is wrong about what is a value relative to their shared dispositions, because he is not valuing as he would under ideal conditions. So long as they think that – and they might think it very persistently – they can hold the language of explicit relativity in reserve. It is there as a last resort, if ever they meet with a proven case of ultimate difference. But it will not be much heard, since it is a practical impossibility to prove a case. If the language of absolutism prevails, that is not strong evidence against relativity.

(Those who have heard of the relativity of simultaneity do not manifest this knowledge all the time. They speak as the ignorant do, and no harm done. They'll resort to the language of relativity when it matters, say in discussing the exploits of the interstellar navy.)

Does the language of absolutism prevail? Not really. With some of us it does. Others of us resort to the language of relativity at the drop of a hat. Yet this too is poor evidence. The eager relativists may have been confused by philosophy. For who can escape it?

So what version should we prefer, absolute or relative? – Neither; instead, I commend a *wait-and-see* version. In making a judgement of value, one makes many claims at once, some stronger than others, some less confidently than others, and waits to see which can be made to stick. I say X is a value; I mean that all mankind are disposed to value X; or anyway all nowadays are; or anyway all nowadays are except maybe some peculiar people on distant islands; or anyway . . . ; or anyway you and I, talking here and now, are; or anyway I am.[19] How much am I claiming? – as much as I can get away with. If my stronger claims were proven false – though how that could be proven is hard to guess – I still mean to stand by the weaker ones. So long as I'm not challenged, there's no need to back down in advance; and there's no need to decide how far I'd back down if pressed. What I mean to commit myself to is *conditionally relative*: relative if need be, but absolute otherwise.

What is the modal status of the equivalence? The equivalence between value and what we are disposed to value is meant to be a piece of philosophical analysis, therefore analytic. But of course it is not obviously analytic; it is not even obviously true.

It is a philosophical problem how there can ever be unobvious analyticity. We need not solve that problem; suffice it to say that it is everybody's problem, and it is not to be solved by denying the phenomenon. There are perfectly clear examples of it: the epsilon-delta analysis of an instantaneous rate of change, for one. Whenever it is analytic that all A's are B's, but not obviously analytic, the Moorean open question – whether all A's are indeed B's – is

19 See the discussion of 'anyway' in Frank Jackson, 'On Assertion and Indicative Conditionals', *Philosophical Review* 88 (1979), pp. 565–589.

intelligible. And not only is it intelligible in the sense that we can parse and interpret it (that much is true even of the question whether all A's are A's) but also in the sense that it makes sense as something to say in a serious discussion, as an expression of genuine doubt.

Besides unobvious analyticity, there is equivocal analyticity. Something may be analytic under one disambiguation but not another, or under one precisification but not another. Examples abound. Quine was wrong that analyticity was unintelligible, right to doubt that we have many clear-cut cases of it. If differing versions of a concept (or, if you like, different but very similar concepts) are in circulation under the same name, we will get equivocal analyticity. It is analytic under one disambiguation of 'dog' that all dogs are male; under one disambiguation of 'bitch' that all bitches are canine. It is analytic under some precisifications of 'mountain' that no mountain is less than one kilometre high. When analyticity is equivocal, open questions make good conversational sense: they are invitations to proceed under a disambiguation or precisification that makes the answer to the question not be analytic. By asking whether there are mountains less than one kilometre high, you invite your conversational partners to join you in considering the question under a precisification of 'mountain' broad enough to make it interesting; yet it was analytic under another precisification that the answer was 'no'.[20] So even if all is obvious, open questions show at worst that the alleged analyticity is equivocal.

I suggest that the dispositional theory of value, in the version I have put forward, is equivocally as well as unobviously analytic. I do not claim to have captured the one precise sense that the word 'value' bears in the pure speech, uncorrupted by philosophy, that is heard on the Clapham omnibus. So far as this matter goes, I doubt that speakers untouched by philosophy are found in Clapham or anywhere else. And if they were, I doubt if they'd have made up their minds exactly what to mean any more than the rest of us have. I take it, rather, that the word 'value', like many others, exhibits both semantic variation and semantic indecision. The best I can hope for is that my dispositional theory lands somewhere near the middle of the range of varia-

20 See my 'Scorekeeping in a Language Game', *Journal of Philosophical Logic* 8 (1979), pp. 339–359.

tion and indecision – and also gives something that I, and many more besides, could be content to adopt as our official definition of the word 'value', in the unlikely event that we needed an official definition.

I've left some questions less than conclusively settled: the matter of absolute versus relative versus wait-and-see versions, the details of 'ideal conditions', the question of admitting values *de se*, the definition of valuing as second-order versus highest-order intrinsic desiring. It would not surprise or disturb me to think that my answers to those questions are only equivocally analytic – but somewhere fairly central within the range of variation and indecision – and that the same could be said of rival answers. Even if no version of the dispositional theory is unequivocally analytic, still it's fair to hope that some not-too-miscellaneous disjunction of versions comes out analytic under most reasonable resolutions of indeterminacy (under some reasonable precisification of 'most' and 'reasonable'.)

If the dispositional theory is only unobviously and equivocally analytic, why think that it's analytic at all? – Because that hypothesis fits our practice. (The practice of many of us, much of the time.) It does seem that if we try to find out whether something is a genuine value, we do try to follow – or rather, approximate – the canonical method. We gain the best imaginative acquaintance we can, and see if we then desire to desire it. In investigating values by the canonical method, we ignore any alleged possibility that values differ from what we're disposed to value. The dispositional theory explains nicely why we ignore it: no such possibility exists.

Now this should sound an alarm. Phenomenalism, behaviourism, and the like might be supported in exactly the same way: we ignore the possibility that our method of investigation deceives us radically, and the alleged explanation is that no such possibility exists. But in those cases, we know better. We know how systematic hallucination might deceive its victim about the world around him, and how a clever actor might deceive everyone he meets about his inner life (and, in both cases, how it might be that experience or behaviour would remain deceptive throughout the appropriate range of counterfactual suppositions). And it doesn't just strike us that such deception is possible *somehow*. Rather, we can imagine just how it might happen. We can give a story of deception all the detail it takes to make it convincing. So we must confess that our method of gaining knowledge of the outer world and the inner lives does consist in part of ignoring genuine possibilities – possibilities that cannot credibly be denied.

The case of value is different, because the convincing detail cannot be supplied. Yes, you might think that perhaps the genuine values somehow differ from what we are disposed to value, even under ideal conditions. (Charles Pigden has noted that a misanthrope might think it because he thinks mankind is irremediably depraved.) The conjecture is not unthinkable; the dispositional theory is not *obviously* analytic; counterexamples are not *obviously* impossible. That is not yet much evidence of possibility. Better evidence would be a detailed story of just how it might happen that something – something specific – is after all a value that we are not disposed to value, or a non-value that we are disposed to value. But I have no idea how to flesh out the story. Without 'corroborative detail', insistence that there exist such possibilities is 'bald and unconvincing'. This time, nothing outweighs the niceness of explaining the ignoring by denying the possibilities allegedly ignored.

But is it realism? Psychology is contingent. Our dispositions to value things might have been otherwise than they actually are. We might have been disposed, under ideal conditions, to value seasickness and petty sleaze above all else. Does the dispositional theory imply that, had we been thus disposed, those things would have been values? That seems wrong.

No: we can take the reference to our dispositions as rigidified. Even speaking within the scope of a counterfactual supposition, the things that count as values are those that we are *actually* disposed to value, not those we would have valued in the counterfactual situation. No worries – unless seasickness actually *is* a value, it still wouldn't have been a value even if we'd been disposed to value it.

This is too swift. The trick of rigidifying seems more to hinder the expression of our worry than to make it go away. It can still be expressed as follows. We might have been disposed to value seasickness and petty sleaze, and yet we might have been no different in how we used the word 'value'. The reference of 'our actual dispositions' would have been fixed on different dispositions, of course, but our way of fixing the reference would have been no different. In one good sense – though not the only sense – we would have meant by 'value' just what we actually do. And it would have been true for us to say 'seasickness and petty sleaze are values'.

The contingency of value has not gone away after all; and it may well disturb us. I think it is the only disturbing aspect of the dispositional theory. Conditional relativity may well disturb us too, but that is no separate problem. What comfort would it be if all mankind just *happened* to be disposed alike? Say, because some strange course of cultural evolution happened to be cut short by famine, or because some mutation of the brain never took place? Since our dispositions to value are contingent, they certainly vary when we take *all* of mankind into account, all the inhabitants of all the possible worlds. Given the dispositional theory, trans-world relativity is inevitable. The spectre of relativity within our own world is just a vivid reminder of the contingency of value.

If wishes were horses, how would we choose to ride? What would it take to satisfy us? Maybe this new version of the dispositional theory would suit us better: values are what we're *necessarily* disposed to value. Then no contingent 'value' would deserve the name; and there would be no question of something being a value for some people and not for others, since presumably what's necessary is *a fortiori* uniform (unless different dispositions to value are built into different people's individual essences, an unlikely story).

What kind of necessity should it be? Not mere deontic necessity – values are what we're disposed to value on pain of being at fault, where the fault in question turns out to consist in failing to be disposed to value the genuine values. That dispositional theory is empty. Its near relatives are nearly empty. And it won't help to juggle terms; as it might be, by calling it 'rational necessity' and then classifying the disposition to value genuine values as a department of 'rationality'. Probably not nomological necessity either – small comfort to think that we were disposed to disvalue seasickness only because, luckily, our neurons are not subject to a certain fifth force of nature that would distort their workings in just the wrong way. It had better be necessity *simpliciter*, so-called 'metaphysical' necessity.

If we amend the dispositional theory by inserting 'necessarily', we can be much more confident that the 'values' it defines would fully deserve the name – if there were any of them. But it is hard to see how there possibly could be. If a value, strictly speaking, must be something we are necessarily disposed to value, and if our dispositions to value are in fact contingent, then, strictly speaking, there are no values. If Mackie is right that a value (his term is 'objective good') would have to be

sought by anyone who was acquainted with it, not because of any contingent fact that this person, or every person, is so constituted that he desires this end, but just because the end has to-be-pursuedness somehow built into it,

then he is also right to call values 'queer' and to repudiate the error of believing in them.[21] (Replacing 'sought' by 'valued' would not change that.) If we amend the dispositional theory, requiring values to be all that we might wish them to be, we bring on the error theory. The fire is worse than the frying pan.

Is it, after all, out of the question that our dispositions to value might be necessary? If the theory of mind I favour is true, then the platitudes of folk psychology do have a certain necessity – albeit conditional necessity – to them.[22] There are states that play the functional roles specified in those platitudes, and it is in virtue of doing so that they deserve their folk-psychological names. It is not necessary that there should be any states in us that deserve such names as 'pain', 'belief', or 'desire'. But it is necessary that if any states do deserve those names, then they conform to the platitudes. Or rather, they conform well enough. Now suppose that some of the platitudes

---

21 J. L. Mackie, *Ethics: Inventing Right and Wrong* (Penguin, 1977), p. 40. But note that the queerness Mackie has in mind covers more than just the to-know-it-is-to-love-it queerness described in this passage.

22 See my 'An Argument for the Identity Theory', *Journal of Philosophy* 63 (1966), pp. 17–25; and D. M. Armstrong, *A Materialist Theory of the Mind* (Routledge and Kegan Paul, 1968).

of folk psychology specified exactly what we were disposed, under ideal conditions, to desire to desire. And suppose those platitudes were non-negotiable: if a system of states did not satisfy them, that would settle that those states did not conform well enough to folk psychology to deserve the mental names it implicitly defines. Then there would be things we were necessarily disposed to value – on condition that we had mental lives at all!

The suggestion is intelligible and interesting, but too good to be true. For one thing, it only spreads the trouble. Instead of losing the risk that nothing deserves the name of value, we gain the added risk that nothing deserves commonplace folk-psychological names. *Pace* the Churchlands, it's not really credible that there might turn out to be no beliefs, no desires, no pains, . . .[23] For another thing, it proves too much. It denies outright that it's possible for someone to differ from others in his dispositions to value. Yet this does seem possible; and we can flesh out the story with plenty of 'corroborative detail'. This cunning and subtle villain once was as others are; he gained excellent imaginative acquaintance with many values, and valued them accordingly. Now he has gone wrong, and cares not a fig for what he once valued; and yet he has forgotten nothing. (He certainly has not stopped having any mental life deserving of the name.) He hates those who are as he once was, and outwits them all the better because of his superb empathetic understanding of what they hold dear. Could it not happen? – not if the present suggestion were true. So the present suggestion is false. Yet it was the only hope, or the only one I know, for explaining how there might be things we are necessarily disposed to value. The dispositions are contingent, then. And, at least in some tacit way, we know it. If the story of the subtle villain strikes you as a possible story, that knowledge thereby reveals itself.

But if we know better, it is odd that we are disturbed – as I think many of us will be – by a dispositional theory of value, unamended, according to which values are contingent. It feels wrong. Why might

23 As argued in Frank Jackson and Philip Pettit, 'In Defence of Folk Psychology', *Philosophical Studies* 59 (1990), pp. 31–54.

that be? – Perhaps because a large and memorable part of our discussion of values consists of browbeating and being browbeaten.[24] The rhetoric would fall flat if we kept in mind, all the while, that it is contingent how we are disposed to value. So a theory which acknowledges that contingency cannot feel quite right. You might say that it is unfaithful to the distinctive phenomenological character of lived evaluative thought. Yet even if it feels not right, it may still be right, or as near right as we can get. It feels not quite right to remember that your friends are big swarms of little particles – it is inadequate to the phenomenology of friendship – but still they are.

I suggested earlier that my version of the dispositional theory of value might be equivocally analytic. So might the amended version, on which values are what we are necessarily disposed to value. Between these two versions, not to mention others, there might be both semantic variation and semantic indecision. If so, it is part of a familiar pattern. One way to create indeterminacy and equivocal analyticity is to define names implicitly in terms of a theory (folk or scientific), and later find out that the theory is wrong enough that nothing perfectly deserves the names so introduced, but right enough that some things, perhaps several rival candidates, deserve the names imperfectly. Nothing perfectly deserves the name 'simultaneity', since nothing quite fits the whole of our old conception. So the name will have to go to some imperfect deserver of it, or to nothing. What it takes to deserve this name, not perfectly but well enough, was never officially settled. One resolution of the indeterminacy makes it analytic that simultaneity must be frame-independent; another, that it must be an equivalence relation; a third, that it must be both at once. The third brings with it an error theory of simultaneity.[25]

I suggest that (for some of us, or some of us sometimes) the amended dispositional theory best captures what it would take for something to perfectly deserve the name 'value'. There are no perfect

24 See Ian Hinckfuss, *The Moral Society: Its Structure and Effects* (Australian National University Discussion Papers in Environmental Philosophy, 1987).
25 See Hartry Field, 'Theory Change and the Indeterminacy of Reference', *Journal of Philosophy* 70 (1973), pp. 462–481.

deservers of the name to be had. But there are plenty of imperfect deservers of the name, and my original version is meant to capture what it takes to be one of the best of them. (But I do not say mine is the only version that can claim to do so. Doubtless there are more dimensions of semantic variation and indeterminacy than just our degree of tolerance for imperfection.) Strictly speaking, nothing shall get the name without deserving it perfectly. Strictly speaking, Mackie is right: genuine values would have to meet an impossible condition, so it is an error to think there are any. Loosely speaking, the name may go to a claimant that deserves it imperfectly. Loosely speaking, common sense is right. There are values, lots of them, and they are what we are disposed *de facto* to value.

Then is my position a form of realism about values? – Irrealism about values strictly speaking, realism about values loosely speaking. The former do not exist. The latter do.

What to make of the situation is mainly a matter of temperament. You can bang the drum about how philosophy has uncovered a terrible secret: there are no values! (Shock horror: no such thing as simultaneity! Nobody ever whistled while he worked!) You can shout it from the housetops – browbeating is oppression, the truth shall make you free.[26] Or you can think it better for public safety to keep quiet and hope people will go on as before. Or you can declare that there are no values, but that nevertheless it is legitimate – and not just expedient – for us to carry on with value-talk, since we can make it all go smoothly if we just give the name of value to claimants that don't quite deserve it. This would be a sort of quasi-realism, not the same as Blackburn's quasi-realism.[27] Or you can think it an empty question whether there are values: say what you please, speak strictly or loosely. When it comes to deserving a name, there's better and worse but who's to say how good is good enough? Or you can think it clear that the imperfect deservers of the name are good enough, but only just, and say that although there are values we are still

26 See Hinckfuss, *op. cit.*

27 Simon Blackburn, *Spreading the Word: Groundings in the Philosophy of Language* (Oxford University Press, 1984), Chapter 6.

terribly wrong about them. Or you can calmly say that value (like simultaneity) is not quite as some of us sometimes thought. Myself, I prefer the calm and conservative responses. But so far as the analysis of value goes, they're all much of a muchness.

8

The trap's dilemma

The Bicentennial year is a fit time to recall an early contribution to 'regional philosophy'.[1] In the year 1879 Edward Kelly put forward this ingenious argument.

I would like to know what business an honest man would have in the police. A man that knows nothing about roguery would never enter the force and take an oath to arrest brother, sister, father, or mother if required and to have a case and conviction if possible. Any man knows it is possible to swear a lie. And if a policeman loses a conviction for the sake of [not] swearing a lie he has broken his oath. Therefore he is a perjurer either way.[2]

At first glance, Kelly's example seems to fit right into present-day discussion of moral dilemmas, as follows. If the unfortunate policeman has taken an oath that obligates him to swear a lie under certain circumstances, and if those circumstances arise, then he has no right course of action. Either he takes a second oath to tell the whole truth and nothing but, and then he breaks it by lying; or else he doesn't, and thereby breaks his first oath to do everything possible to secure a conviction. Kelly's conclusion also looks familiar: it is because of his previous wrongdoing that the policeman afterward has no right

First published *The Australasian Journal of Philosophy* **66** (1988), 220–223. Reprinted with kind permission from *The Australasian Journal of Philosophy*.

1 See Richard Sylvan, 'Prospects for Regional Philosophies in Australasia', *Australasian Journal of Philosophy* 63 (1985), pp. 188–204.
2 Unpublished at the time; later published in Max Brown, *Australian Son* (Melbourne, 1948), p. 297, and elsewhere. Slightly copy-edited here.

course of action. An honest man would never have taken the first oath.

I think this first glance is misleading. Kelly's example is different, in two important ways, from the run of present-day examples. That is why a scrap of barroom wit deserves attention in this journal. However I shall leave the two differences in abeyance, and first ask the inevitable question: does Kelly's conclusion follow?

A man can be honest at one time and not at another. Kelly's conclusion seems to be that no policeman was honest when he entered the force. That conclusion does not follow. If an honest man is one who shuns oath-breaking, then it is safe to say that an honest man would not take the first oath if he thought it certain, or highly probable, that to fulfill his first oath he would have to take and break a second. But must an honest man foresee and shun even the slightest risk of being forced into oath-breaking? Suppose first that the policeman foresaw a risk of dilemma, and estimated that the risk would be negligible – he was confident, wrongly as it turned out, that he would never need to swear a lie in order to secure a conviction. Or suppose he thought, contrary to what 'any man knows', that swearing a lie would not be possible; or anyway, that swearing a *convincing* lie would not be possible. Or suppose the policeman was none too clever when he took the first oath, and the idea that swearing a lie might someday be needed to secure a conviction just never crossed his mind. In the first case it seems that the policeman at the time of the first oath may have been, if not infinitely averse to oath-breaking, at least averse enough to count as honest. In the second and third cases, it seems there is no trace of dishonesty at the time of the first oath. An honest man can at least enter the force, if he is sufficiently optimistic or stupid.

But a harder, and interesting, question concerns honesty at the time of the *second* oath, if the policeman is eventually put to the test. Whether he was honest when he entered the force, years ago perhaps, is neither here nor there. Now that the only way not to break the first oath is to take and break a second oath, it is impossible not to be an oath-breaker. (And the policeman knows this.) Does that mean it is now impossible to be honest? We would think (1) that honesty is a trait of character, (2) that there can be no absolutely necessary connection between outer circumstances and inner character, and (3) that an honest man will never (knowingly) break an oath. But (1), (2), and (3) cannot be true together. We are forced to distinguish: to be *honest in character* is, in part, to be very averse to oath-breaking; to be *honest in deed* is, in part, never to (knowingly) break an oath. Given the distinction, it is hard to say which of the two best deserves the simple name: honesty. The surprise is that these are not the same thing, and furthermore that no amount of honesty in character is a certain guarantee of honesty in deed. Bad fortune is independent of honesty in character, perhaps, but it may necessitate dishonesty in deed.

The first big difference between Kelly's example and present-day discussion has now appeared. The present-day discussion mostly concerns dilemmas in which no course of action is right, or no alternative is good. What Kelly claims is different. He says that there is no way for the policeman to be honest. Kelly's example is a dilemma not in deontological or consequential ethics, but in the theory of the virtues.

Perhaps you've already thought that it wasn't much of a dilemma; because the policeman's first oath is morally null and void, either from the start or from the time it turned out to require him to swear a lie. (Maybe some part of its content retains some force, but not the part that makes the dilemma.) The easy answer to the non-problem about what course of action is right is that the policeman ought to break his first oath and testify truthfully or not at all. Yes indeed! But this easy answer about what's *right* does not even address Kelly's point about what's *honest*.

If you think rightness should be written into the very definition of honesty, so that there's nothing dishonest about breaking an oath that would be wrong to fulfill, then you can ignore the difference between a moral dilemma about what's right and a dilemma about what's honest. It is an ancient idea that we can blur distinctions in this way. Myself, I think it a bad idea. In the first place it defies ordinary language: we can perfectly well say that sometimes it's wrong to do what's honest, so that even if there's nothing to do that's honest, still there may be something to do that's right. More important, if we blur the many virtues into some sort of nondescript overall rightness, we beg the question against a plurality of incommensurable values.

We may call Kelly's example a dilemma about 'obligation'; but only if we use the word in a strict and narrow sense, saving it for the sort of obligation that is undertaken by an oath, and not applying it indiscriminately to all manner of right conduct and pursuit of good. The policeman's misfortune is that his first oath, plus the circumstances, have put him under what we may call the *first obligation*: to do what is needed to secure a conviction. The first obligation requires him, for one thing, to take the second oath; and when he does, that will put him under what we may call the *second obligation*: to tell the whole truth and nothing but. The first obligation requires him, for another thing, to lie. So after he has taken the second oath, his dilemma is that he is under two opposite obligations arising from two different oaths. Such conflict of obligations is a familiar mainstay of present-day discussion.

But notice that even before he takes the second oath (if he ever does) the policeman already has a problem: whatever he does, he will break some oath, he will not be honest in deed, he will leave some obligation unfulfilled. And notice that his dilemma at this point is *not* a conflict of obligations. So far, his only obligation is the first obligation. He has no conflicting obligation. He is *going* to have a conflicting obligation, if he takes the second oath, but he doesn't have it yet. He is obligated to put himself under a conflicting obligation, but his obligation to become obligated is not yet an obligation *simpliciter*.

Here is the second interesting and unfamiliar feature of Kelly's example. If present-day discussion has led us to identify moral dilemmas with conflicts of obligations (insofar as they involve obligation at all) we are misled by the proverbial one-sided diet. It turns out that we have a different kind of dilemma: not a conflict between obligations in being, but rather an obligation in being versus an obligation to become obligated.

(You might say that even before he takes the second oath, the policeman already has an obligation to testify truthfully; this obligation conflicts with the first obligation; so we already have a conflict of obligations. I reply (1) that this looks like the nondescript sense of obligation that we wanted to set aside in order to concentrate not on what's right but what's honest; and (2) that we could stipulate that the prevailing customs are such that truthful testimony is not obligatory apart from the second oath; and (3) that even if there is a simple conflict between the first obligation and an obligation to testify truthfully, this dilemma is not the same as the one that Kelly presents, even if the policeman is in both dilemmas at once.)

Kelly's example illustrates a little-known point about the interpretation of deontic logic.[3] A system of deontic logic has a sentential operator O which expresses deontic necessity. This is understood in the usual way in terms of accessible possible worlds: $O\phi$ is true at world w iff ϕ is true at all worlds deontically accessible from w. The accessible worlds are those which are in some sense 'ideal'; what exactly that means will vary from one intended interpretation to another. Also, we often impose a restriction to worlds in which certain fixed circumstances obtain: we have a certain time t in mind, and we limit ourselves to worlds that match the history of w up to t. For instance if t is the time when the policeman is choosing whether to take and then break the second oath, we thereby restrict ourselves to worlds where he has already taken the first oath, and where the circumstances are such that he can secure a conviction only by swearing a lie. Let us interpret O in such a way as to tie deontic necessity to the obligations (in the narrow sense) of the policeman: say that an ideal world is one at which, at time t and thereafter, the policeman never fails to fulfill any of his obligations. That means that, in view of the first obligation and the fixed circumstances, every accessible world is one where he takes and then breaks the second oath. But also, in view of the second obligation, no accessible world is one where he takes and then breaks the second oath. So there are no accessible worlds at all. That means that anything whatever is deontically necessary; $O\phi$ is true for any ϕ.

It is customary to read O as 'it is obligatory that . . .', especially

---

3 I learned it not from Kelly, however, but from Ernest Loevinsohn: personal communication, circa 1975.

when we have in mind the idealness that consists in perfect fulfillment of obligations. The surprise is that this customary reading for O is not quite right. It is deontically necessary to fulfill obligations that one is obligated to undertake but has not yet undertaken; but it is not yet obligatory to fulfill them. For instance in Kelly's example it is deontically necessary that the policeman tell the whole truth and nothing but; however until he swears the second oath – which he may never do – that is not yet, strictly speaking, obligatory. What is deontically necessary thus exceeds what is obligatory. The customary reading is safe enough if we use it with care and understand its limitations – just as it's safe enough to go on reading the hook as 'implies', so long as we know the difference – but still it is not strictly and literally correct. Deontic logic is not, strictly speaking, the logic of obligation.

9

Evil for freedom's sake?

Christianity teaches that whenever evil is done, God had ample warning. He could have prevented it, but He didn't. He could have
stopped it midway, but He didn't. He could have rescued the victims
of the evil, but – at least in many cases – He didn't. In short, God is
an accessory before, during, and after the fact to countless evil deeds,
great and small.

An explanation is not far to seek. The obvious hypothesis is
that the Christian God is really some sort of devil. Maybe He is
a devil as popularly conceived, driven by malice. Or maybe He
is unintelligibly capricious. Or maybe He is a fanatical artist who
cares only for the aesthetic quality of creation – perhaps the abstract beauty of getting rich variety to emerge from a few simple
laws, or perhaps the concrete drama of human life with all its
diversity – and cares nothing for the good of the creatures whose
lives are woven into His masterpiece. (Just as a tragedian has no
business providing a happy end out of compassion for his characters.) But no; for Christianity also teaches that God is morally
perfect and perfectly benevolent, and that He loves all of His
creatures; and that these things are true in a sense not a million

First published in *Philosophical Papers* **22** (1993), 149–172. Reprinted with kind permission from *Philosophical Papers*.

I am much indebted to many people for helpful discussion and correspondence;
especially Marilyn Adams, Robert M. Adams, Jonathan Bennett, John Bishop, Calvin
Normore, Alvin Plantinga, Susanna Siegel, and Peter van Inwagen.

miles from the sense in which we attribute morality, benevolence, or love to one another.

We turn next to the hypothesis that God permits evil-doing for the sake of its good effects. And indeed we know that sometimes good does come of evil, and doubtless in more ways than we are able to discover. But omnipotence is not bound by laws of cause and effect. God can make anything follow anything; He never has to allow evil so that good may come. Cause-and-effect theodicy cannot succeed. Not all by itself, anyway; the most it can be is part of some theodicy that also has another chapter to explain why God does not pursue His good ends by better means.

A hypothesis that God allows evil for the sake of some good might work if there was a logical, not merely a causal, connection between allowing the evil and gaining the good. Therefore Christians have often gone in for free-will theodicy: the hypothesis that God allows evil-doing for the sake of freedom. He leaves His creatures free because their freedom is of great value; leaving them free logically implies allowing them to do evil; then it is not inevitable, but it is unsurprising, that evil sometimes ensues. In this paper, I shall examine free-will theodicy, consider some choices, and consider some difficulties to which various choices lead.

I. SOME PRELIMINARY DISCLAIMERS

I am an atheist. So you might suspect that my purpose is to debunk free-will theodicy, and every other theodicy besides, so as to provide – at last! – a triumphant knock-down refutation of Christianity. Not so. I am convinced that philosophical debate almost always ends in deadlock, and that this case will be no exception.[1] When I argue that free-will theodicy meets with difficulties, I mean just what I say, no more and no less. I am not saying, and I am not slyly hinting, that

---

1 That may suggest an 'anything goes' attitude toward philosophical questions that I neither hold nor approve of. I would insist that when debate over a philosophical question – say, the question whether I have hands – ends in deadlock, it does *not* follow that there is no truth of the matter; or that we don't know the truth of the matter; or that we ought to suspend judgement; or that we have no reason for thinking one thing rather than the other.

these so-called difficulties are really refutations. In fact, I wish free-will theodicy success, or at least some modicum of success. I don't want to have a proof that all the Christians I know are either muddle-heads or devil-worshippers. That conclusion would be as incredible as it is unfriendly. But I won't mind concluding that a Christian must believe one or another of various things that I myself find unbeliev-able. For of course I knew that all along.

I shall, accordingly, suspend disbelief on several points. I shall not make heavy weather over God's supposed omnipotence, despite my own conviction that a principle of recombination of possibilities disallows any absolutely necessary connections between God's will and the world that obeys His will.[2] Likewise I shall not make heavy weather over God's supposed necessary existence. I shall not make heavy weather over God's supposed moral perfection, despite my own conviction that values are diverse and incommensurable and conflict in such ways that even God could not pursue some without betraying others. (It is a real loss if God is not a fanatical and diaboli-cally ruthless artist. It can't just be outweighed by the goods that He pursues instead, for lack of any determinate weights to be compared.) I shall not make heavy weather – well, not for long – of assuming incompatibilism, or even of assuming the Molinist doctrine of middle knowledge.

My topic is circumscribed. I ask what free-will theodicy can ac-complish single-handed, not what it can contribute to a mixed the-odicy that combines several approaches. Further, my topic is evil-doing – not the entire problem of evil. I do not ask why God permits natural evil; or, more urgently, why He permits, and perhaps perpe-trates, the evil of eternal damnation. I put these questions aside as too hard.[3] Neither do I ask why God did not create the best possible

---

2 See David Lewis, *On the Plurality of Worlds* (Oxford, Blackwell, 1986), 86–92.

3 It seems that many find the second question too hard. Seldom does an analytic philosopher of religion defend the eternal torment of the damned. Among those who discuss the question at all, Richard Swinburne, 'A Theodicy of Heaven and Hell' in *The Existence and Nature of God*, ed. by Alfred Freddoso (Notre Dame, Indiana, Notre Dame Press, 1983) is typical: he offers no 'theodicy of Hell' but only a reason why the damned may not enjoy the delights of Heaven. But Peter Geach rises to the challenge: in *Providence and Evil* (Cambridge, Cambridge

world. To that question, I am content with the answer that, maybe, for every world there is another still better, so that none is best.[4]

II. THEODICY VERSUS DEFENCE

Alvin Plantinga, our foremost modern authority on free-will theodicy, would recoil from that name for his subject. He has taught us to distinguish 'theodicy' from 'defence'.[5] 'Theodicy', for Plantinga, means an audacious claim to know the truth about why God permits evil. And not just a trivial bit of the truth – God permits evil for the sake of some good or other – but something fairly substantive and detailed. One who claims to know God's mind so well (especially if he claims to know without benefit of revelation) will seem both foolhardy and impudent.

'Defence', on the other hand, means just any hypothesis about why omniscient, omnipotent, benevolent God permits evil. Its sole purpose is to rebut the contention that there is no possible way that such a thing could happen. To serve that purpose, the hypothesis need not be put forward as true. It need not be at all plausible. Mere possibility is enough.

Plantinga aims only at defence. So why does he invest so much effort and ingenuity in the hypothesis that God permits evil for freedom's sake? I think an easier hypothesis would serve his purpose. As follows. We are partly right, partly wrong in our catalogue of

University Press, 1977), he claims that 'someone confronted with the damned would find it impossible to wish that things so evil should be happy' (139). Grant that they shouldn't be happy; but why wouldn't it be best to destroy them? Wouldn't 'the work of the Divine Artist . . . be permanently marred if the surd or absurd element of sin were a permanent element of it'? (140) In reply Geach speculates that time forks, Hell in one fork and Heaven in the other; so that the blessed in Heaven cannot say that Hell was, or is, or will be. But why does this leave the work of the Artist – the *entire* work – unmarred?

4 George Schlesinger, 'The Problem of Evil and the Problem of Suffering', *American Philosophical Quarterly* 1 (1964), 244–247; Peter Forrest, 'The Problem of Evil: Two Neglected Defences', *Sophia* 29 (1981), 49–54.
5 Alvin Plantinga, *God, Freedom, and Evil* (New York, Harper & Row, 1974), 10, 27–29; Plantinga, 'Self-Profile' in *Alvin Plantinga*, ed. by James Tomberlin and Peter van Inwagen (Dordrecht, Reidel, 1985), 35, 42.

values. The best things in life include love, joy, knowledge, vigour, despair, malice, betrayal, torture, ... God in His infinite love provides all His children with an abundance of good things. Different ones of us get different gifts, all of them very good. So some are blessed with joy and knowledge, some with vigour and malice, some with torture and despair. God permits evil-doing as a means for delivering some of the goods, just as He permits beneficence as a means for delivering others.

Why not? The hypothesis isn't true, of course. And it isn't plausible. But a defence needn't be true and needn't be plausible; possibility is enough. And not epistemic possibility, or 'real' possibility given the actual circumstances and laws of nature; just 'broadly logical' possibility. That's an easy standard. If somehow it could be made to explain why God permits evil, the hypothesis that pigs fly would be good enough for mere defence.

I myself think that a false value judgement, however preposterous, is possibly true.[6] But suppose you disagree, and deny that value judgements are contingent. No matter. What you deny is a disputed metaphysical thesis. Plantinga incorporates a disputed metaphysical thesis into his own free-will defence – the thesis that there are truths about how unactualized free choices would have come out – without stopping to prove that it is possible because it is true. Evidently he takes for granted that whether or not it's true, still it is possible in the relevant sense. So why may I not follow his precedent?

Defence is too easy; knowing God's mind is too hard. I think the topic worth pursuing falls in between, and has no place in Plantinga's scheme of theodicy versus defence. *Pace* Plantinga, I'll call that topic 'theodicy', but I don't mean the know-it-all theodicy that he wisely disowns. Rather I mean tentative theodicy, even speculative theodicy. The Christian needn't hope to end by knowing for sure why God permits evil. But he can hope to advance from a predicament of

---

6 That follows from my meta-ethical position, subjectivism with bells and whistles. See David Lewis, 'Dispositional Theories of Value', *Aristotelian Society Supplementary Volume* 63 (1989), 113–137 (reprinted in this volume as Chapter 7). It's necessary to consider the value judgement taken in an 'unrigidified' form (see 132–133) but there's nothing wrong with that.

not having a clue to a predicament of indecision between several not-too-unbelievable hypotheses (maybe still including the hypothesis: 'none of the above').[7] The job is to devise hypotheses that are at least somewhat plausible, at least to the Christian, and to find considerations that make them more plausible or less. Robert M. Adams has written that 'the atheological program . . . need not be one of rational coercion. It might be a more modest project of rational persuasion, intended not to coerce but to attract the minds of theists and agnostics, or perhaps to shore up the unbelief of atheists.'[8] Right; and the same, *mutatis mutandis*, goes for theodicy.

III. SIGNIFICANT FREEDOM

If free-will theodicy is to explain the evil-doing that actually goes on, and if it is to be plausible that our freedom is of great enough value to be worth the evil that is its price, then we can't just suppose that God leaves us free to choose what cereal to eat for breakfast. We'd better suppose that God permits evil for the sake of *significant* freedom: freedom in choices that matter. Free choice of breakfast is insignificant and worthless.

But choices that matter needn't be between good and evil. They might be momentous choices between incommensurable goods. Example, half-fictitious: a splendid painting has gradually been covered with dirt. By luck, the dirty painting is splendid in its own way. There's no saying which is better, the old clean painting or the new dirty painting; they're too different. Will you have the painting cleaned? Either choice is tragic, neither is evil.

If freedom in such choices as this is significant enough, unlike free choice of breakfast, then God need not permit evil for freedom's sake. He can leave us free to choose between goods, but not free to choose evil. (Just as He leaves us free to stand or to walk, but not to fly.) To make free-will theodicy explain the evil that actually goes

---

7 See Sylvain Bromberger, 'An Approach to Explanation' in *Analytic Philosophy: Second Series*, ed. by R. J. Butler (Oxford, Blackwell, 1965) on the distinction between kinds of predicaments.

8 Adams, 'Plantinga on the Problem of Evil' in *Alvin Plantinga*, 240.

on, you have to say that this is not freedom enough. It would be well (but it isn't compulsory) to say why not.

Plantinga, after he notes that free choice of breakfast is insignificant, goes on to define significant freedom as freedom with respect to an action such that either it is wrong to perform it and right to refrain, or else *vice versa*.[9] That is too weak, if we hope to explain all the evil-doing that takes place. Christians, and some others too, believe in wicked thoughts. Example: spending an hour silently composing an eloquent diatribe against God. Insofar as thoughts are voluntary – and to a substantial extent they are – thinking a wicked thought is an action it's wrong to perform. So God could grant us plenty of significant freedom, in Plantinga's sense, if He left our thoughts free but rigidly controlled our behaviour. You have to say that this too is not freedom enough. We need to explain not only why God permits thoughtcrime but also why He permits evil behaviour.

The same point goes for victimless evil-doing in general, even when it is behaviour rather than secret thought. Some might think it wicked to utter a blasphemous diatribe aloud, even if there are none to hear it save the incorruptible and the already-corrupted; but none of the audience will be harmed. And all will agree that some evil-doing is victimless because an attempt to do harm fails.

It cannot be said that harm is ever the inevitable consequence of evil-doing. For omnipotence, no merely causal consequence is inevitable. God could put each of His free creatures in a playpen. He could make freedom safe by making all evil victimless. He could have so arranged things, for instance, that no matter what evil Stalin freely did, no harm would come of it. And Stalin needn't have known the playpen was there. Insofar as the intrinsic character of Stalin and his evil deeds went, the playpen needn't have made the slightest difference. Stalin's freedom to do evil – significant freedom in the sense of Plantinga's definition – would have been undiminished.[10]

9 *God, Freedom, and Evil*, 30

10 Steven Boer, 'The Irrelevance of the Free-Will Defence', *Analysis* 38 (1978), 110–112, suggests that the question why evil sometimes causes harm belongs to the department of theodicy that is concerned with the problem of natural evil. If so,

So why didn't God put Stalin in a playpen? – An answer is not far to seek. It seems that Stalin's freedom would have been much less significant if nothing much had been at stake. Outside the playpen as he actually was, Stalin's freedom gained its significance from two factors taken together. One was the good or evil intrinsic character of the actions he was left free to perform or refrain from. The other factor was the extent to which good and bad outcomes – the well-being of millions – depended on his choice. Plantinga's definition of significant freedom should be expanded to include the second factor. Without a solution to the playpen problem free-will theodicy does not explain the sort of evil that actually takes place.

(Still, why should the value of the freedom depend on how much is at stake? – Here's one answer, but whether it should appeal to Christians I do not know. Christianity teaches that man is made in God's image; and also that God is not only the creator, but also the sustaining cause of the world. All that is good in the world, as well as all that isn't, depends at every moment on God's will for its continued existence. And likewise much that was good depended on Stalin's will for its continued existence, and so perished. Thus Stalin had his little share of the power that makes God what He is; and he wouldn't have had, if his significant freedom had just been the freedom to misbehave in his playpen.)

God's answer to a prayer from the Gulag:

No, I will not deliver you. For I resolved not to; and I was right so to resolve, for otherwise your fate would not have been in Stalin's hands; and then Stalin's freedom to choose between good and evil would have been less significant. If you had been spared just because Stalin freely relented, that would have been a very good thing. I knew it wouldn't happen. But it was not for *me* to prevent it, and I would be preventing it if I stood by ready to release you if Stalin didn't. So here you stay!

the playpen problem falls outside our present topic. However, I note that in that case, we must dismiss the hypothesis that natural evil is the evil-doing of Satan and his cohorts. (See *God, Freedom, and Evil*, 58–59.) For why does the evil-doing of Satan and his cohorts cause harm? God could have put Satan and his cohorts in the playpen along with Stalin.

If what I've said about the playpen problem is right, this is where free-will theodicy leads. Absurd? Monstrous? – I rather think not, though I'm of two minds about it. It's uncomfortable, for sure.

I ask a final question. Why should we not do as God does, and leave victims to their fates so as not to make the freedom of evil-doers less significant? – Not unanswerable. One answer: There are other considerations that enter into the decision, notably how we shall use our own significant freedom. Another answer (suggested by John Bishop in conversation): If the victims had been protected by the power of God Almighty, that would have put the evil-doer in altogether too much of a playpen. But if we do our fallible best, the evil-doer is in a very imperfect playpen and his freedom remains significant enough. I think the two answers succeed, but they leave a residual question I don't know how to answer. Why is the significance of the evil-doer's freedom a weightless consideration for us, not merely an outweighed consideration?

IV. COMPATIBILISM

Compatibilism says that our choices are free insofar as they manifest our characters (our beliefs, desires, etc.) and are not determined via causal chains that bypass our characters. If so, freedom is compatible with predetermination of our choices via our characters. The best argument for compatibilism is that we know better that we are sometimes free than that we ever escape predetermination; wherefore it may be for all we know that we are free but predetermined.

Incompatibilism says that our choices are free only if they have no determining causes outside our characters – not even causes that determine our choices via our characters. The best argument for incompatibilism rests on a plausible principle that unfreedom is closed under implication. Consider the prefix 'it is true that, and such-and-such agent never had any choice about whether', abbreviated 'Unfree'; suppose we have some premises (zero or more) that imply a conclusion; prefix 'Unfree' to each premise and to the conclusion; then the closure principle says that the prefixed premises imply the prefixed conclusion.[11] Given determinism, apply closure to the implication that takes us from preconditions outside character – long ago, perhaps – and deterministic laws of nature to the predetermined choice. Conclude that the choice is unfree. Compatibilists must reject the closure principle. Let's assume that incompatibilists accept it. Else why are they incompatibilists?

I'll speak of 'compatibilist freedom' and 'incompatibilist freedom'. But I don't ask you to presuppose that these are two varieties of freedom. According to incompatibilism, compatibilist freedom is no more freedom than counterfeit money is money.

It seems that free-will theodicy must presuppose incompatibilism. God could determine our choices via our characters, thereby preventing evil-doing while leaving our compatibilist freedom intact. Thus He could create utopia, a world where free creatures never do evil.

Plantinga once responded to compatibilist opponents as if their objection were a terminological quibble. The hypothesis is that God permits evil so that our actions may be not determined. If you find 'free' a tendentious word, use another word: 'unfettered', say.[12] But of course the issue is one of value, not terminology. The opponents grant the value of compatibilist freedom. But they think that if God

---

11 The closure principle is a generalization of the 'Rule Beta' that plays a leading role in Peter van Inwagen's defence of incompatibilism in *An Essay on Free Will* (Oxford, Oxford University Press, 1983); it first appears on page 94. The closure principle says that the logic of 'Unfree' is a 'normal' modal logic; see Brian Chellas, *Modal Logic: An Introduction* (Cambridge, Cambridge University Press, 1980), 114–115. We can see from Chellas's Theorem 4.3(4) that the closure principle is equivalent, *inter alia*, to this combination of four principles:

RE: if '*A* iff *B*' is valid, so is 'Unfree *A* iff Unfree *B*',
N: 'Unfree *T*' is valid, where *T* is an arbitrary tautology,
M: 'Unfree (*A* & *B*)' implies 'Unfree *A* and Unfree *B*', and
C: 'Unfree *A* and Unfree *B*' implies 'Unfree (*A* & *B*)'.

The compatibilist must therefore challenge one of the four, most likely C: and Michael Slote has done so in 'Selective Necessity and the Free-Will Problem', *Journal of Philosophy* 79 (1982), 5–24.

12 Plantinga, *God and Other Minds* (Ithaca, Cornell University Press, 1967), 135. But later he concedes that this was too short a way with compatibilism: 'Self-Profile', 45–47, and 'Reply to Robert M. Adams', 371–372, both in *Alvin Plantinga*. My complaint here applies only to his earlier view.

permits evil for the sake of incompatibilist freedom, what He gains is worthless.

Yet for purposes of mere 'defence' it needn't be true, or even plausible, that incompatibilist freedom has value. It is enough that it be possible. Plantinga's short way with the compatibilists would have been fair if, but only if, it was common ground that a false and implausible value judgement is nevertheless possible.

Before we turn back to the free-will theodicy that does presuppose incompatibilism, let's consider the compatibilist alternative a little further. Suppose God did determine our choices via our characters, preventing evil-doing while leaving us free. How might He do it? By a wise choice of initial conditions and uniform, powerful, simple laws of nature? – That might be mathematically impossible.[13] The problem might be overconstrained. It might be like the problem: find a curve which is given by an equation no more than fifteen characters long, and which passes through none of the following hundred listed regions of the plane.

Rather, God might attain utopia by elaborate contrivance. Instead of uniform and powerful laws of nature, He could leave the laws gappy, leaving Him room to intervene directly in the lives of His creatures and guide them constantly back to the right path. Or (if indeed this is possible) His laws might be full of special quirks designed to apply only to very special cases. Either way, despite our compatibilist freedom, God would be managing our lives in great detail, making extensive use of His knowledge and power.

John Bishop has suggested that 'the value of fully autonomous mutual loving relationships' would be lacking in a world where this happens.[14] (Think of analogous contrivance in the relationship of two people!) Freedom – compatibilist freedom, perhaps – is an integral part, but only part, of this larger value. In this way, Bishop arrives at

---

13 Remember how much the laws of nature must be 'fine-tuned' before they even permit life. See John Leslie, *Universes* (London, Routledge, 1989), 4–6, 27–65.

14 John Bishop, 'Compatibilism and the Free Will Defence', *Australasian Journal of Philosophy* 71 (1993), 104–120. Note that Bishop's theodicy offers another solution to the playpen problem – one that is not available within free-will theology narrowly construed.

something akin to free-will theodicy that is available even under compatibilism. The story is for Bishop to tell, and I will not pursue it further. Except to note that Bishop fears it must end in heterodoxy: the loving relationship between God and His creatures will be unspoiled only if God gives away some of His power over them, and becomes no longer omnipotent.

Though I am in fact a compatibilist, from this point on I concede incompatibilism for the sake of the argument. I'll say 'freedom' for short to mean incompatibilist freedom.

We've come this far: there is nothing God can do to make sure that there will be (significantly) free creatures who never do evil. Because whatever act of God makes sure that you choose not to do evil *ipso facto* renders you unfree in so choosing. To show this, apply the closure principle to the implication that runs from God's act, plus the conditional that if God so acts then you will not do evil, to the conclusion that you do not do evil.

It proves helpful to restate this, lumping together all God's acts and all His omissions. A (*maximal*) option for God is a maximally specific, consistent proposition about which acts He does and doesn't do. These options partition the possible worlds where God exists. At any such world, God (*strongly*) actualizes just one of His options: that is, He acts and refrains from acting in such a way that this option, and no other, is true. In a derivative sense, He actualizes other propositions: all and only those that are implied by the option He actualizes. (Implied sometimes with the aid of the necessary connections between God's will and the world that comprise His omnipotence.) And in a still more derivative sense, He actualizes the things that exist, and the events that occur, according to the propositions He actualizes.

We cannot blame God because He has not actualized significant freedom without evil-doing. He could not have actualized that: He had no option that implied it.

V. GOD THE UNLUCKY

At this point we may picture God as an unlucky gambler. He confronted a range of options. Some were mediocre: no free creatures, or at least no significant freedom. Others offered Him a gamble on how His creatures would use their freedom. If He gambled, He might lose. Or He might win: His free creatures might freely shun all evil, and that would be very good indeed. Wisely weighing the prospects of winning and losing, He chose to gamble. He lost. Lost rather badly, to judge by the newspapers; but we don't really know quite how much worse it could have been. Tough luck, God!

(Our commiseration for God's bad luck seems scarcely consonant with worship of Him as a Supreme Being. However, the mysteries of the Trinity may go some way to reconcile dissonant stances toward one and the same God.)

Be that as it may, the picture of God as an unlucky gambler is wrong. Or anyway it is heterodox, which is the same for present purposes. For it overlooks God's foreknowledge. An ordinary gambler makes a decision under uncertainty; he doesn't know how any of the gambles on offer would turn out. When he finds out he has lost, it's too late to change his mind. He can only regret having gambled as he did. God, however, does know the outcome of at least one of His options: namely, the one that He will in fact actualize. He knows all along just what He will and won't do, and just how His free creatures will respond. So if He gambles and loses, He knows all along that He will lose. If He regrets His gamble, His regret does not come too late − it comes as early as early can be. Then nothing forces Him to go ahead with it. He has the power, and it is not too late, to actualize some other option instead.

You may well protest: if He did switch to some other option, how would He gain the foreknowledge that made Him regret His original choice? − Fair enough. My point should be put as a *reductio* against the supposition that God is an unlucky gambler who regrets His gamble. Suppose for *reductio* that God actualizes a certain option O; and O turns out badly; and the prospect for some other option is better than O is when O turns out badly. Then God knows by foreknowledge that O turns out badly, so He prefers some other option to O. Then He actualizes another option instead of O. Contradiction.

God is not, we may conclude, an unlucky gambler who regrets

His gamble. He may yet be an unlucky gambler who does not regret His gamble, even though He lost. How might that be?

God might know that the gamble He lost still, even when lost, surpasses the expected value[15] of all the other gambles He might have tried instead, as well as the mediocre options in which He doesn't gamble at all. That could be so if He lost, but much less badly than He might have done. He would have no cause for regret if He took one of the gambles with the best expected value (or near enough[16]) and the actual outcome was no worse than the expected value. But on this hypothesis gambling on significant freedom is a much more dangerous game than we would have suspected just on the basis of the evil-doing that actually happens. That makes it all the harder to believe that freedom is worth the risk.

Or instead, God might not regret the gamble He lost because, somehow, He knows that if He had tried any other gamble, He would still have lost, and lost at least as badly as He actually did.

VI. MOLINISM

We might think, with de Molina and Suarez, and Plantinga in at least some of his writings, that God has not only foreknowledge but also 'middle knowledge'.[17] Not only does He know what the free creatures who actually exist, in the predicaments in which they actually

---

15 Or some vague approximation to an expected value. I don't suppose an incompatibilist will think that free choices have well-defined probabilities; but neither will he want to abandon altogether the idea that some free choices are more likely than others, and so contribute more weightily to the prospect of a certain gamble on freedom.

16 Maybe God is a satisficer; maybe it is not part of His benevolence, rightly understood, that He must actualize the very best of His options. See Robert M. Adams, 'Must God Create the Best?' *Philosophical Review* 81 (1972), 317–332, reprinted in Adams, *The Virtue of Faith* (Oxford, Oxford University Press, 1987). The more of a satisficer God is, of course, the easier it will be for Him not to regret a gamble that turns out badly.

17 See Robert M. Adams, 'Middle Knowledge and the Problem of Evil,' *American Philosophical Quarterly* 14 (1977), 109–117, reprinted in *The Virtue of Faith*; Anthony Kenny, *The God of the Philosophers* (Oxford, Oxford University Press, 1979), 61–71; and Plantinga, 'Self-Profile', 48–50.

find themselves, will actually do; He also knows what the free creatures would have done had they found themselves in different predicaments, and He even knows what would have been done by free creatures who do not actually exist.

If this is so – and if, in addition, God has middle knowledge about chance systems other than free creatures, for instance radium atoms – then God is no gambler. He confronts not a decision problem under uncertainty, not even a decision problem under partial uncertainty alleviated by His foreknowledge, but rather a decision problem with perfect information. He knows just how each of His options would turn out. He can reason step-by-step, using His middle knowledge of free creatures (and chancy nature) at every step. 'If I were to create Satan, he would rebel; if then I were to create Adam and Eve, Satan would tempt Eve; if so, Eve would succumb, and would in turn tempt Adam. . . . ' In short: so-and-so option would result in such-and-such world.[18]

Under Molinism, God is in the best position imaginable to govern the world wisely. The option He actualizes may yet turn out badly: the free creatures may do evil. But God will have no regrets. He will have known all along that none of His other options would have turned out better (anyway, not enough better to make His chosen option wrong).

The counterfactual conditionals that God knows by His middle knowledge – call them *counterfactuals of freedom*, ignoring henceforth the ones about the radium atoms – must be contingent truths. It is always possible for the antecedent to be true and the consequent false, making the whole counterfactual false. Being contingent, there are various combinations of them that might be true. Some especially unfortunate patterns of counterfactuals yield what we may call, approximately following Plantinga, a pattern of *depravity*: God has no

---

18 This is not the fallacy of counterfactual transitivity. Instead, it repeatedly invokes the inference

If it were that A, then it would be that B;
if it were that A & B, then it would be that C;
therefore if it were that A, then it would be that B & C

which is uncontroversially valid.

option such that, if He were to actualize it, there would then exist significantly free creatures and none of them would ever freely do evil. If so, evil would indeed be the inescapable price of freedom.[19]

19 Let $O(W)$ be the option that God strongly actualizes at world W, assuming that W is a world where God exists. We say that God *can actualize* world W if the following counterfactual is true (here at our actual world): if it were that $O(W)$, then W would be actualized. If, in addition, $O(W)$ holds at no world except W and hence strictly implies that W is actualized, we say that God *can strongly actualize* W; if not, we say that God *can weakly actualize* W. These definitions differ from Plantinga's, but they are equivalent; see the statement and proof of 'Lewis's Lemma', in his 'Self-Profile', 50–51.

Assume that God is able to leave something unsettled. What God leaves unsettled comes out differently at different possible worlds, but not because of any difference in what God does. That is: God has an option O that holds at two different worlds V and W, so that $O(V) = O(W) = O$. Then one or both of these two worlds is a world that He cannot actualize, either weakly or strongly. Else we would have two true counterfactuals with the same antecedent and conflicting consequents: if it were that O, V would be actual; if it were that O, W would be actual; but V and W cannot both be actual. That would mean that O was not an entertainable supposition, contrary to the assumption that it is one of God's options. Thus we refute 'Leibniz's Lapse', the thesis that for any world (or any world in which God exists), God can actualize that world.

(Susanna Siegel has observed that the 'lapse' may be badly named. For Leibniz could invoke his principle of sufficient reason to argue that God is *un*able to leave anything unsettled. In that case it would be no lapse for Leibniz to conclude that God is, after all, able to actualize any world.)

Note that this refutation of Leibniz's lapse does not require us to say anything specific about *what* it is that God can leave unsettled, and *why* He might want to leave it unsettled. But one case to keep in mind is the case that He might leave a creature's action unsettled, because He values incompatibilist freedom. Note also that the refutation does not presuppose Molinism. If the difference between worlds V and W concerns the action of a free creature, Molinism says that *one* of the conflicting counterfactuals is true and anti-Molinism says that neither is true; but what matters for the refutation is just that they can't *both* be true.

Call a world *utopian* if it contains significantly free creatures, none of whom ever freely do evil. Once we know that there are some worlds that God cannot actualize, we are in a position to speculate that every utopian world is one of these unactualizable worlds. That is a weak version of the hypothesis of depravity.

Plantinga's own version of the hypothesis, in *The Nature of Necessity*, 186–189, is stronger by a quantifier shift. His hypothesis is that *every* possible creature P

Given Molinism and the hypothesis of depravity, we have a free will theodicy that is immune to our *reductio* against regret. God gambles and loses without any regret, knowing that He would have done no better (or not enough better to matter) if He had actualized any other option. Insofar as it affords a way around the problem of regret, Molinism makes free-will theodicy easier. In other ways, though, Molinism makes more trouble than it cures.

Not every so-called counterfactual is really contrary to fact. Counterfactuals of freedom come in two kinds: the *fulfilled*, with true antecedents, and the unfulfilled. Consider a fulfilled counterfactual: if Judas had the chance, he would betray Christ for thirty pieces of silver. Counterfactuals obey *modus ponens*. So apply the closure principle to the implication

Judas has the chance;
If Judas had the chance, he would betray Christ;
Therefore Judas betrays Christ.

Ex hypothesi Judas had a free choice about whether to betray Christ; but presumably he never had any choice about whether to be offered the chance. Therefore Judas must have had a free choice about whether the counterfactual of freedom was to be true. And that's just as we might have thought: when Judas freely betrayed Christ, he thereby rendered true the counterfactual of freedom.

Unfulfilled counterfactuals of freedom are very different. They're not rendered true by the free choice of the agent, since they concern choices that never actually take place. Some of them even concern agents who never actually exist. It's peculiar – but consistent, good enough for mere defence – that the two kinds of counterfactuals of freedom should work so very differently.

What does make unfulfilled counterfactuals of freedom true? Are they subject to God's will? – If so, it seems that God would have

suffers from trans-world depravity: that is to say (almost), there is no world God can actualize where *P* exists and is significantly free and never freely does evil. (I omit another unimportant strengthening, and I omit Plantinga's use of essences as surrogates for *possibilia*.)

117

options of actualizing free creatures and also actualizing counterfactuals of freedom such that those creatures would freely shun evil. That goes against the hypothesis of depravity, and thereby wrecks our way around the problem of regret. Further, if God did both these things, then the alleged free creatures would not be free after all, by the closure principle. We conclude that counterfactuals of freedom can be subject to God's will *only* if they remain unfulfilled! God's supposed power to see to it that an agent would freely do so-and-so if put to the test is a 'finkish' power: God has it only on condition that the agent is *not* put to the test. It seems absurd that God's powers should be finkish in this way – the conclusion is a *reductio*. Therefore unfulfilled counterfactuals of freedom are not subject to God's will.[20]

Are they true in virtue of what things and what fundamental properties do and don't exist, and how these things and properties are arranged in patterns of instantiation? In John Bigelow's phrase, does their truth supervene on being?[21] No; for unless God's omnipotence is limited in still other respects, any truth that supervenes on being is subject to His will. So there can be nothing that makes unfulfilled counterfactuals of freedom true. They just *are* true, and that's that.[22]

---

20 Compare C. B. Martin's idea of a finkish disposition: as it might be, the solubility of something that would instantly cease to be soluble if ever it were put into solvent. Martin discussed finkish dispositions years ago in Sydney, and in 'Powers and Conditionals', presented at the University of North Carolina in 1968. I agree with Martin that finkish dispositions are possible, and that they refute a simple conditional analysis of dispositions. What I deem absurd is not finkishness *per se*, but finkishness applied to God's powers.

21 See John Bigelow, *The Reality of Numbers* (Oxford, Oxford University Press, 1988), 133; and 'Real Possibilities', *Philosophical Studies* 53 (1988), 38, where supervenience on what things exist turns into supervenience on what things exist and *how they are arranged* (i.e. arranged in patterns of instantiation). Bigelow's principle is a weakened form of C. B. Martin's principle that truths require truthmakers; see D. M. Armstrong, 'C. B. Martin, Counterfactuals, Causality, and Conditionals' in *Cause, Mind, and Reality: Essays Honoring C. B. Martin*, ed. by John Heil (Dordrecht, Kluwer, 1989).

22 *A fortiori*, for what it's worth, they violate the analysis I advanced in *Counterfactuals* (Oxford, Blackwell, 1973). For on my analysis, the truth of counterfactuals is supervenient on being.

VII. SELECTIVE FREEDOM

A final difficulty with Molinism is that it seems to give God a winning strategy whereby He can, after all, see to it that His significantly free creatures never do evil. He needn't just decide, once and for all, whether His creatures are to be free. He can make a creature free only some of the time. He always knows, by foreknowledge or middle knowledge as the case may be, whether a creature would do evil if left free on a given occasion. So He can grant freedom selectively, when and only when He knows the creature will not misuse it.

This strategy of selective freedom, if it worked, would circumvent depravity. In other words, the hypothesis of depravity says that the strategy can't work. But what would go wrong if God tried it?

Perhaps this. The counterfactuals of freedom say what the free creatures would do in various circumstances; and among the circumstances are God's granting and withholding of freedom. They just might say that the more God withholds freedom so as to prevent evil, the more evil would be done on the remaining occasions when creatures are left free. For example, we could have a pattern of counterfactuals saying that a certain man would do evil on the first, and only the first, of the days when he is left free. It is useless, then, for God to withhold his freedom on day one – that would only put off the evil day. Given this pattern, the only way God can prevent him from doing evil is to withhold freedom on all the days of his life. Selective freedom doesn't work.

There might be a similar pattern involving many men, at separate times and places. Instead of the days of one man's life, we might have a succession of isolated islands. In that case, however, the pattern of counterfactuals that frustrates the strategy of selective freedom will be much more peculiar. It will be a pattern of occult counterfactual dependence that somehow overcomes barriers to any normal sort of causal interaction. The islands, at the times in question, might even be outside one another's light cones.

Not plausible, except as a last resort for heroic faith. But consistent, good enough for mere defence.

119

Set aside these peculiar patterns of counterfactual dependence. Then the hypothesis of depravity is false; the strategy of selective freedom would work; and free-will theodicy fails. Or so it seems – unless we can come up with some other objection to the strategy of selective freedom. Several objections are worth considering. I take them in order of increasing strength.

First objection. If God grants freedom selectively, He deceives us. Often we will think we are free when we are not. Deception is wrong.

Reply. At worst He misleads us, permitting us to jump rashly to a false conclusion. And maybe not even that. Why shouldn't we be able to figure out that selective freedom is a good strategy for God – if indeed it is – and conclude that God may well be following it? And if that's still not enough, why shouldn't God reveal to us that we are not always free?[23]

Second objection. God ought to follow a uniform policy, leaving us free either always or never. Fairness requires Him to treat like cases alike.

Reply. I am not sure it is the essence of fairness to treat like cases alike. Maybe uniformity is just a by-product of treating each case correctly. Or maybe it is just a means to the end of making the law predictable to those who care to study the precedents and rely on the rule of *stare decisis*. (In which case uniformity loses its point when previous cases are kept secret.)

Anyway, the cases God would treat differently are not alike. They differ in respect of counterfactuals of freedom.

Third objection. Augustine says that 'as a runaway horse is better than a stone which does not run away because it lacks self-movement and sense perception, so the creature is more excellent which sins by free will than that which does not sin only because it has no free will.'[24] Maybe free evil-doing is good in its own right, not just the price of trying for freedom without evil. Then God should not withhold freedom just because He knows that it would be misused.

---

23 A charge of deception gives us a third solution to the playpen problem. Again I reply that outright deception is not required to create a playpen.
24 Cited in Plantinga, *God, Freedom, and Evil*, 27.

That substitutes the worst outcome for the second-best – the stone for the horse.

Reply. That value judgement, if credible, would surely smooth the path of free-will theodicy. But stop to think how an unfree man is better than a stone; and stop to think of the victims beneath the horse's hooves. What we have here, I suggest, is a taste of the aesthetic theodicy that we set aside at the beginning: God the fanatical artist.

Fourth objection. John Bishop's point reappears. To secure freedom without evil by the strategy of selective freedom, God would have to manage our lives in great detail, making plenty of use of His superior knowledge and power. Even when He left us free, a larger value that subsumes the value of freedom would be lost. Such overbearing contrivance on God's part could have no place in a 'fully autonomous mutual loving relationship' between God and his creatures.

Reply. As before, I don't dispute Bishop's point. But I note that it is not exactly free-will theodicy, and I note Bishop's concern that it must end in heterodoxy.

Final objection. If God resolves to leave me free when and only when He knows that I would not misuse my freedom to do evil, then whatever 'freedom' He sometimes gives me is bogus freedom. Assume for *reductio* that on a certain occasion God left me free to do evil because He knew that I would not do evil. Then what if I had done evil after all? If I was really free, that ought to be an *entertainable* supposition: we ought to be able to reason hypothetically under the supposition that I did evil after being left free, without ending in contradiction. Yet it seems that if I had done evil, God would have foreseen it; so he would not have left me free, so I would not have done evil after all; so the counterfactual supposition that I did evil does end in contradiction. So I was not really left free.

Reply. There is another, and no less plausible, course of hypothetical reasoning that does not end in contradiction. Hold fixed my freedom, rather than God's success in predicting me. God made up His mind, once and for all, come what may, to leave me free. His resolve is firm. (It must be, else His strategy of selective freedom would indeed be bogus.) So if I did evil after all, God might be astonished to turn out wrong, but I'd still be free. If He foresaw that I'd shun evil, then if I did evil He would have been mistaken.

Objection to the reply. God is essentially infallible. If He made even one mistake, He would not be God at all. Whatever happened, God could not lack His essence. So the alternative course of hypothetical reasoning just considered also ends in contradiction: the contradiction that God is infallible and yet turns out mistaken, or more simply the contradiction that God is not God. So again it turns out not to be an entertainable supposition that I do evil; again, my 'freedom' under the strategy of selective freedom is bogus.

Defence of the reply. Not so; or not indisputably so. (Here, as elsewhere, I expect argument to end in deadlock.) Counterfactual suppositions contrary to essence are sometimes entertainable. For instance, the supposition that Descartes is material and the supposition that he is immaterial both are entertainable. Presumably one supposition or the other is contrary to Descartes' essence.[25] Yet it makes sense to reason hypothetically about what would be the case under either supposition, and the reasoning need not end in contradiction. Further, even when an entertainable supposition is not itself contrary to essence, still it may happen that what would be the case given that supposition is contrary to essence. For instance, consider the counterfactuals:

If all creatures were material, Descartes would be material.

If material things couldn't think, Descartes would be immaterial.

25 I myself would say that suppositions contrary to essence are entertainable because essence is a flexible matter; it's no contradiction that a being is, loosely speaking, God but is not, strictly speaking, God because of one lapse from omniscience; just as it is no contradiction that a glass is, loosely speaking, empty but is not, strictly speaking, empty because of one remaining drop of beer. Not essentialism *per se*, but only an especially rigid version of essentialism stands in the way of supposing counterfactually that Descartes lacks his essence, or that God lacks His. Nor need we explain this in terms of my theory of counterparts; the same flexibility is available on rival approaches to modal metaphysics, except for one approach that lacks adherents. See my *On the Plurality of Worlds*, Ch. 4.

Presumably one consequent or the other is contrary to Descartes' essence; yet both counterfactuals seem non-vacuously true, and neither antecedent is contrary to essence. So even if the consequent 'God is mistaken' is contrary to God's essence, the supposition that I did evil may yet be entertainable.

The logical situation is confusing because it involves a counterfactual within a counterfactual. So it may be helpful to spell it out more fully. Let *OH*, the *outer* hypothesis, be that God can tell whether or not I would do evil if left free, foresees that I would not do evil if left free, follows the strategy of selective freedom, and accordingly leaves me free. Let *IH*, the *inner* hypothesis, be that I nevertheless freely do evil. We take as a premise that unless my 'freedom' were bogus, *IH* would be entertainable; so we have

(1) If it were that *OH*, then not:
    if it were that *IH*, then a contradiction would obtain.

And we trivially have

(2) If it were that *OH*, then:
    if it were that *IH*, then I would freely do evil.

And it seems that we also have

(3) If it were that *OH*, then: if it were that *IH*, then:
    God would foresee that I would do evil if left free; and

(4) If it were that *OH*, then: if it were that *IH*, then:
    God would still follow the strategy of selective freedom.

From (3) and (4) we have

(5) If it were that *OH*, then: if it were that *IH*, then:
    God would not leave me free and so I would not freely do evil.

From (2) and (5) we have

(6) If it were that *OH*, then:
    if it were that *IH*, then: a contradiction would obtain.

From (1) and (6) we have

123

(7) If it were that OH, then a contradiction would obtain.

This means that *OH* – a sample instance of selective freedom – is not an entertainable supposition. That completes the objection. The reply denies (3) and says that what's true instead is

(3′) If it were that *OH*, then: if it were that *IH*, then:
  God would wrongly think that I wouldn't do evil if left free.

And from (3′) there follows no difficulty for the hypothesis *OH*. The objection to the reply uses God's essential infallibility to support

(8) If it were that *OH*, then: if it were that *IH*, then:
  God would not wrongly think anything;

and from (3′) and (8) we obtain (6) and proceed as before. The defence of the reply questions (8), finding precedent for (3′) in other true counterfactuals with consequents contrary to essence.

We might think, wrongly, that (3) is guaranteed by counterfactual logic; namely, by the same principle that yields: 'if we had ham, then if we had eggs we'd have ham and eggs'. (If *A*, then: if *B* then *A&B*.) This ham-and-eggs principle would indeed yield (3), since the consequent of (3) follows from *OH* and *IH* together. For *OH* says in part that God can tell whether I would do evil if left free; *IH* says in part that I freely do evil, and hence implies that I would do evil if left free; these together imply that God would foresee that I would do evil if left free. But the ham-and-eggs principle would equally yield (3′). For *OH* says in part that God foresees that I would not do evil if left free, and *IH* implies that I would do evil if left free, so together they imply that He's wrong. Anyway, the ham-and-eggs principle, plausible though some of its instances may be, is invalid. Maybe if we had ham, our having ham would depend on our not having eggs; so maybe if we had ham, it would be that: if we had eggs we'd have eggs and no ham.[26] The principle is useless to support either (3) or (3′). They must stand or fall on their own merits.

26 On the analysis I offer in *Counterfactuals* – which, however must remain bracketed so long as we suspend disbelief about Molinism – the ham-and-eggs principle amounts to assuming, roughly, that any closest B-world to any closest A-world to ours must be an A&B-world. The analogy of similarity distance to spatial distance

Our present discussion retraces part of the famous dispute over fore-knowledge and freedom. Suppose I freely accept a gift of $1000, ignoring putative reasons why I should decline it. God foresaw that I would. If I had declined – an entertainable supposition – then God certainly would not have known ahead of time that I would accept. But what would have happened? God's foreknowledge that I would accept, taken as a whole, is a 'soft' fact: if I had done otherwise, it would have been otherwise, so it does not limit my freedom. But we can divide it into two parts. On the one hand, there is the content of a past belief: it was a belief that I was going to accept the gift. On the other hand, there is the fact that this was God's belief, and constituted part of His infallible foreknowledge. Which part is the soft part? Opinion may well divide.

Perhaps we should hold fixed that the believer was infallible God, and say then that it is the content of His belief that is soft: if I had later declined the gift, He would all along have expected me to decline. 'I am able to make some proposition to have been known by God that is not [in fact] known by God, and conversely' said Richard of Campsall in the fourteenth century;[27] and in our time, Plantinga has taken a similar view.[28]

Or perhaps instead we should hold fixed the content of the past belief, and say that what is soft is that this belief belonged to infallible God. He expected me to accept, so if I had declined He would have suffered a lapse in His essential infallibility, so He would not, strictly speaking, have been God at all. So said Robert Holkot in the sixteenth century;[29] and in our time, Marilyn Adams has taken a similar view.[30]

quickly reveals counterexamples. Then why is the ham-and-eggs principle plausible offhand? Maybe we mistake the double counterfactual

If it were that A, then: if it were that B . . .

for a single counterfactual with a conjunctive antecedent

If A and B, then. . . .

27 Campsall's *Notabilia*, 7, in *The Works of Richard of Campsall* ed. by Edward A. Synan (Toronto, Pontifical Institute of Mediaeval Studies, 1982), Vol. II, 40.
28 'On Ockham's Way Out', *Faith and Philosophy* 3 (1986), 235–269.
29 According to Calvin Normore, personal communication.
30 'Is the Existence of God a "Hard" Fact?', *Philosophical Review* 76 (1967), 492–503.

We should take care how we state the two opinions, lest they seem harder to believe than they really are. The opinion that if I had declined, then God's past expectation would have been different from what it actually was does not mean that I have the power to change the past. There is no question of God's past expectations being first one way and then the other! As Campsall also said, 'I am able to bring about that God has known from eternity that which He never [in fact] has known.'[31] If I had declined the gift, God would always have expected me to decline. The only 'change' I can make, if indeed we may call it that, is to put the actual past in place of a might-have-been past that never was.

And the opinion that if I had declined, then God would have been mistaken does not necessarily mean that I have it in my power to cause God to have made a mistake long ago. I wasn't around then to cause anything. Unless God's foreknowledge works by backward causation – maybe so, maybe not – I cannot influence God's thoughts long ago. I can only influence an extrinsic description of those thoughts – knowledge or error? – in relation to what comes afterward. A parallel: I don't cause someone to have set an all-time record long ago just by acting today to stop you from breaking his record.

If we put a human predictor in place of God, and we ask again what would have been the case if I had declined the $1000, the answer will depend on the predictor's *modus operandi*. First case: the predictor is a time traveler. He saw me accept the $1000, then departed to the past taking his knowledge with him. His foreknowledge is causally downstream from its object. Then I want to hold fixed that the time traveler has foreknowledge, and say that if I had declined, the time traveler would have known that I was going to decline. If God's foreknowledge is like the time traveler's, if it does work by backward causation, then I agree with the first opinion: if I had declined, God would have expected me to. In that case, also, I conclude that Molinist free-will theodicy has nothing to fear from selective freedom, because indeed such 'freedom' would be bogus.

Second case: the predictor is an expert psychologist, who knows past conditions and regularities of cause and effect. His foreknowledge

31 *Notabilia*, 8, in *The Works of Richard of Campsall*, 41.

and its object are separate effects of common causes. Then I want to hold the past fixed, and say that if I had declined, I would have violated some one of the regularities the psychologist relied on.[32] If God's foreknowledge is like the psychologist's, then I stand by my reply to the final objection and persist in saying that Molinist free-will theodicy has a problem with selective freedom.

But God's way of gaining foreknowledge cannot be much like either the time traveler's way or the psychologist's way – not if God's way provides middle knowledge as well. So I conclude, most inconclusively, that we just don't know whether my reply to the final objection succeeds, and hence don't know whether selective freedom is bogus freedom or genuine. Some will want to play on by debating which side bears the burden of proof. Myself, I think this pastime is as useless as it is undignified.

32 For contrary views, see Plantinga, 'On Ockham's Way Out'; and Terence Horgan, 'Counterfactuals and Newcomb's Problem', *Journal of Philosophy* 78 (1981), 331–356.

10

Do we believe in penal substitution?

Imagine that an offender has a devoted and innocent friend. The offender has been justly sentenced to be punished for his offence. But the friend volunteers to be punished in his place.[1] If the friend undergoes the punishment that the offender deserved, does that render it permissible (or even obligatory) to leave the offender unpunished? Is that any reason at all in favour of sparing the offender?

Mostly we think not. It is unheard of that a burglar's devoted friend serves the burglar's prison sentence while the burglar himself goes free; or that a murderer's still-more-devoted friend serves the murderer's death sentence. Yet if ever such a thing happened, we surely would hear of it – for what a newsworthy story it would be! Such things do not happen. And not, I think, because a burglar or a murderer never has a sufficiently devoted friend. Rather, because the friend will know full well that, whatever he might wish, it would be

First published in *Philosophical Papers* 26 (1997), pp. 203–209. Reprinted with kind permission from *Philosophical Papers*.

I thank Bruce Langtry, Megan McLaughlin, Alan Hájek, John Bishop, Ormond College, and the Boyce Gibson Memorial Library.

1 A. M. Quinton once argued, in 'On Punishment', *Analysis* 14 (1954), pp. 133–142, that punishment of the innocent is logically impossible, simply a contradiction in terms. Maybe so. Nevertheless, since abuse of language makes for easier communication than circumlocution or neologism, I shall speak of the innocent volunteer being punished. I trust that the reader will understand: I mean that the volunteer undergoes something that would have constituted punishment if it had happened instead to the guilty offender.

futile to offer himself as a substitute for punishment. The offer would strike the authorities as senseless, and they would decline it out of hand.

Even if the friend managed to substitute himself by stealth, and arranged for it to be found out afterward that he had been punished in place of the offender, the scheme would fail. Once the authorities learned that the offender had gone unpunished, they would get on with the job. However much they might regret their mistake in punishing the innocent friend, they could not undo that mistake by failing to punish the guilty offender. That would merely add a second mistake to the first.

We can say, if we like, that the offender 'owes a debt of punishment'. But the metaphor is misleading. As we mostly conceive of them, the condition of owing a debt and the condition of deserving to be punished are not alike. In the case of debt, what is required is that the creditor *shall not* suffer a loss of the money he lent; what happens to the debtor is beside the point. Whereas in the case of a 'debt of punishment', what is required is that the debtor *shall* suffer a loss; there is no creditor. (Society? – Not really. The creditor is supposed to be the one who suffers a loss if the debt is not paid. But sometimes, what with the cost of prisons, society will suffer more of a loss if the debt *is* paid.) This is common ground between alternative conceptions of the function of punishment. Perhaps the guilty ought to suffer a loss simply because it is better that the wicked not prosper; or as an expression of our abhorrence of their offences; or as a means to the end of reforming their characters; or as a means to the end of depriving them of the resources – life and liberty – to repeat their offences; or as a means of deterring others from similar offences. Punishment of innocent substitutes would serve none of these functions. (Not even deterrence, since the deception that would be required to make deterrence effective could not be relied upon.)

What function would we have to ascribe to punishment in order to make it make sense to punish an innocent substitute? – A compensatory function. Suppose that the offender's punishment were seen mainly as a benefit to the victim, a benefit sufficient to undo whatever loss the offender had inflicted upon him. Then the source of the benefit wouldn't matter. If the offender's innocent friend provided the benefit, the compensatory function would be served, no less than if the offender himself provided it.

But our actual institutions of punishment are not designed to serve a compensatory function. A murderer's victim cannot be compensated at all, yet we punish murderers just the same. A burglar's victim can be compensated (so long as the victim is still alive), and may indeed be compensated, but not by the punishment of the burglar. How does it benefit the victim if the burglar serves a prison sentence? The victim, like anyone else, may be pleased to know that wrong-doing has met with its just reward; but this 'compensation', if such it be, could not (without deception) be provided by the punishment of the burglar's innocent friend.

We can imagine a world in which the punishment of burglars really is designed to serve a compensatory function, and in such a way as to make sense of substitution. But when we do, the differences from actuality are immense. Suppose, for instance, that the burglar was required to serve a sentence of penal servitude as the victim's personal slave. Then a compensatory function would indeed be served; and punishing an innocent substitute could serve that function equally well. Or suppose the burglar was to be hanged before the victim's eyes. If the victim took sufficient pleasure in watching a hanging, that might compensate him for the loss of his gold; and if he enjoyed hangings of the innocent no less than hangings of the guilty, then again punishment of a substitute could serve a compensatory function.

A one-sided diet of mundane examples might convince us that we do not believe in penal substitution; we agree, in other words, that the substitutionary punishment of the innocent friend is never any reason to leave the offender unpunished. But of course we do not all agree to this. For many among us are Christians; and many among the Christians explain the Atonement as a case of penal substitution. They say that when Christ died for our sins, He paid the debt of punishment that the sinners owed; and thereby He rendered it permissible, and thereby He brought it about, that the sinners (those of them that accepted His gift) were spared the punishment of damnation that they deserved.

Although these Christians do believe in penal substitution in the context of theology, they do not seem to believe anything out of the ordinary in the context of mundane criminal justice. We do not hear of them arguing that just as Christ paid the debt of punishment owed by all the sinners, so likewise other innocent volunteers can pay the lesser debts of punishment owed by burglars and murderers. ('Innocent' not in the sense that they are without sin, but only in the sense that they are not guilty of burglary or murder.) Why not? I think we must conclude that these Christians are of two minds about penal substitution. Their principles alter from one case to another, for no apparent reason.

My point is not new (though neither is it heard as much as we might expect). Here is a recent statement of the point by Philip Quinn:

In [medieval legal] codes, the debt of punishment for even such serious crimes as killing was literally pecuniary; one paid the debt by paying monetary compensation. What was important for such purposes as avoiding blood feud was that the debt be paid; who paid it was not crucial. . . . But our intuitions about the proper relations of crime and punishment are tutored by a very different legal picture. Though a parent can pay her child's pecuniary debts, a murderer's mother cannot pay his debt of punishment by serving his prison term. . . . So to the extent that we think of serious sins as analogous to crimes and respect the practices embedded in our system of criminal law, we should expect the very idea of vicarious satisfaction for sin to seem alien and morally problematic.[2]

However, the heart of the rebuke against those Christians who explain the Atonement as a case of penal substitution is not that they are out of date and disagree with our 'intuitions'. Rather, it is that they disagree with what they themselves think the rest of the time.

An impatient doubter might say that it is pointless to rebuke these Christians for their on-again-off-again belief in penal substitution. The prior problem lies elsewhere. Even if their (sometime) principle of penal substitution were right, and even if they themselves accepted

2 Philip Quinn, 'Aquinas on Atonement', *Trinity, Incarnation and Atonement*, ed. R. Feenstra and C. Plantinga (University of Notre Dame Press, 1989), pp. 171–72. See also Eleonore Stump, 'Atonement According to Aquinas', *Philosophy and the Christian Faith*, ed. T. Morris (University of Notre Dame Press, 1988), pp. 61–63.

it single-mindedly, still they would be misapplying it. For in the case of the Atonement, the supposed substitution is far from equal. Evil though it is to be put to death by crucifixion, even if the death is temporary and foreseen to be temporary, still the eternal damnation of even one sinner, let alone all of them, is a far worse evil. How can the former be a fair exchange for the latter, even if we grant in general that such exchanges make sense?

But to this question the Christians have an answer. They may say, with scriptural support, that what happened to Christ on the cross was something very much worse than crucifixion. He 'bore our sins', whatever that means, and He found Himself forsaken by God.[3] Perhaps these evils, if not the crucifixion itself, were an equal substitute for the deserved damnation that the sinners escaped in return.

An alternative answer is on offer. Perhaps Christ paid only some small part of the debt of punishment that the sinners owed; only just enough so that, if they had paid it for themselves, it would have been the penance required as a constitutive element of sincere repentance. Thereby He made it possible for them to repent, and when they repented the rest of their debt was forgiven outright.[4]

So we can see, at least dimly, how our doubter's inequality objection might be fended off. And if it is, we are back where we were before: the real problem is with the very idea that someone else can pay the sinners' debt of punishment.

Those Christians who explain the Atonement as a case of penal substitution, yet do not in general believe in the principle they invoke, really are in a bad way. Yet the rest of us should not be overbold in rebuking them. For we live in the proverbial glass house. *All*

---

3 How could Christ have been forsaken by God when He *was* God? – perhaps God the Son found Himself forsaken by the other persons of the Trinity.

4 See Richard Swinburne, 'The Christian Scheme of Salvation', *Philosophy and the Christian Faith*, ed. T. Morris (University of Notre Dame Press, 1988), pp. 15–30. Although Swinburne's theory of the Atonement is not the standard penal substitution theory – it is rather a theory of *penitential* substitution – Swinburne by no means abandons the idea of substitution. 'God . . . can help us atone for our sins by making available to us an offering which *we* may offer as *our* reparation and penance . . . ' (p. 27, my emphasis).

132

of us – atheists and agnostics, believers of other persuasions, the lot – are likewise of two minds about penal substitution.

We do not believe that the offender's friend can serve the offender's prison sentence, or his death sentence. Neither can the friend serve the offender's sentence of flogging, transportation, or hard labour. But we do believe – do we not? – that the friend can pay the offender's fine. (At least, if the offender consents.) Yet this is just as much a case of penal substitution as the others.

Or is it? You might think that the proper lesson is just that the classification of fines as punishments is not to be taken seriously. Consider a parking space with a one-hour limit. If you want to park there for an hour, you pay a fee by putting a coin in the meter. If you want to park there for two hours, you pay a fee at a higher hourly rate; the fee is collected by a more cumbersome method; and the fee is called a 'fine'. But what's in a name? The function served is the same in either case. The fee helps pay the cost of providing the parking place; and, in a rough and ready way, it allocates the space to those who want it more in preference to those who want it less. Since those who want it more include some who want to make a gift of it instead of using it themselves, and since some of these may want to make a gift of two-hour rather than one-hour use, the payment of others' 'fines' fits right in. Paying someone else's 'fine' for two-hour parking is no more problematic than buying someone else a pot of beer. It has little in common with the penal substitution we mostly do not believe in.

Agreed. But set aside these little 'fines' that are really fees. Some fines are altogether more serious. They are as much of a burden as some prison sentences. (If given the choice 'pay the fine or serve the time', some would choose to serve the time.) They convey opprobrium. They serve the same functions that other punishments serve. They do not serve a compensatory function, since the fine is not handed over to the victim. Yet if the offender is sentenced to pay a fine of this serious sort, and his friend pays it for him, we who do not otherwise believe in penal substitution will find that not amiss – or anyway, not very much amiss.

You might think that in the case of fines, but not in other cases, we accept penal substitution because we have no practical way to prevent it. Suppose we had a law saying that a cheque drawn on someone else's bank account would not be accepted in payment of a fine. Anyone sentenced to pay a fine would either have to write a cheque on his own bank account or else hand over the cash in person. What difference would that make? – None.

If the friend gives the offender a gift sufficient to pay the fine, we have a *de facto* case of penal substitution. Whoever may sign the cheque, it is the friend who mainly suffers the loss that was meant to be the offender's punishment. What happens to the offender? – His debt of punishment is replaced by a debt of gratitude, which may or may not be any burden to him; he gets the opprobrium; if the friend has taken the precaution of withholding his gift until the fine has actually been paid, he may need a short-term loan; and there his burden is at an end. Whereas what happens to the friend, according to our stipulation of the case, is that he suffers a monetary loss which is as much of a burden as some prison sentences. The transfer of burden from the offender to the friend may not be quite complete, but plainly the friend is getting much the worst of it.

How to prevent *de facto* penal substitution by means of gifts? Shall we have a law that those who are sentenced to pay fines may not receive gifts? (Forever? For a year and a day? Even if the gift was given before the case came to trial? Before the offence was committed? If the recipient of a generous gift afterward commits an offence and uses the gift to pay his fine, could that make the giver an accomplice before the fact?) Such a law would be well-nigh impossible to get right; to enforce; or to square with our customary encouragement of generosity even toward the undeserving. We well might judge that what it would take to prevent *de facto* penal substitution in the payment of fines would be a cure worse than the disease.

Here we have the makings of an explanation of why we sometimes waver in our rejection of penal substitution. It would go like this. In the first place, we tolerate penal substitution in the case of fines because it is obviously impractical to prevent it. Since, in the case of punishment by fines, the condition of being sentenced to punishment is the condition of owing a debt – literally – the metaphor of a 'debt of punishment' gets a grip on us. Then some of us persist in applying this metaphor, even when it is out of place because the 'debt of punishment' is nothing like a debt in the literal sense. That is how we fall for such nonsense as a penal substitution theory of the Atonement.

Well – that might be right. But I doubt it: the hypothesis posits too much sloppy thinking to be credible. The worst problem comes right at the start. If we were single-mindedly against penal substitution, and yet we saw that preventing it in the case of fines was impractical, we should not on that account abandon our objections to penal substitution. Rather we ought to conclude that fines are an unsatisfactory form of punishment. (Serious fines, not the little 'fines' that are really fees.) We might not abandon fines, because the alternatives might have their own drawbacks.[5] But our dissatisfaction ought to show. Yet it does not show. The risk of *de facto* penal substitution ought to be a frequently mentioned drawback of punishment by fines. It is not. And that is why I maintain that all of us, not just some Christians, are of two minds about penal substitution.

If the rest of us were to make so bold as to rebuke the Christians for their two-mindedness, they would have a good *tu quoque* against us. A *tu quoque* is not a rejoinder on behalf of penal substitution. Yet neither is it intellectually weightless. It indicates that both sides agree that penal substitution sometimes makes sense after all, even if none can say how it makes sense. And if both sides agree to that, that is some evidence that somehow they might both be right.

---

5 Might we console ourselves with the thought that, although penal substitution has not been prevented, cases of it are at least not frequent? – That might not be much of a consolation. For if cases are rare, those few cases that do occur will seem all the more outrageous.

11

Convention: Reply to Jamieson

Jamieson produces nine examples. Eight are said to be conventions according to our common, established concept of convention but not according to my analysis thereof in *Convention*.[1] The ninth is said to be clearly not a convention according to our common concept, but an unsettled case under my analysis. Since Jamieson proposes no rival analysis, the best way of proceeding will be to respond to his examples one by one. Some I judge to be simply mistaken, either about our common concept or about my analysis. In considering these examples we will do well to bear in mind three things: (1) that we may be guided by preferences and expectations to which we give no conscious thought; (2) that under my analysis conventionality is relative to a population; and (3) that conditional preferences must be distinguished from conditionals about preferences. Others of Jamieson's examples are more instructive, and do exhibit genuine usages that do not fall under my analysis. I think these might best be regarded as derivative usages, related in familiar ways to the central concept given by my analysis; not as evidence for a revised analysis of the central concept,[2] and not as evidence for different and unrelated senses of the

First published in *The Canadian Journal of Philosophy* **6** (1976), 113–120. Reprinted with kind permission from *The Canadian Journal of Philosophy*.

1 *Convention: A Philosophical Study* (Harvard University Press, 1969). Jamieson's article is in Vol. V, no. 1 (Sept. 1975) of *The Canadian Journal of Philosophy*.

2 There is one important revision that is desirable on other grounds, but has no bearing on the cases considered by Jamieson. I have adopted it, at Jonathan Ben-

word "convention." Thus I gladly concede that we may properly call something a convention, although it does not meet the defining conditions I gave, because we hope that it will come to meet them, or we wish that it did, or we contemplate the possibility that it might have, or we believe that it used to, or we pay lip service to the fiction that it does.

The Third Hague Convention of 1907. This "convention" was an explicit agreement to refrain from undeclared warfare; it was futile, for most subsequent wars among the parties were undeclared. There prevails no general regularity to refrain, and *a fortiori* no convention according to my analysis. It may be, for all I know, that this agreement is called a convention because it is one in some technical sense that has grown up among international lawyers; but alternative explanations also are available.

One possibility is that people call it a convention because its proper name suggests that it is one, much as they might mistakenly call the Holy Roman Empire an empire, or the Podunk Municipal Street Railway (which has for many years operated only buses) a railway.

For another possibility, consider the pretender to the throne. His followers still call him a king, although in fact he is no longer a king. It isn't that they call him a king in some special sense in which he still really is one; that would be useless as an expression of fealty. His adherents wish to express the sentiment that he should be, and one day will be again, a king in the ordinary sense. Others, less loyal or more willing to face the facts, may nevertheless find it courteous or prudent or expedient to speak as the loyalists do. Similarly, our Third Hague Convention was first called a convention, presumably, by people who hopefully thought that a general regularity of refraining from undeclared war had begun. Some who call it a convention even now may still think so – a long-term general regularity may have its few exceptions, and it is barely possible that the exceptions so far comprise a short-run fluctuation. Others, perhaps most, may not

nett's suggestion, in "Languages and Language," in Keith Gunderson, ed. *Minnesota Studies in the Philosophy of Science*, Volume VII (University of Minnesota Press, 1975).

share such hopes but may think it impolitic to admit that the cause is lost. Others may call it a convention simply to avoid misunderstanding or pointless dispute with those who call it so for other reasons.

Numbering pages in the upper right. A disregarded "convention" in some office to number pages in the upper right would not be so called because it is a convention in some special technical sense, nor because of its misleading proper name. But it might well be called a convention by way of wishful thinking or propaganda. If someone said that it was a convention there to number pages in the upper right, he would be indulging in some sort of hopeful pretense. Very likely he would hope that by pretending that the convention prevailed already he would improve its chances of prevailing in the future.

Eating soup with a spoon. It is a convention among us to eat soup with a spoon, although certainly it seldom occurs to us to eat soup any other way. We use the spoon by habit. It's not true, however, that we use the spoon because other ways don't occur to us, for if alternatives did come to mind we would reject them. We would find that we preferred to carry on using the spoon. But the explanation in terms of habit does not compete with the explanation I require in terms of expectation and preference. Both are right. We use the spoon by habit, and we use the spoon because we expect others to use spoons and we prefer to eat soup as others do. It is only because of the preference and expectation that the habit persists and succeeds in governing our unthinking use of the spoon. If ever I expected others to pour soup into their mouths through funnels, or if ever I preferred to be different, alternatives would at once occur to me and probably I would manage to overcome force of habit. In using the spoon unthinkingly because of habit, I also use it because of the causal factors that permit the habit to operate without interference; and among these factors are the expectations and preferences that constitute my participation in a convention.

Jamieson would find it obscure and unilluminating if I explained conventions partly by appeal to unconscious preferences and expectations. So would I, if I had to rely on the sort of unconscious states that are posited in psychoanalytic theory: preferences and expectations, for instance, that would fail to produce many of their proper manifestations in consciousness and behavior even if put to the test, and that can be discovered only by lengthy and ill-understood special techniques. But in fact I do not need unconscious states of that sort; I need only rely on preferences and expectations that stand ready to manifest themselves as soon as a relevant choice or question arises. Is it so that at this very moment, as I write, Jamieson prefers being given a can of frosty ice-cold Foster's lager to being given a poke in the eye with a burnt stick? In all probability he does, but in all probability he has never in his life given any conscious thought whatever to this preference. The preference is unconscious, not in the obscure psychoanalytic sense, but in a sense in which almost all of our preferences are almost always unconscious. I see no reason to steer clear of attitudes that are unconscious in this commonplace sense. The only reason Jamieson suggests is that perhaps we can only determine whether certain unconscious preferences and expectations obtain by determining whether some regularity is a convention. But he does not say why he thinks that might be so. I find it unlikely.

Use of quotation marks. If asked to explain the prevailing convention for use of quotation marks in philosophical writing, it would be perfectly correct for me to reply that there is *no* convention: different writers use different systems. But I grant that Jamieson's answer seems just as correct: *two* (or more) competing conventions are followed, neither one universally. To explain how these seemingly contrary answers – none or two – both can seem right, we must find ambiguity somewhere. In fact I think that there are two ambiguities working together.

First ambiguity: it may happen that we apply a word mostly to the occupants of a status, but sometimes instead to the candidates for that status. Such occupant-candidate ambiguity, though by no means universal, is widespread. We can say, for instance, that several solutions to a problem were proposed, and that it turned out that three were solutions and the rest were not. There were several candidates for the status of solution, but only three occupants. In the case at hand, there are two or more leading candidates for the status of convention, none of which yet occupies that status. Indeed, even if there were a well established convention by now, we might still say truly that a rival

139

convention had been advocated, discussed, and rejected. In calling that rival a convention we would mean only that it had been a candidate for the status of convention.

Second ambiguity: disregarding mere candidacy, it may be that although there is no convention in the entire population of philosophers nevertheless there are various conventions in various subpopulations. If you say that a regularity R is a convention in population P, you might mean that all members of P (or almost all) participate in the convention; or you might mean only that some of them do. The former was my official usage in *Convention*, but the latter usage is no doubt equally correct. As a convenient but artificial stipulation, I would suggest saying in the latter case that the regularity R is a convention *within* the population P: then a convention *within* P is a convention in some population included in P. In the case at hand no quotation convention prevails in the entire population of philosophers, but two or more prevail within that population.[3]

Single-spacing of addresses. I agree that there is a convention that outside addresses on envelopes are to be single-spaced; that is to say, I agree that such a convention prevails in some substantial population. But it would be wrong to take for granted that the members of this population must be all and only those among us who address envelopes. Some of us have no conditional preference for spacing as others do; some do not single-space, and others cultivate the habit of single-spacing only because some addresses on some envelopes don't fit unless single-spaced. Such a one belongs to a population *within* which the convention prevails, but not to any population in which it prevails. On the other hand, there might be someone who does want the addresses on his envelopes to be spaced in whatever way is usual, but who never addresses envelopes for himself; he employs programmed machines, trained chimps, coerced slaves, or intimidated

3 This is not to say that *all* users of any one system comprise a population in which there is a convention to use that system. I share Jamieson's suspicion that most philosophers lack the conditional preferences for conformity that my analysis ascribes to participants in a convention. I would guess that the sub-populations of philosophers in which there are established quotation conventions might be quite small.

secretaries to address his envelopes for him, carefully seeing to it that the programming, training, coercion, or intimidation are such as to result in single-spacing. It is the boss in such a case, not his machine or chimp or slave or secretary, who belongs to the population in which the convention prevails. I may add that if there are such bosses, then the convention should not be described as a convention to single-space, but rather as a convention to see to it somehow that addresses on one's envelopes are single-spaced.

Currency and barter. Jamieson complains that "surely it is not a necessary condition for something to be a convention in a population that members of the population have knowledge about what would be the case in some hypothetical situation"; he thinks such a condition would be too stringent because the required hypothetical knowledge would often be lacking. For instance, he notes without dissent my claim that we have a convention to exchange goods and services for U.S. currency and that one alternative to this convention would be barter of goods and services. But he says that this alternative does not meet my standards for knowledge of relevant conditional preferences, since we do not know what people would prefer if a system of barter became established. I think we have more hypothetical knowledge in this case than Jamieson thinks. (I further note that if even one alternative, perhaps not this one, meets my requirements, that is enough to satisfy clause (5) of my analysis.) Nevertheless I agree with Jamieson that it would be unwise to require much knowledge about hypothetical situations as a condition for something to be a convention.

Fortunately, I imposed no such requirement. What I did require was knowledge of conditional preferences. Jamieson wonders whether conditional preferences are (A) preferences among conditionals or (B) conditionals about preferences. His objection is based on supposing that they are the latter. But they are not, and neither are they the former. Rather, conditional preferences are (C) actual preferences among certain (ordinarily) non-conditional states of affairs. You prefer X to Y, conditionally on Z, iff you prefer the combination of Z and X to the combination of Z and Y. For instance, you prefer to conform to some possible regularity rather than not, on condition that others do, iff you prefer the state of affairs in which

141

they conform and so do you to the state of affairs in which they conform but you do not.

It is essential to distinguish conditional preferences from conditionals about preference, since they may disagree. Consider Odysseus as he prepared to sail past the Sirens. On condition that he could hear their song, he preferred to be tied to the mast. That is, he preferred to hear the song and be tied rather than to hear the song and not be tied. But he knew well that if the condition were met his preferences would change: if he heard the song, he would then prefer not to be tied.

We must also distinguish conditional preferences from preferences among conditionals, since these too may disagree. At least that is so if the conditionals are truth-functional;[4] the question is more complicated if other conditionals are considered, but I doubt that there is any way to construe conditionals on which conditional preferences and preferences among conditionals always agree.

Marriage in Malabar. I do not know how many of the so-called "conventions" that obtain in primitive societies really are conventions according to our common, established concept; those who have called them so might have the facts wrong. Neither do I know how far Jamieson is right in his provincial opinion that members of primitive societies have not considered alternatives to existing regularities. But even if the Nayar have never considered alternatives to their actual marriage customs, that does not settle whether their customs are conventions under my analysis. In the first place, they need not have knowledge about what their preferences would be in some counterfactual situation; knowledge of conditional preferences is not knowledge of conditionals about preferences. In the second place, they need not consider alternatives in order to have expectations and preferences, and even knowledge of one another's expectations and preferences, regarding those alternatives. The requisite attitudes might

---

4 A die will be thrown; I stand to win $2 if the 6 is up, $1 if the 5 is up, and nothing otherwise. I suppose the die to be fair and care only about the money I may win, so my preferences follow the computable expected payoffs. X holds iff a 2 or 6 is up, Y iff a 1 or 5 or 6 is up, and Z iff a 3, 4, 5, or 6 is up. I prefer X to Y conditionally on Z, but I prefer the conditional $Z \supset Y$ to the conditional $Z \supset X$.

perfectly well remain unconscious (in the commonplace, not the psychoanalytic, sense).

Sleeping in beds. Sleeping in beds (rather than trees) is not a good example of a non-arbitrary convention, since it is not a convention at all either according to our common concept or according to my analysis. However, there are other examples of conventions that are preferable to their alternatives; indeed, I mentioned some in *Convention*. I don't mind if Jamieson wishes to call such conventions non-arbitrary, since he seems not to disagree with what I meant when I said that any convention is arbitrary.

Procreation by copulation. Jamieson thinks, and so do I, that it is clearly not a convention among us to procreate by means of copulation rather than artificial insemination. (What difference does he see, I wonder, between this non-convention and the alleged convention of sleeping in beds?) He asks what keeps procreation by copulation from wrongly counting as a convention under my analysis. I reply, as Jamieson expects, that it is clause (5) that saves the day: it is not true, nor is it common knowledge among us, that we have a general preference for general conformity to some alternative regularity (such as the use of artificial insemination) conditional on at least almost-general conformity to that alternative.

Jamieson finds this reply wanting. Although he finds it clear that procreation by copulation is not a convention, he apparently finds it quite uncertain whether or not clause (5) is satisfied. He asks how to determine what is common knowledge about what almost everyone would prefer if most people procreated by artificial insemination. Fortunately this difficulty does not arise. Clause (5) concerns conditional preferences, not conditionals about preference. Jamieson is right that we need not know or care what people would prefer in some strange counterfactual situation. We are concerned with people's actual, present preferences, whether or not those preferences would have been the same if circumstances had been different. We do know that there are many people whose actual preferences are contrary to the requirements of clause (5): they prefer the state of affairs in which they copulate although most others use artificial insemination to the state of affairs in which they use artificial insemination along with the others. That is enough (if artificial insemination is the only alternative we need to consider) to settle that procreation by copulation is not a convention under my analysis.

Indeed, it is more than enough. People need not have preferences contrary to those required by clause (5); it is enough if many people lack the required preferences because they have no preferences one way or the other. Further, even if everyone had the required preferences, clause (5) would not be satisfied unless those preferences were a matter of common knowledge. If people's preferences on these matters are hard to ascertain, all the better. Absence of common knowledge one way or the other is enough to settle the case correctly.

Conventional behavior. This completes a review of Jamieson's nine cases. I turn now to another topic that he briefly mentions: analysis of the notion of conventional behavior. Jamieson wisely avoids saying that the analysis which he criticizes in connection with my work is actually my analysis; indeed, I do not remember ever proposing any analysis of conventional behavior, nor will I propose one now. *Contra* Jamieson, I suspect that there may be some sort of connection between conventional behavior and behavior that conforms to conventions. Whether one behaves conventionally is certainly not simply a matter of *whether* one conforms to conventions; but it may be at least partly a matter of *which* conventions one conforms to.

Jamieson's own analysis of conventional behavior is clearly wrong. According to Jamieson, "if it is said that Smith's behavior is conventional . . . what is being said is that Smith's behavior is ordinary, there is nothing unusual about it." But it might truly be said of some Smith that his behavior is extraordinary, that there is something quite unusual about it: Smith behaves very much more conventionally than anyone else.

12

Meaning without use: Reply to Hawthorne

Surely it is our use of language that somehow determines meaning. But if we try to say how, we must face the fact that only a tiny part of our language, or any human language, is ever used. There are many reasons why a meaningful sentence might never be suited to serve anyone's conversational purposes, and so might go unused. For instance, take length. Even the most abominable stylist will never write a sentence more than, say, a hundred words long. (Never? – Well, hardly ever.) But almost all of the infinitely many meaningful sentences of English, all but a finite minority, are longer than a hundred words. Almost all are longer than a thousand words, almost all are longer than a million words . . . So almost all sentences have meaning without use.

Years ago, Stephen Schiffer raised the meaning-without-use problem against my own account of use and meaning, which ran as follows. A *language* L is a function that assigns truth conditions to certain verbal expressions, called the *sentences* of L; one of them is *true* in L or *false* in L according as the truth condition assigned to it by L is satisfied or not. To be *truthful* in L is to avoid uttering any sentence of L unless it is true in L; to be *trusting* in L is to expect others to be truthful in L. We (or any population) use L iff, by convention, we are truthful and trusting in L. (A convention is a regularity in the population that is sustained, in a certain way, by expectation of others'

First published in *The Australasian Journal of Philosophy* **70** (1992), 106–110. Reprinted with kind permission from *The Australasian Journal of Philosophy*.

conformity. The details need not concern us here.) The *meaning* of a sentence, for us, is the truth condition assigned to that sentence by the language we use. That, I said, is how use determines meaning.[1]

Now for the problem. If a sentence of L is never uttered at all, *a fortiori* it is never uttered falsely in L; if it is expected never to be uttered at all, *a fortiori* it is expected never to be uttered falsely in L. So for the unused part of L – which is almost all of L – truthfulness and trust in L go trivial. And this is so whether or not L gets the truth conditions right. Let L_1 be our actual language, the one that does get the truth conditions right. Let L_2 be a different language that agrees with L_1 on all the sentences we ever use: all we might ever utter, and all we do not expect others never to utter. On the unused sentences, however, L_1 and L_2 may differ wildly. They may assign conflicting truth conditions to the same unused sentences, or they may disagree about which unused expressions are sentences at all. Yet we are truthful and trusting in L_1 and L_2 alike: trivially so in the differing unused parts, non-trivially and conventionally so in the used part that L_1 and L_2 have in common. It is not perfectly clear how my analysis classifies a case where truthfulness and trust are partly trivial and only partly conventional. Maybe we use both L_1 and L_2, maybe we use neither. But, either way, L_1 and L_2 are on a par. Our truthfulness and trust do not distinguish them. So I have not explained why the correct meanings of unused sentences, and the correct ascription of sentencehood to unused expressions, are those given by L_1 rather than L_2.

In reply to Schiffer I proposed this solution. Let us say that trust in L is more than just the expectation that sentences of L will not be uttered falsely in L. Say rather that one is *trusting* in L with respect to sentence S to the extent that one's conditional subjective probability

---

1 David Lewis, 'Languages and Language', *Minnesota Studies in the Philosophy of Science* 7 (1975) pp. 3–35; reprinted in David Lewis, *Philosophical Papers*, Vol. I (Oxford: Oxford University Press, 1983). A generally similar account appeared in David Lewis, *Convention* (Cambridge, MA: Harvard University Press, 1969; Oxford: Blackwell, 1986); however, that account lacked the appeal to 'trust in L' that figures in the present discussion. Here I simplify the story by ignoring indexicality, ambiguity, non-indicative moods, sub-sentential linguistic expressions, and hyperintensional differences of meaning.

that S will be uttered, given that S is true in L, exceeds one's unconditional probability that S will be uttered. Equivalently, to the extent that the 'likelihood ratio'

$$\frac{\text{Probability (S is uttered / S is true in L),}}{\text{Probability (S is uttered / S is false in L)}}$$

which measures the extent to which the truth of S in L is confirmed when S is uttered, exceeds one-to-one. Even if all these probabilities are minute – even if they are literally infinitesimal – still comparisons between them make sense. Trust thus defined does not go trivial just because one expects S never to be uttered, so long as the probability of utterance is not quite zero. Even for the unused sentences, we have one remaining vestige of use: non-trivial, conventional, trust in L, consisting of a difference between minute probabilities. It is this vestigial trust, so I said, that distinguishes our actual language L_1 from the impostor L_2.

John Hawthorne now revives the issue.[2] He says that my solution fails because the subjective probability of utterance of the unused sentences is exactly zero. Then even the redefined version of trust in L goes trivial. The compared probabilities are all zero, and the likelihood ratio goes undefined, regardless of whether L gets the truth conditions right or wrong. (He needn't say we have zero probabilities always, for every unused sentence and every member of the population. But if we have them sometimes, that is bad enough.) I do not agree. I suppose I am typical among language-users; and although I find it improbable that a hundred-word sentence will be uttered, I find it more improbable that a thousand-word sentence will be uttered, and still more improbable that a million-word sentence will be uttered, and so on *ad infinitum*. This would make no sense if, after a point, the probabilities were zero exactly. But it does make sense. So they are not zero; just very, very small.

Why think otherwise? One bad reason – not given by Hawthorne, I hasten to add – is based on an operational definition of subjective probability. What would you pay for a bet whereby you win a rich

2 John Hawthorne, 'A Note on Languages and Language', *Australasian Journal of Philosophy* 68 (1990) pp. 116–118.

reward if a certain very long sentence is ever uttered? (And uttered not for the sake of winning the bet.) Exactly nothing, if the sentence is long enough. But that needn't mean that the probability is zero. It just means that there is no coin so worthless as not to exceed the minute expected value of the bet. Or perhaps it means that the bet is not worth the trifling effort it would take to buy it. Other operational tests are more revealing. If forced to choose, would you not take the bet which you win if a certain thousand-word sentence is uttered instead of the bet which you win if a certain million-word sentence (without countervailing advantages) is uttered? But would you not take the second bet instead of a bet on some still worse sentence?

Anyhow, subjective probability should not be tied by definition to particular operational tests. Rather, it is a theoretical concept, defined implicitly by its role in decision theory. This theory contains constitutive constraints of rationality, and one aspect of rationality is a modicum of open-mindedness whereby genuine possibilities do not get probability zero. (Infinitesimal, maybe, when infinitely many alternatives seem more or less equiprobable. But infinitesimal isn't zero.) Utterance of a very long sentence is a genuine possibility, in the sense that matters. If the sentence is long enough, its utterance may be a physical impossibility, to be sure; but mere physical impossibilities are not entitled to probability zero, since we cannot know the laws of nature with absolute certainty.

So I disagree with Hawthorne: trust in L, taken in the sense of likelihood ratios, does not go trivial. But I disagree still more with my earlier self. It's all very well to define trust in terms of likelihood ratios, but doing so does not solve the meaning-without-use problem. To that extent, Hawthorne is right.

Consider some very long sentence. Let it be not only long but complicated: clauses within clauses within phrases within clauses . . . , and abundantly interlaced with cross references to 'the latter', 'the former', 'the aforementioned', 'condition (b*)', and so on *ad nauseam*. Of course you don't expect to hear this sentence uttered. The subjective probability is minute. But what if you did hear it? Would you think this was a successful job of truth-in-L-telling? Not likely! You'd think the speaker was trying to win a bet or set a record, or feigning madness or raving for real, or doing it to annoy, or filibustering, or making an experiment to test the limits of what it is humanly possible to say and mean. You wouldn't think he was even trying to be truthful in L. Still less would you think he was trying effectively, armed with skill enough to overcome the complexities of the sentence. In short, the lion's share of your subjective probability would go to hypotheses under which the utterance of the sentence had little to do with whether it was true in L. And likewise now, when you haven't heard the sentence uttered, the lion's share of your minute subjective probability that it will be uttered goes to these same hypotheses. Whether the sentence is uttered is probabilistically independent, near enough, of whether it is true in L. The likelihood ratio is one-to-one, or near enough. It does not go undefined. We can tell whether you are trusting in L. But the likely answer, for a great many unused sentences, is that you are not.[3]

So if, as before, L_1 gets the truth conditions of unused sentences right and L_2 gets them wrong, we cannot hope to distinguish L_1 from L_2 as the language in which we are truthful and trusting. They will be on a par. And the same will be true, for similar reasons, if L_2 differs from L_1 about which expressions are sentences at all. The meaning-without-use problem is with us still.

But it has an obvious solution: extrapolation. First, use somehow determines meaning for the fragment of the language that is actually used. There are rules of syntax and semantics that generate the right sentences with the right meanings within the used fragment. These rules also generate other, longer sentences, with meanings, outside the used fragment. Use determines some meanings, those meanings determine the rules, and the rules determine the rest of the meanings. Thus use determines meaning, in part directly and in part indirectly, for the entire language.[4]

---

3 It won't help much to restrict attention to utterances in 'serious communication situations', a move that I consider at one point in 'Languages and Language'. That sets aside the cases of filibustering, etc., but leaves the case of an ineffective attempt at truthful communication.

4 Once we have the rules, we may use them to correct or refine our assignment of truth conditions within the used fragment, if we do so with enough restraint not to overthrow the basis from which we extrapolated the rules. *Correction* (here I am indebted to John Hawthorne): suppose the extrapolated rules assign truth condition

Hawthorne has not overlooked the obvious solution, of course, and neither did my earlier self. But we were both scared off it by Kripkenstein's challenge (formerly Goodman's challenge).[5] As follows: the used fragment does not determine the rules. There are many different systems of rules – different grammars – that yield just the same sentences with just the same meanings inside the used fragment, but that differ wildly when they go beyond it. Extrapolation, which means going on according to the same rules, is radically underdetermined.

We should not have been scared off. The obvious solution is right. True, there are many grammars. But they are not on equal terms. Some are 'straight' grammars; for example, any grammar that any linguist would actually propose. Others are 'bent', or 'gruesome', grammars; for example, what you get by starting with a straight grammar for English and adding one extra rule, which states that every expression with more than forty occurrences of the word 'cabbage' is a sentence meaning that God is great. We have no difficulty in telling the difference. (Except insofar as bentness admits of degree,

T to sentence S; and suppose it is common knowledge that nobody has any way to tell whether T obtains; or that everybody already knows that T obtains; or that everybody already knows that T does not obtain. If the rules are right, the truth condition for S cannot be manifest in a pattern of truthfulness and trust, even if S is in the used fragment. If there is any such pattern it should be disregarded. S should be assigned its truth condition indirectly, in virtue of the extrapolated rules. *Refinement* (here I am indebted to M. J. Cresswell): suppose two languages L_1 and L_2 have the same sentences and differ only slightly, as follows, in the truth conditions they assign. Wherever T_1 and T_2 are truth conditions assigned to the same sentence by the two languages, T_1 and T_2 will coincide except in some case that all those in the population take to be quite improbable. (Example: the population consists of devout theists; S means in L_1 that Max likes cookies; S means in L_2 that God knows that Max likes cookies; and similarly for other sentences.) Then it may happen that the population is, by convention, truthful and trusting both in L_1 and L_2 to (near enough) equal degrees. But use of the extrapolated rules might favour L_1 over L_2. (Parsing S in accordance with these rules, we find words that mean 'Max', 'likes', and 'cookies', but no word that means 'God' or 'knows'.)

5 Ludwig Wittgenstein, *Philosophical Investigations* (Oxford: Blackwell, 1958), especially sections 185–242; Saul Kripke, *Wittgenstein on Rules and Private Language* (Cambridge, MA: Harvard University Press, 1982); Nelson Goodman, *Fact, Fiction, and Forecast* (Cambridge, MA: Harvard University Press, 1955), ch. II.

and some grammars are only a little bit bent. But this is a complication we can ignore.) We can reasonably hope that all straight grammars that agree on the used fragment will agree everywhere. We have no ironclad guarantee of this, but also no cause for alarm. After all, the used fragment is large and varied. The wild differences are between straight and bent grammars. The notion of extrapolation presupposes the distinction between straight and bent. It means going on according to the same straight rules. It is not radically underdetermined. We can speak of extrapolation with a clear conscience.[6]

The lesson of Kripkenstein is not that extrapolation is an illegitimate notion. What is illegitimate, rather, is a simple-minded analysis of extrapolation, one that does without the bent-straight distinction by overlooking bent rules altogether. Something else that is illegitimate, at least for those of us who have not embraced circularity, is an overall plan of analysis that postpones the bent-straight distinction to a later chapter and yet uses it in an early chapter. If we must rely on the bent-straight distinction to reach an analysis of meaning, we may not afterward analyse straightness in terms of straightforward (short, simple, non-disjunctive) expressibility in our language. Likewise, *mutatis mutandis*, if we must rely on the bent-straight distinction still earlier to reach an analysis of the content of thought. If that means carrying more baggage of primitive distinctions or ontological commitments than some of us might have hoped, so be it.[7] But thinking that Kripkenstein proscribes talk of extrapolation is like thinking that Zeno stops us going from place to place.

6 Maybe there is a grammar somehow written into the brain. And conceivably it is a bent grammar, so that the language it generates differs, somewhere outside the used fragment, from the language we get by straight extrapolation. Schiffer has asked: does straight extrapolation give the right answers even then? I think so. If not, then whenever we resort to extrapolation to answer questions of syntax and semantics, we are engaged in risky speculation about the secret workings of the brain. That seems wrong.

7 For catalogues of baggage available to be carried, see my 'New Work for a Theory of Universals', *Australasian Journal of Philosophy* 61 (1983) pp. 343–377; and D. M. Armstrong, *Universals: An Opinionated Introduction* (Boulder: Westview Press, 1989).

13

Illusory innocence?

Peter Unger, *Living High and Letting Die: Our Illusion of Innocence*, Oxford University Press, 1995.

While driving on a deserted road, far away in the bush, you come upon a stranger with a wounded leg. The leg is in a bad way. Unless the stranger reaches a hospital right away, amputation may be unavoidable. You have business of your own to attend to. Taking the stranger to hospital would cost you time and bother. Further, for reasons we need not stop to explain, it would cost you quite a lot of money. Further, you would have to commandeer resources that belong to someone else, knowing full well that the owner would not consent. Still, what else can you do? You do what most of us would do, and take the stranger to hospital.

Another day, you find in your mailbox a printed letter from UNICEF. It tells you, credibly, that in some distant and poverty-stricken place, children are dying for lack of emergency medical assistance. It asks you for a contribution. The treatment required is cheap, and sending your contribution is easy. Saving a distant child's life would cost you far less time, less bother, less money than saving the wounded stranger's leg. And you know that your contribution would make a difference: UNICEF has not enough money to pay for all the lifesaving work it would do if it could, so the more

First published in *Eureka Street* **5** (1996), 35–36. Reprinted with kind permission from *Eureka Street*.

contributions, the more saved lives. Understanding all this, you do what most of us would do: nothing. You send no contribution, you discard the letter without further thought. . . . You let more die instead of fewer.

Most of us would think it seriously wrong to refuse to come to the aid of the wounded stranger. Yet we would think it not very seriously wrong, perhaps not wrong at all, to refuse to come to the aid of the distant child. Sending the contribution that would save the child's life strikes us not as doing what one must, but as a commendable act of optional generosity. Very strange! Because, after all, the cases are much alike. Insofar as they differ, it would seem that you have more reason to aid the child than to aid the stranger: the benefit is more, a life instead of a leg, and the cost is less.

The remarkable contrast in what we think about the two questions poses an urgent question. Or rather, two questions: (1) Could our commonsensical ethical opinions possibly be right? (2) Whether right or whether wrong, what psychological mechanism causes us to respond so very differently to the two cases? The two questions are well worth a book, and that is the book Peter Unger has given us. And a very fine book it is: carefully argued, imaginative, fearless. Whether also it is correct in its conclusions remains to be seen.

Unger's answer to the ethical question is uncompromising: our commonsensical opinions are *not* right. Failing to aid the distant child *is* seriously wrong. When we think otherwise we are under an ethical illusion.

Unger does not rest his argument upon any contentious system of utilitarian ethics. Rather, the case of the wounded stranger is taken to reveal the basic values that we already accept. Then we have only to ask how those same values apply to the case of the distant child. Unger's conclusion may come as a surprise; yet it is meant to have the authority of established ethical common sense. Unlike some of the utilitarians with whom he is *de facto* allied, Unger is not trying to reform the foundations of ordinary morality. He is claiming instead that we are terribly, disastrously wrong about what ordinary morality requires of us. In case of the distant child – and in very many similar cases – ordinary morality is far less lenient than we like to think.

If Unger were arguing that each of us ought to send UNICEF

$100 every year, or even $1000, his argument would be hard to resist. But his conclusion is far more extreme than that. Willing contributors are few, distant children dying for lack of medical assistance are many; and so the need for lifesaving contributions is inexhaustible. An argument that is cogent once is cogent twice over. If indeed it is seriously wrong not to save the life of one distant child – even more seriously wrong than it would be not to save the wounded stranger's leg – then why is it not equally wrong not to save the life of the next distant child? And the next, and the next . . . ? There is nothing to shut the argument off after you have saved one life. Or after you have sent your $100 for the year – enough, Unger informs us, to save many lives. Or after you have sent $1000. Or after you have sent whatever contribution would be your fair share if, somehow, the burden of paying for lifesaving medical care were being fairly divided among all the world's affluent. When you have so little left that it becomes doubtful whether you can live to give again another day, then the argument shuts off. But only then. Talk about giving until it hurts!

If we follow unflinchingly where argument leads – as Unger does – the conclusions that await us are still more extreme. If you give all you have and all you earn, keeping back only enough to provide for your own survival, that is not enough. If you could give more by devoting yourself single-mindedly to the pursuit of wealth, you should do that too. And you should give not only all that you can earn (beyond subsistence), but also all that you can beg, borrow, or steal. For did you not agree that you might have to commandeer someone else's property in order to take the wounded stranger to hospital? And is it not more important to save a life than to save a leg?

What is required of you, if Unger's argument is right, turns out to be very much more than just a substantial annual contribution to UNICEF. It is a life devoted entirely to serving those endangered distant children. If it were the life of a saint, or of an outlaw robbing the rich to give to the poor, it might have its attractions. But if it is the life of an unscrupulous money-grubber, toiling away at dirty business so as to serve the distant children in the most efficient possible way, it is altogether repellent. You are not asked to give

154

away your life so that the distant children may live. But neither are you asked to give away just a few trivial luxuries. You may well be asked to give away most of what makes your life worth living. And this in the name of our ordinary morality, in the name of the basic values we already accept!

Somewhere we have crossed the line into a *reductio ad absurdum*. The conclusions that supposedly follow from our ordinary morality are so violently opposed to what we ordinarily think that, somehow, the argument must have gone astray. It is hard to see just what has gone wrong. But even if we cannot diagnose the flaw, it is more credible that the argument has a flaw we cannot diagnose than that its most extreme conclusion is true.

But if the argument for the extreme conclusion is flawed, that does not mean that we are left with a cogent argument for something less extreme, more comfortable, and more credible. More likely we are left with nothing. However much we might welcome an argument that we are required to contribute $100 annually – say – that is not what we have been offered. Flawed is flawed. Unless somehow the flaw resulted only because we pushed Unger's argument too far, it will not automatically go away just because we stop short.

Well then, what is the flaw? The lesson of the *reductio ad absurdum* is just that something must have gone wrong somewhere. To arrive at an answer – an admittedly tentative answer – we do best to approach the question indirectly, by way of Unger's answer to the second, psychological question: what causes us to respond so differently to the case of the wounded stranger and the case of the distant child? Here is Unger's explanation.

'Often we view the world as comprising just certain *situations*. Likewise we view a situation as including just *certain people*, all of them well grouped together within it. . . . Often we view a certain serious problem as being a problem for only those folks viewed as being (grouped together) in a particular situation; and, then, we'll view the bad trouble as *not* any problem for all the world's other people.' (p. 97) It is easy to see how this phenomenon of 'separation' might apply to our pair of contrasting cases. When you decide that you must do what it takes to save the wounded stranger's leg, you and he have met face to face, far away from anyone else; no wonder

155

you and he are grouped together psychologically within a salient situation. Nothing like that happens in the case of the distant child. If you limit your aid to those who are grouped together with you in a psychologically salient situation, of course you will go to far greater lengths to save the stranger's leg than you will to save the child's life.

Unger illustrates the phenomenon of separation with a plethora of examples. But his examples are fantastic, and often comical as well, and so it is harder than it ought to be to appreciate their lessons. I substitute my own contrasting pair of examples.

The first is a true story. When London was under attack by German missiles, the British devised a trick. They could have deceived the Germans into thinking that the missiles were hitting too far north. The Germans would have adjusted their aim to make the missiles hit further south. Instead of killing more people in densely populated London, the missiles would have killed fewer people – but different people – in the less densely populated southern suburbs. Sources differ about whether the deception was tried. Anyhow, it was opposed: the Home Secretary was averse to 'playing God.' Many of us would think the government had no alternative to playing God: whether they intervened to stop the deception or whether they let it go forward (or whether they acted to bring about the deception or whether they prevented it by inaction), the allocation of danger depended in any case on them. Their only choice was whether to play God in a more or less lethal fashion. If we describe their choice that way, aversion to playing God is beside the point. The right choice seems clear: to try the deception.

Contrast that case with another, set this time in the near future. Transplant surgery has been perfected, but there are not nearly enough organs to go around. Shall we snatch some young and healthy victims and cut them up for parts? For each one we kill, many will be saved. By snatching involuntary organ donors rather than letting them live, we would play God in a less rather than a more lethal fashion. Then should we do it? Of course not. The idea is monstrous.

Why the difference in our response to the two cases? Both times, what we have is a plan to sacrifice a few to save many. When the few are suburbanites and the many are Londoners, many of us

156

(though not all) approve. When the few are the donors and the many are those who need transplants, all of us (near enough) disapprove.

Unger's psychological hypothesis provides an answer. The Londoners and the suburbanites, and the rest of the British as well, are all in it together. Wherever the missiles may happen to be aimed, all of Britain is under attack. Those who would be sacrificed and those who would be saved are all involved in the same salient situation. Not so in the other case. Those who need organs are united by a shared predicament. But those who could be butchered to provide the needed organs are most naturally viewed just as uninvolved bystanders. Why should others' need for spare organs be seen as *their* problem? (Just because their organs could solve it?) So separation explains why we approve (insofar as we do) of diverting the German missiles; and why we disapprove of snatching the lifesaving organs.

Unger casts separation as the villain of his story: the malign psychological force that generates 'distorted' moral responses and prevents us from seeing what our ordinary morality really requires of us. But here Unger is resorting to mere *obiter dicta*, very exceptional in what is otherwise a tightly argued book.

I am inclined to think that Unger is right, and importantly right, about the psychology of separation; but wrong when he treats this phenomenon he has uncovered as a distorting force that clouds our moral judgement. On the contrary, separation might be a central, if underappreciated, feature of our ordinary morality.

Unger has made it his task to find out what is required of us by the basic values we actually accept. (To repeat: he is not trying to rebuild morality *a priori* on new foundations.) If he goes in search of our accepted values, and what he finds are judgements shaped by the phenomenon of separation, why doubt that he has found just what he was seeking? Why assume that he has instead found a veil of illusion that conceals our basic values from our view?

If indeed separation is a legitimate feature of our ordinary morality, and if separation breaks the parallel between the case of the wounded stranger and the case of the distant child, then we have diagnosed the flaw in Unger's argument. It has not been shown that failure to save the child's life is as seriously wrong as failure to save the stranger's leg. It has not even been shown that it is wrong at all. We can go on disagreeing about whether failing to respond to UNICEF's solicitations is seriously wrong or mildly wrong or not at all wrong. Doubtless we *will* go on disagreeing. Unger's argument, if flawed as I suggest that it is, is powerless to settle the matter.

14

Mill and Milquetoast

1. TOLERATION

We are fortunate to live under institutions of toleration. Opinions that many of us deem false and pernicious are nevertheless held, and even imparted to others, with impunity. This is so in part because we hold legal rights to freedom of thought and freedom of expression. Not only do these legal rights exist; they enjoy widespread support. Any effort to revoke them would be widely opposed. Those whose opinions were threatened with suppression would find many allies, even among those who most deplored their opinions.

But legal rights are far from the whole story. The institutions of toleration are in large part informal, a matter not of law but of custom, habits of conduct and thought. Even when the law lets us do as we like, many of us do not like to do anything that would make people suffer for the opinions they hold, or hinder their expression of their opinions. We may choose our friends and our casual acquaintances as we please, and we are certainly free to shun those whose opinions we find objectionable; but many of us exercise

First published in *The Australasian Journal of Philosophy* **67** (1989), 152–171. Reprinted with kind permission from *The Australasian Journal of Philosophy*.

I thank audiences on several occasions for helpful discussions. Thanks are due especially to D. M. Armstrong, Geoffrey Brennan, Keith Campbell, Philip Kitcher, Martin Krygier, Stephanie Lewis, Michael Mahoney, H. J. McCloskey, Thomas Nagel, T. M. Scanlon, D. W. Skubik, and Kim Sterelny.

this freedom half-heartedly, or with a bad conscience, or not at all. An editor or a bookseller has plenty of discretion to assist in the spreading of some opinions and not others, and might weigh many different considerations in deciding what to publish or what to sell; but might very well think it wrong to give any weight at all to whether an author's opinions are true or false, beneficial or dangerous.

Not only do customs of toleration complement legal rights; to some extent, the customs may even substitute for the rights. Doubtless it is a good idea to entrench toleration by writing it into the constitution and the statutes. But the measure of toleration need not be legalistic. The real test is: what can you get away with? What opinions can you express without fear of reprisal? To what extent can you reach your audience, if it wants to be reached? What can you read or hear without fear of reprisal? If the samizdat circulate freely, and you needn't be a hero to write or produce or read them, that is not yet good enough. But it is very much more than nothing. A country where banned books become contraband best-sellers is worse off than a country where books cannot be banned at all; but their difference is not great when we compare them both with a country where banned books really do disappear.

Toleration need not be everywhere to be effective. An atheist is not welcome everywhere – who is? – and if he cannot find toleration in the place he most wants to be, to that extent he suffers for his opinions. But if there are many and varied places where an atheist is perfectly welcome, then he doesn't suffer much. Likewise, it is essential that there should be some magazines where atheism may be published; it matters little that there are many others where it may not. Even a handful of urban and rural bohemias can go a long way toward making toleration available to those who have need of it. So if an intolerant majority do not bestir themselves to clean up the bohemias, then even they are participating in the institutions of toleration.

2. MILL'S PROJECT

That is what toleration is. Now, what is it good for? In his *On Liberty*, Mill undertakes to give it a utilitarian defence.[1] That is, he undertakes to show that its expected benefits outweigh its expected costs. But he is no simplistic Benthamite: 'I regard utility as the ultimate appeal on all ethical questions; but it must be utility in the largest sense, grounded on the permanent interests of man as a progressive being.' (p. 14) So whatever commitments Mill may incur elsewhere, here we needn't worry whether matters of human flourishing somehow translate into a common currency of pleasure and pain.

All the same, we had better not take utility in *too* large a sense. 'I forego any advantage from the idea of an abstract right as a thing independent of utility.' (p. 14) So it will not do to claim that the infringement of such 'abstract' rights is itself one cost to be weighed in the balance as a component of 'utility', whether with infinite weight (as a 'side constraint') or just as one consideration among others.

There seems to be another rule to Mill's game, unannounced but manifest in his practice. Let us make it explicit. It is the rule of *neutralism*. Suppose we have a dispute, say between believers and atheists, and suppose the believers want to suppress what they take to be the false and dangerous opinions of the atheists. Some utilitarian atheist might defend toleration thus: in the first place there is no God, therefore no harm can come of holding beliefs offensive to God. Nor can the spread of atheism do harm in any other way. Therefore suppressing atheism has no benefits to match its costs. Therefore toleration would be better. This defence is utilitarian, sure enough; but unMillian. The Millian defender of toleration makes his case without taking sides in the dispute. Of course he may argue from factual premises – no utilitarian could go far without them! – but not from factual premises that are part of the very dispute between the suppressors and the suppressed. It is Mill's ambition to defend toleration even when questions remain disputed, therefore it will not do to

---

1 John Stuart Mill, *On Liberty* (London: J. W. Parker & Son, 1859); page references here are to the edition edited by C. V. Shields (Indianapolis: Bobbs-Merrill, 1956).

require some settlement of the dispute before the case for toleration can be completed.

The neutralism of Mill's practice goes further. Some utilitarian might say to the believers that according to their opinion toleration maximises utility because God is offended more by the cruelty of inquisitors than by the impudence of atheists; and might argue to the atheists that according to their opinion toleration maximises utility because there is no God to be offended. This playing both sides of the street is a valid argument by separation of cases: *A* or *B*, if *A* then toleration maximises utility, if *B* then toleration maximises utility, therefore toleration maximises utility in either case. But however valid it may be, this too is unMillian. In a Millian defence of toleration, not only must the factual premises be common ground between the two sides; also a uniform and non-disjunctive argument must be addressed to both. The Millian invites both sides to assent to a single, common list of the benefits of toleration and costs of suppression. This common list is supposed to have decisive weight in favour of toleration. One or the other side may have in mind some further costs and benefits that obtain according to its own disputed opinions, perhaps including some that count in favour of suppression; but if so, these considerations are supposed to be outweighed by the considerations on the neutral common list.

Why do I ascribe a rule of neutralism to Mill? Only because I never see him violate it. Not because he states and defends it – he does not. And not because it is in any way essential to his project of defending toleration by appeal to utility. On the contrary. To decide whether he himself should think that toleration maximises utility, Mill must sum up all the relevant costs and benefits according to his own opinions. To persuade me that toleration maximises utility, he must sum them up according to my opinions (perhaps my original opinions, or perhaps my new opinions after he is done persuading me). It is irrelevant whether the opinions are disputed or undisputed. But Mill is not doing his private sums, nor is *On Liberty* addressed to some one person in particular. It is meant to persuade an audience with varied opinions. It's hard to play both sides of the street when you're writing for both sides at once! Better for Mill if he can address the whole of his case to the whole of his audience. He can do so, if a neutral common list suffices to outweigh whatever other disputed costs and benefits there may be. Hence the rule of neutralism. It makes no sense as a constraint on utilitarian argument *per se*, but plenty of sense as part of Mill's strategy of persuasion.

3. SELF- AND OTHER-REGARDING

The main principle of *On Liberty*, second only to the ultimate appeal to utility in the largest sense, is that 'the sole end for which mankind are warranted . . . in interfering with the liberty of action of any of their number is self-protection.' (p. 13) It is notoriously difficult to get clear about the requisite line between self- and other-regarding action. But it is worth a digression to see why the principle and the difficulty need not concern us here.

First, and decisively, because the protection of self-regarding conduct is in any case derived from the ultimate appeal to utility. It has no force of its own to justify toleration if the direct appeal to utility fails.

Second, in addition, because if an opinion is not held secretly, but is expressed in a way that might persuade others, that *is* other-regarding: both because of the effect that the opinion may have on the life of the convert and because of what the convert might do, premised on that opinion, which might affect third parties.

Mill is confusing on this point. 'The liberty of expressing and publishing opinions may seem to fall under a different principle, since it belongs to that part of the conduct of an individual which concerns other people; but, being almost of as much importance as the liberty of thought itself and resting in great part on the same reasons, is practically inseparable from it.' (p. 16) What kind of argument is this? Other-regarding conduct is not in general protected by reason of inseparability from private thought, as will be plain if someone's religion demands human sacrifice.

4. MILL'S TALLY

I do not believe that a utilitarian defence of toleration, constrained by Mill's rule of neutralism, has any hope of success. I make no fundamental objection to broadly utilitarian reasoning, at least in such matters as this. It's just that I think the balance of costs and benefits will too easily turn out the wrong way. When we tally up the benefits of toleration that can be adduced in a neutral and uniform way, they will just not be weighty enough. They will fall sadly short of matching the benefits of suppression, calculated according to the opinions of the would-be suppressors.

I begin the tally with the items Mill himself lists.

Risk of error. True and beneficial opinion might be suppressed in the mistaken belief that it is false and harmful.

Mill says just 'true' and 'false'; the utilitarian argument requires that we say 'beneficial' and 'harmful'; there's no guarantee that these coincide, but for simplicity let's suppose they do.

Mixture. Truth and error may be found combined in one package deal, so that there's no way of suppressing the error without suppressing truth as well.

Dead dogma (reasons). Unless received opinion 'is suffered to be, and actually is, vigorously and earnestly contested, it will . . . be held in the manner of a prejudice, with little comprehension of its rational grounds.' (p. 64)

Dead dogma (meaning). Further, 'the meaning of the doctrine itself will be in danger of being lost or enfeebled, and deprived of its vital effect on the character and conduct . . . cumbering the ground and preventing the growth of any real and heartfelt conviction from reason or personal experience.' (p. 64)

Mill counts deadness of dogma as a harm only in case received opinion is true. But perhaps he should also think it worse, from the standpoint of human flourishing, that error should be held as dead dogma rather than in a real and heartfelt and reasoned way.

Mill's guess about what will happen if received opinion is vigorously contested seems remarkably optimistic. Will there be debate at all, and not just warfare? If there is debate, will it help the debaters think through their positions, or will they rather throw up a cloud of sophistries? If they think things through, will they discover unappreciated reasons or bedrock disagreement?

5. THE TALLY EXTENDED

Mill's list so far seems too short. Why not borrow from the next chapter of *On Liberty* also? Then we could add –

Individuality. If diversity is of value, and thinking for oneself, and thoughtful choice, why aren't these things of some value even when people think up, and thoughtfully choose among, diverse errors?

Building character. The more chances you get to think and choose, the better you get at it; and being good at thinking and choosing is one big part of human flourishing. Freedom as a social condition offers exercises which conduce to freedom as a trait of character. Practice makes perfect.

This too seems more a piece of armchair psychology than a firm empirical result. Travelers' tales suggest that the hard school of the east sometimes does better than the free and easy west at building just such character as Mill rightly values. If we like guessing, we might guess that when it comes to building character, freedom and competent repression both take second place – what does best is repression bungled, with gratuitous stupidity and cruelty. That speculation seems at least as likely as Mill's – but responsible utilitarian calculation should put little faith in either one.

We noted that truth and error might be found combined in a package deal. Then if we suppress the error, we lose truth as well. But the same thing can happen even if the error we suppress is unmixed with truth.

Transformation. Future thinkers may turn our present errors into truth not just by filtering out the false parts but in more complicated ways. They may find us standing on our heads, and turn us on our feet. They may attend to old questions and give them new answers. They may borrow old ideas and transplant them into new and better settings. They may put the old errors to use in metaphors and analogies. If we suppress errors that might have been the germ of better things to come, we block progress. Does progress conduce to utility? – We may hope so, at least if it is 'utility in the largest sense, grounded on the permanent interests of man as a progressive being'.

Mill's lists of harms and benefits feature the highfaluting, interesting, speculative ones. He omits the obvious.

The insult of paternalism. If I paternalise over you, and in particular if I prevent you from being exposed to some seductive heresy, my action is manifestly premised on doubt of your competence, and on confidence in my own. You are likely to take offence both at my low opinion of you and at my pretension of superiority. No less so, if you acknowledge that I am indeed more competent than you are to govern your life. Bad enough it should be true! Do I have to rub it in?

(This is a different thing from the alleged insult of denying that you have rights. For (1) no similar insult is given when Bentham tells you that natural rights are nonsense upon stilts, yet he denies that you have rights more clearly than any paternalist does; (2) the insult may still be there even if you too are of Bentham's opinion; or (3) if you think that you once had rights but have freely given them away to me.)

More obviously still, there are –

The secret police. To do an effective job of suppression, it is necessary to build a system of informers and dossiers. Once in place, the means of suppression may be taken over and turned to new purposes. They might be used to advance the ambitions of a would-be tyrant – something all would agree (before it began, at least) in counting as a cost.[2]

2 Another possibility is that the means of suppression might be turned to a new purpose which, like the original suppression, serves utility according to the opinions of some but not of others. The Informer of Bray, like the Vicar, might serve his new masters as willingly as he served the old. But this danger, however weighty it might seem to some, is inadmissible under the rule of neutralism.

166

The dungeon. If you wish to express or study proscribed opinions, and someone stops you, you will be displeased that your desires are frustrated. And if you are determined to go ahead, the only effective means of stopping you – the dungeon, the gulag, the asylum, the gallows – may prove somewhat unfelicific.

This completes our neutralist tally, our list of considerations that are meant to be accepted by all parties to disputed questions. One way or another, and even if we receive Mill's armchair psychology with all the doubt it deserves, we still have some rather weighty benefits of toleration and costs of suppression. But of course that's not enough. Mill wins his case only if the benefits of toleration outweigh the costs – and not only according to his own opinions, but according to the opinions of those he seeks to dissuade from suppressing. The cost of toleration, lest we forget, is that dangerous errors may flourish and spread.

6. THE INQUISITOR READS MILL

McCloskey has written that 'many Christian liberals appear to be especially muddled, for, as Christians, they regard eternal salvation and moral living as being of tremendous importance and as being goods as valuable as freedom. Yet many of them deny the state even the abstract right to aid truth, morality, and religion and to impede error and evil, while at the same time they insist on its duty to promote the good of freedom. Their implicit value judgment is so obviously untenable that one cannot but suspect that it has not been made explicit and considered in its own right.' In the same vein, Quine: 'If someone firmly believes that eternal salvation and damnation hinge on embracing his particular religion, he would be callous indeed to sit tolerantly back and watch others go to hell.'[3] To dramatise their point, I imagine the Inquisitor: a thoughtful Christian,

3 H. J. McCloskey, 'The State and Evil', *Ethics* 69 (1959), p. 190; W. V. Quine, *Quiddities: An Intermittently Philosophical Dictionary* (Cambridge, Massachusetts: Harvard University Press, 1987), p. 208.

benevolent by his own lights, far from muddled and far from liberal. Can Mill persuade him to change his intolerant ways?

The Inquisitor, as I shall imagine him, is the very man Mill ought to be addressing. He agrees completely with Mill that the ultimate appeal is to utility in the largest sense. He claims no infallibility. Indeed his faith is infirm, and he is vividly aware that he just might be making a tragic mistake. He is satisfied – too quickly, perhaps – that Mill is an expert social psychologist, who knows whereof he speaks concerning the causes of dead dogma and the causes of excellent character. In short, he grants every item in the neutralist tally of costs and benefits.

His only complaint is that the tally is incomplete. He believes, in fact, that the included items have negligible weight compared to the omitted item. Heresy, so the Inquisitor believes, poisons the proper relationship between man and God. The heretic is imperfectly submissive, or sees God as nothing but a powerful sorcerer, or even finds some trace of fault in God's conduct. The consequence is eternal damnation. That is something infinitely worse than any evil whatever in this life; infinitely more weighty, therefore, than the whole of the neutralist tally. Further, damnation is not just a matter of pain. (Hell-fire is no part of it, just an inadequate metaphor for what really happens.) Damnation is harm along exactly the dimension that Mill wanted us to bear in mind: it is the utter absence and the extreme opposite of human excellence and flourishing.

The Inquisitor also believes that heresy is contagious. The father of lies has fashioned it with all his cunning to appeal to our weaknesses. There is nothing mechanical about it – those never exposed to heretical teachings sometimes reinvent heresy for themselves, those who are exposed may withstand temptation – but still, those who are not exposed are a great deal safer than those who are.

The Inquisitor also believes that if he is ruthless enough in suppressing heresy, he may very well succeed. Not, of course, in eradicating heresy for all time; but in greatly reducing the incidence of exposure, and consequently in saving a great many souls from damnation.

Note well that the Inquisitor does not think that he could save the souls of heretics by forced conversion. He accepts the common wisdom that this cannot be done: forced conversion would be insincere, so it would be worthless in the sight of God. He knows no way to save the heretics themselves. What he could do by suppressing heresy, so he thinks, is to save many of those who are not yet heretics, but would succumb if exposed to heretical teachings.

The Inquisitor does not relish the suffering of heretics. As befits a utilitarian, he is moved by benevolence alone. He hates cruelty. But he heeds the warning: 'if you hate cruelty, remember that nothing is so cruel in its consequences as the toleration of heresy.'[4]

Therefore the Inquisitor concludes, even after discounting properly for his uncertainty, that the balance of cost and benefit is overwhelmingly in favour of suppression. Mill's case for tolerating heresy is unpersuasive. In fact it is frivolous – serious matters are at stake! You might as well oppose the suppression of heresy on the ground that dungeons cost too much money.

Mill has lost his case.

This is not to say that the Inquisitor stumps utilitatianism itself. Mill was trying to bring off a *tour de force*: to abide by his self-imposed rule of neutralism, and yet win the argument against all comers. A more modest utilitarian might proceed in any of three ways.

One way for the utilitarian to deal with the Inquisitor is not to argue with him at all. You don't argue with the sharks; you just put up nets to keep them away from the beaches. Likewise the Inquisitor, or any other utilitarian with dangerously wrong opinions about how to maximise utility, is simply a danger to be fended off. You organise and fight. You see to it that he cannot succeed in his plan to do harm in order – as he thinks and you do not – to maximise utility.

A second way is to fight first and argue afterward. When you fight, you change the circumstances that afford the premises of a utilitarian argument. First you win the fight, then you win the argument. If you can make sure that the Inquisitor will fail in his effort to suppress heresy, you give him reason to stop trying. Though he thinks that successful persecution maximises utility, he will certainly agree that failed attempts are nothing but useless harm.

4 Spoken by the just and wise inquisitor in George Bernard Shaw, *Saint Joan* (London: Constable, 1924), p. 77.

Finally, a modest utilitarian might dump the rule of neutralism. He might argue that, according to the Inquisitor's own opinions, there are advantages of toleration which are more weighty than those on the neutralist tally and which the Inquisitor had not appreciated. Or he might start by trying to change the Inquisitor's mind about the facts of theology, and only afterward try to demonstrate the utility of toleration. He might try to persuade the Inquisitor to replace his present theological opinions by different ones: atheism, perhaps, or a religion of sweetness and light and salvation for all. Or he might only try to persuade the Inquisitor to be more sceptical: to suspend judgement on matters of theology, or near enough that the uncertain danger of damnation no longer outweighs the more certain harms that are done when heresy is suppressed.

7. THE ASSUMPTION OF INFALLIBILITY

Mill does at one point seem to be doing just that – supporting toleration by supporting scepticism. If he did, he would not be observing the rule of neutralism. He would be putting forward not an addition to whatever his reader might have thought before, but rather a modification. And he would be a fine old pot calling the kettle black. Part of his own case rests on far-from-certain psychological premises.

But the appearance is deceptive.[5] Mill's point when he says that 'all silencing of discussion is an assumption of infallibility' (pp. 21–22) is not that we should hesitate to act on our opinions – for instance by silencing discussion we believe to be harmful – out of fear that our opinions may be wrong. For Mill very willingly agrees with the hypothetical objector who says that 'if we were never to act on our opinions, because those opinions may be wrong, we should leave all our interests uncared for, and all our duties unperformed . . . There is no such things as absolute certainty, but there is assurance sufficient

---

5 Here I follow C. L. Ten, *Mill on Liberty* (Oxford: Clarendon Press, 1980), pp. 124–127, in distinguishing Mill's 'Avoidance of Mistake Argument' from his 'Assumption of Infallibility Argument'.

for the purposes of human life. We may, and must, assume our opinion to be true for the guidance of our own conduct.' (pp. 23–24) Mill's real point is that if we are duly modest and do not assume ourselves infallible, we should have confidence in our opinions only when they have withstood the test of free discussion. A sceptic is like a traffic cop: he admonishes us to slow down in our believing. Whereas Mill is like the traffic cop in the tire advertisement: 'If you're not riding on Jetzon tires – slow down!' *That* cop doesn't want us to slow down – he wants us to buy Jetzon tires. Free discussion is the Jetzon tire that gives us license to speed, fallible though we be. To dare to do without Jetzon tires is to overrate your skill as a driver; to do without free discussion is to assume yourself infallible. 'Complete liberty of contradicting and disproving our opinion is the very condition which justifies us in assuming its truth for purposes of action; and on no other terms can a being with human faculties have any rational assurance of being right.' (p. 24) Mill thus assures us that if we *do* meet the condition, then we *are* justified in acting on our opinions.

Our Inquisitor, if he takes Mill's word for this as he does on other matters, will not dare suppress heresy straightaway. First he must spend some time in free discussion with the heretics. Afterward, if they have not changed his mind, then he will deem himself justified in assuming the truth of his opinion for purposes of action; which he will do when he goes forward to suppress heresy, and burns his former partners in discussion at the stake.

Compare Herbert Marcuse, who advocated 'withdrawal of tolerance from regressive movements *before* they can become active; intolerance even toward thought, opinion, and word, and finally, intolerance . . . toward the self-styled conservatives, to the political Right' during the present 'emergency situation'.[6] If tolerance is withdrawn only after Marcuse has enjoyed it for many years, Mill cannot complain that Marcuse has not yet earned the right to act on his illiberal opinions.

6 'Repressive Tolerance' in R. P. Wolff, B. Moore, and H. Marcuse, eds., *A Critique of Pure Tolerance* (Boston: Beacon Press, 1965), p. 109.

8. DANGEROUS OPINIONS

The Inquisitor, apart from his anachronistic utilitarianism, is just an ogre out of the past. Might Mill's defence work well enough, if not against just any imaginable foe of toleration, at least against any we are likely to meet in the present day? I doubt it. To be sure, some of us nowadays are sanguine about dangerous opinions. Whatever harm opinions may do under other conditions, we think they pose no present danger in our part of the world. The neutralist tally is all the defence of toleration *we* need. But others of us think otherwise: they think that some of the people around them hold opinions that are not only false but harmful. I predict that for many pairs of my readers – perhaps a majority of pairs – one of the pair holds some opinion that the other would find profoundly dangerous.

It might be a religious or irreligious opinion that conduces, in the opinion of the other, to contempt for oneself, for other people, for the natural world, or for God.

It might be a political opinion favouring some social arrangement which, in the opinion of the other, is a trap – an arrangement which makes most people's lives degraded and miserable, but which gives a few people both a stake in its continuation and the power to prevent change.

It might be an opinion belittling some supposed danger which, in the opinion of the other, requires us to take urgent measures for our protection. It might be the opinion that we need not worry about environmental hazards, or nuclear deterrence, or Soviet imperialism, or AIDS, or addictive drugs.

It might be an opinion which, in the opinion of the other, is racist or sexist and thereby fosters contempt and oppressive conduct.

It might be a moral opinion (say, about abortion) which, in the opinion of the other, either condones and encourages wickedness or else wrongly condemns what is innocent and sometimes beneficial.

In each of these cases, important matters are at stake. In each case, the stakes involve a great deal of 'utility in the largest sense, grounded on the permanent interests of man as a progressive being.' To be sure, these cases are less extreme than that of the Inquisitor and the heretics. We have no *infinite* outweighing. Still, they are extreme enough. In each case, the disutility that is feared from the dangerous opinion seems enough to outweigh all the advantages of toleration according to the neutralist tally. And this remains so even if we discount all around for uncertainty, duly acknowledging that we are fallible.

In each case, therefore, if effective suppression were feasible, it would seem frivolous for the foe of the dangerous opinion to stay his hand because of any consideration Mill has on offer. If he does stay his hand, it seems as if he lets geniality or custom or laziness stand in the way of his wholehearted pursuit of maximum utility.

9. MORRIS

Take our contemporary, Henry M. Morris. He thinks, for one thing, that 'Evolution is the root of atheism, of communism, nazism, behaviorism, racism, economic imperialism, militarism, libertinism, anarchism, and all manner of anti-Christian systems of belief and practice.'[7] He thinks, for another thing, that in history and the social sciences, 'it is especially important . . . that the teacher gives a balanced presentation of both points of view [evolutionist and creationist] to students. Otherwise the process of education for living becomes a process of indoctrination and channelization, and the school degenerates into a hatchery of parrots.'[8] At any rate, he says both these things, and let us take him at his word. Doubtless he mainly has in mind the 'balanced treatment' versus purely evolutionist teaching. But what he says, and his argument for it, apply equally to the 'balanced treatment' versus the purely creationist teaching we might have expected him to favour. So evolution is dangerous in the extreme, yet it is not to be suppressed – it is not even to be left out of the curriculum for schoolchildren – lest we hatch parrots! ('Parrots', I take it, are the same thing as those who hold their opinions as dead dogma.) How can Morris possibly think that the harm of hatching parrots is remotely comparable to the harm done by 'balanced presentation' that spreads evolutionist ideas? How dare he give this feeble

7 *The Remarkable Birth of Planet Earth* (San Diego: Creation-Life Publishers, 1972), p. 75.
8 *Scientific Creationism* (San Diego: Creation-Life Publishers, 1974), p. 178.

173

Millian reason for tolerating, and even spreading, such diabolically dangerous ideas? Surely, by his own lights, he is doing the Devil's work when he favours balance over suppression.

10. MILQUETOAST

Mill's defence – who needs it? Perhaps the sceptical who, when told any story about the harmful effects of dangerous opinions, will find it too uncertain to serve as a basis of action? Or perhaps the apathetic, who may believe the story but not think the harm really matters very much? No, because the sceptical and the apathetic will be equally unimpressed by Mill's own story about the harmful effects of suppression. Nor would Mill have wanted to address his argument to the sceptical or the apathetic. That is not how he wants us to be. He wants us to have our Jetzon tires exactly so that we *may* speed. He favours vigour, dedication, moral earnestness.

I suggest that Mill's defence of toleration might best be addressed to Caspar Milquetoast, that famous timid soul.[9] Doubtless he too is not the pupil Mill would have chosen, but at least he is in a position to put the lesson to use.

Milquetoast *does* have opinions about important and controversial matters. And he does care. He cares enough to raise his voice and bang the table in the privacy of his own house: asked if he wants *Russian* dressing on his salad, the answer is 'NO!' He isn't *always* timid. (p. 185) But when he is out and about, his main goal is to avoid a quarrel. All else takes second place. He knows better than to talk to strangers on vital topics: asked what he thinks of the Dodgers' chances, he'd 'rather not say, if you don't mind'. (p. 162) And when his barber, razor in hand, asks how he's going to vote, Milquetoast fibs: 'Why-uh-er-I don't get a vote. I've been in prison – stir I mean – and I've lost my citizenship'. (p. 183)

Milquetoast thinks, let us suppose, that it is a dangerous mistake to ignore the threat of Soviet imperialism. He would be hard put to explain why a rosy view of the evil empire is not dangerous enough

9 H. T. Webster, *The Best of H. T. Webster: A Memorial Collection* (New York: Simon and Schuster, 1953), pp. 158–185.

to be worth suppressing. But he knows that this opinion is controversial. He knows that others think that the Soviet threat is bogus, and that the only real threat comes from our efforts to resist the bogus threat. How horrid to have to dispute these matters – as he surely would if he dared to suggest that the dangerous mistake should be suppressed. What to do? – Solution: bracket the controversial opinions. Keep them as opinions, somehow, in some compartment of one's mind, but ignore them in deciding what is to be done. In questions of suppression and toleration, in particular, appeal to uncontroversial considerations only. Conduct the discussion according to Mill's rule of neutralism. Then all hands can perhaps agree that the neutralist tally is right so far as it goes. And without the airing of disagreeable disagreement, we can go no further. Settle the question without acrimony, then, and we must settle it in favour of toleration. Those compartments of the mind that fear the dangerous consequences of the tolerated opinions should hold their tongues, lest they get us into strife.[10]

Milquetoast, of course, is an incompetent maximiser of utility. His conduct may be fortunate enough, if there turn out to be better reasons for toleration than we have yet considered. But his thought is simply shocking – he systematically declines to be guided by the whole of his system of opinions, ignoring the part that would engage him in unpleasant dispute. Nor is he at all keen to improve the quality of his thought by entering into discussion. That is why Mill should not be proud to have Milquetoast as his star pupil.

11. A TREATY OF TOLERATION

To see how toleration can find a better utilitarian foundation, let us return to our story of the Inquisitor and the heretics. The Inquisitor

10 Milquetoast may resemble the sort of liberal portrayed in Thomas Nagel, 'Moral Conflict and Political Legitimacy', *Philosophy & Public Affairs* 16 (1987), pp. 215–240: 'The defense of liberalism requires that a limit somehow be drawn to appeals to *the truth* in political argument' (p. 227). True liberalism 'must depend on a distinction between what justifies individual belief and what justifies appealing to that belief in support of the exercise of political power' (p. 229). But of course Nagel's liberal is moved not by timidity but by high principle.

thinks that the heretics hold a dangerous opinion – dangerous enough to be well worth suppressing, despite all the considerations on the neutralist tally. Because the Inquisitor thinks this, he in turn is a danger to the heretics. Not only does he menace their personal safety; also, if the heretics think that the spreading of their word will benefit all who embrace it, then they must see the Inquisitor as bringing disutility to all mankind. And the more there are of the orthodox, who think as the Inquisitor does, the worse it will be. It would be best, indeed, if none were left who might someday reinfect mankind with the old darkness. Important matters are at stake. And now let us suppose that the heretics, no less than the Inquisitor, are wholehearted pursuers of utility as they see it. (Utility in the largest sense.) In this way the heretics think that the Inquisitor, and all of the orthodox, hold a dangerous opinion – dangerous enough to be well worth suppressing, despite all the considerations on the neutralist tally.

I suppose that some such rough symmetry is a common, though not a necessary, feature of situations in which someone thinks that someone else's opinion is dangerous enough to be worth suppressing.

Devoted as both sides are to utility, and disagreeing as they do about where utility is to be found, what is there to do but fight it out? According to the Inquisitor's opinion, the best outcome will be victory: to vanquish the heretics and suppress their heresy. If this outcome is within reach, going for it is required. Not only is toleration not required by any appeal to utility; it is forbidden. Any restraint or mercy would be wrong. It would be self-indulgent neglect of 'the permanent interests of man as a progressive being', since the foremost of these interests is salvation. Suppose further that there is no hope of changing the Inquisitor's mind about the causes of salvation and damnation. Then there is no way – Millian or unMillian – to persuade him that it is a utilitarian mistake to suppress heresy. He has done his sums correctly, by his lights; we cannot fault them. Of course we can, and we should, fault his premises. They are both false and harmful. But there is no further mistake about what follows.

Likewise, *mutatis mutandis*, according to the heretics' opinion.

If one side has victory within reach, the utilitarian defence of toleration fails. But now suppose instead that the two sides are more or less equally matched. Victory is not so clearly within reach. Neither side can have it just for the asking. Resort to war means taking a gamble. One side or the other will win, and then the winners will suppress the dangerous opinions of the losers. Orthodoxy will triumph and heresy will vanish, at least for a time. Or else heresy will triumph and orthodoxy will vanish. Who can tell which it will be?

In deciding what he thinks of a state of toleration, the Inquisitor must compare it not just with one possible outcome of war but with both. Toleration means that both creeds go unsuppressed, they flourish side by side, they compete for adherents. Many are lost, but many are saved. How many? – It depends. The fear is that the heretics will not scruple to advance their cause by cunning deceit; the hope is that truth will have an inherent advantage, and will benefit from God's favour. Let us suppose that the Inquisitor takes a middling view of the prospect, not too pessimistic and not too optimistic. Then just as he finds victory vastly better than toleration, from the standpoint of salvation and therefore from the standpoint of utility, so he finds defeat vastly worse. According to the Inquisitor's opinion, the triumph of heresy would be a catastrophic loss of utility. The considerations on the neutralist tally have negligible weight, given the enormous amount of utility at stake. Even the pleasures of peace and the horrors of war have negligible weight. But the risk of defeat is far from negligible.

Likewise, *mutatis mutandis*, according to the heretics' opinion.

The Inquisitor's fear of defeat might outweigh his hope of victory. It might seem to him that suppression of orthodoxy would be more of a loss than suppression of heresy would be a gain (more lasting, perhaps); or he might take a pessimistic view of the gamble of war, and think it more likely than not that the heretics would win. Or he might take a moderately optimistic view of how many souls could be won under toleration. One way or another, he might have reason to prefer mutual toleration, unsatisfactory stalemate though it be, to war. His reason is a utilitarian reason. But it rests entirely on what he takes to be the weighty benefits and harms at stake – not the lightweight benefits and harms on the neutralist tally.

It might happen for the heretics likewise that the fear of defeat

177

outweighs the hope of victory. If both sides think defeat more likely than victory, one side must be mistaken, but even a thoughtful utilitarian might well make such a mistake. If both sides think defeat would be more of a loss than victory would be a gain, there needn't be any mistake on either side – except, of course, the underlying mistake that one or both are making all along about what conduces to utility.

Or the heretics also might hope to do well at winning souls under toleration. The orthodox and the heretics can expect alike to win the most souls, if they believe alike that truth, or the creed God favours, will have the advantage. Their expectations are opposite, and one side or the other will be disappointed, but they can face competition with a common optimism.

It may happen, then, that each side prefers toleration to defeat more than it prefers victory to toleration, and therefore prefers toleration to the gamble of fighting it out.[11] Then we have a utilitarian basis for a treaty of toleration. Conditional toleration – toleration so long as the other side also practices toleration – would be an equilibrium. It would be the best that either side could do, if it were what the other side was doing. Toleration is everyone's second choice. The first choice – to suppress and yet be tolerated, to gain victory without risking defeat – is not available; the other side will see to that. The third choice is the gamble of war, and we have supposed that both sides find the odds not good enough. War would be another equilibrium, but a worse one in the opinions of both sides. The worst choice is unconditional unilateral toleration, which means letting the other side have their way unopposed.

In such a case, with two equilibria and a preference on both sides for one over the other – toleration over war – it is neither automatic nor impossible that both sides will find their way to the equilibrium

11 I shall be speaking almost as if there were a conflict of opposed aims. Strictly speaking, there is not. Both sides are, *ex hypothesi*, wholehearted in their pursuit of utility. But their fundamental disagreement about how to pursue their common aim is no different, strategically, from a fundamental conflict of aims. We may speak for short of a gain for one side, versus a gain for the other. But what that really means is a gain for utility according to the opinion of one side, versus a gain for utility according to the opinion of the other.

they both prefer. They might get there formally, by bilateral negoti-
ation and agreement.[12] They might get there by unilateral initiatives
and invitations to reciprocate. They might drift there, gradually de-
veloping a tacit understanding. They might get there under the influence of non-utilitarian reasons, and only afterward find that they had
reached the outcome that maximised utility by the lights of both
sides. They might have been there all along, in accordance with
ancient custom. In each case, I will say that they have arrived at a
treaty of toleration – maybe explicit and formal, maybe tacit.

Some treaties need to be sustained by trust and honour, lest a
cheater gain advantage. It is hard to see how such a treaty could work
between strict utilitarians; because if a utilitarian thinks it will maximise utility if he gains the upper hand, and if he thinks he can gain
the upper hand by breaking his sworn word, then that is what he
must do. But if there are no opportunities for secret preparation and
a surprise breakout, then unutilitarian means of commitment are not
required. The utility of the treaty is incentive enough to keep it.
Neither side wants to withdraw toleration, lest the other side should
have nothing to lose by withdrawing its reciprocal toleration. Often
enough, contractarian and utilitarian defences of social institutions are
put forward as rivals. Not so this time – here we have a contract for
utilitarians.

The hopes and fears of the two sides may or may not be such as
to permit a treaty of toleration. If they are, toleration may or may not
be forthcoming – war is still an equilibrium, it takes two to make the
switch. But now a utilitarian friend of toleration has a case to make.
This time, it is a case meant not for the sceptical or the apathetic, not
for the dismayed irreligious bystanders, not for Milquetoast, but for
the Inquisitor himself.

It is a thoroughly utilitarian case, but it is unMillian because it
flouts the rule of neutralism. It plays both sides of the street. We say

12 Formal treaties of toleration, specifically between Catholic and Protestant powers,
played a great part in the origins of the institutions of toleration we know today.
But we can very well question whether those treaties were equilibria in the pursuit
of utility in the largest sense, or whether they were just an escape from the horrors
of war in the short term.

to the Inquisitor that a treaty of toleration affords his best hope for preventing the suppression of orthodoxy; we say to the heretics that it affords their best hope for preventing the suppression of heresy. Thereby we say to both that it affords the best hope for maximising utility, according to their very different lights. But there is no common list of benefits and costs. On the contrary, what we offer to each side as the greatest benefit of toleration is just what the other must see as its greater cost.[13]

12. CLOSING THE GAP

While a utilitarian defence of some sort of toleration has been accomplished, or so I claim, it seems not yet to be the right sort. This grudging truce between enemies, who would be at each other's throats but for their fear of defeat, is a far cry from the institutions of toleration we know and love. Our simple story of the orthodox and the heretics differs in several ways from the real world of toleration.

> *Cheerful toleration.* If we want to uphold a treaty of toleration, and doing our part means letting harmful error flourish, then we have to do it; but we don't have to like it. Why should we? Whereas we are proud of our institutions of toleration, and pleased to see the spectrum of diverse opinions that flourish unsuppressed. Without the ones we take to be harmful errors, the diversity would be less and we would be less well pleased. Our feelings are mixed, of course. We do not wholeheartedly welcome the errors. But we do to a significant, and bizarre, degree.

13 Unfortunately, a parallel case might be made out for a treaty that not only enjoins toleration between the orthodox and the heretics, but also bans proselytising. That might offer the orthodox their best hope for preventing the slow and peaceful extinction of orthodoxy, and likewise offer the heretics their best hope for preventing the slow and peaceful extinction of heresy. It would be bad for toleration, since each side would have to sustain the treaty by curbing its own zealots. But while this might be a third equilibrium, preferred both to war and to toleration with proselytising, it needn't be. Only if neither side has much confidence in its powers of persuasion will it be an equilibrium at all, let alone a preferred one.

Thoughtless toleration. In the story, the defence depends on the details of the strategic balance between the two sides. Whereas in the real world, we never stop to think how the fortunes of war might go before we take for granted that toleration is better.

Tolerating the weak. In particular, we tolerate the weak. If our Inquisitor had the chance to nip heresy in the bud, long before there was any chance that the heretics might have the strength to win and suppress orthodoxy, of course he would do it. Whereas we treasure the liberty of the weak, and proclaim that the minority of one means as much to us as any other minority.

Tolerating the intolerant. There is no sense in making a treaty with someone who declares that he will not abide by it. If we tolerate harmful error as a *quid pro quo*, so that others will reciprocate by tolerating beneficial truths, why continue after they announce that they will not reciprocate? Whereas we tolerate the intolerant, no less than the tolerant. We do it; and almost everyone who cares for toleration thinks we ought to do it. After Marcuse said that the time had come to withdraw tolerance, his books were no harder to buy than they were before.

Tolerating the extra-dangerous. In the story, the utilitarian defence may depend also on the exact balance of good and harm that we expect from the several opinions that will be protected by a treaty of toleration. The more danger heresy seems to pose, the less likely our Inquisitor is to conclude that a treaty with the heretics might be advantageous. Whereas we, for the most part, favour tolerating all dangerous opinions alike, without seeking exceptions for the very most dangerous.

One difference between our simple story and the real world, of course, is that in the real world we are not all utilitarians. We may be content to mind our own business, and insist that it is not our business to protect mankind against the harm done by dangerous opinions. Or we may be devotees of the 'abstract rights' forsworn by Mill; then we may think that the rights of others constrain us not to serve utility by suppressing dangerous opinions, no matter how high the stakes. (Or they may constrain us to renounce only the harshest methods of suppression. But if only the harshest methods could succeed, we will not need any very weighty utilitarian reasons to dissuade us from trying the ineffective milder methods.)

These differences certainly work in favour of toleration – cheerful and thoughtless toleration, and toleration even of the weak, the intolerant, and the extra-dangerous. But let us not rely on them. Let us rather stay with the fiction of a population of wholehearted utilitarians, so that we may retain as much common ground with Mill as possible. Even so, I think we can close the gap between toleration as we find it in the simple story and toleration as we find it in the real world. We need not abandon the idea of a treaty of toleration. Instead, we must find the right way to extend the idea from our simple two-sided case to a complicated case, many-sided and always changing.

In the real world, there are many different factions. They differ in their opinions, they differ in their opinion about one another's opinions, and they differ in strength. As time goes by, factions wax and wane, and split and merge. The weak may suddenly gang up in a strong alliance, or an alliance may break up and leave the former allies weak. The people who comprise the factions change their minds. Circumstances also change. As the complicated situation changes, understanding of it will lag. Nobody will know very well who deplores whose opinions how much, and with how much strength to back up his deploring. In this complicated world, no less than in the simple case, some will find the opinions of others dangerous, and worthy of suppression; and some will think their own opinions beneficial, and will seek to protect them from suppression. Many would think it worthwhile to tolerate the most deplorable opinions, if they could thereby secure reciprocal toleration from others. They would welcome toleration by treaty. But how can they arrange it?

There might be a vast network of little treaties, each one repeating in miniature our story of the treaty between the orthodox and the heretics. Each faction would have protection from its treaty partners, and if it had chosen its partners well, that would give it the protection it needs. Each faction would extend toleration so far as its treaties require, and no farther. Two factions would enter into a treaty only when both thought it advantageous, given the strategic balance between them, their estimate of the fortunes of war, and their estimate of the potential for good or harm of the opinions that would be protected. The weak, who can offer no reciprocal toleration worth seeking, and the fanatically intolerant, who will not offer reciprocal toleration, would of course be left out of the network of treaties. Those whose opinions were thought to be extra-dangerous also would tend to be left out, other things being equal. A treaty would end when either side thought it no longer advantageous, or when either side thought (rightly or wrongly) that the other side was breaking it.

The trouble is plain to see. It would be enormously difficult for any faction to see to it that, at every moment in the changing course of events, it had exactly the treaties that would be advantageous. There would be abundant opportunities to be mistaken: to overestimate one threat and underestimate another; to be taken by surprise in a realignment of alliances; to see violation where there is compliance or compliance where there is violation; to think it open season on some weakling, unaware that your treaty partner regards that weakling as an ally. Too much care not to tolerate deplorable opinions without an adequate *quid pro quo* is unwise, if it makes the whole arrangement unworkable. Then the desired protection cannot be had.

There might instead be one big simple treaty, loose in its terms, prescribing indiscriminate toleration all around. Exceptions to a treaty of toleration – for the weak, for the intolerant, or for the extra-dangerous – seem at first to make sense. But they threaten to wreck the treaty. As new opinionated factions arise, and old ones wax and wane and merge and split, there will be occasion for endless doubt and haggling about what the exceptions do and don't cover. If some suppression is a violation and some falls under the exceptions, then the first can be masked as the second and the second can be misperceived as the first; all the more so, if most of the cases that arise are unclear ones. Then who can know how well the treaty is really working? How confident can anyone be that his own toleration will be reciprocated in the cases that matter? It will be all too easy to doubt whether it makes good sense to remain in compliance.

Therefore, beware exceptions. Keep it simple, stupid – that which is not there cannot go wrong.[14] First, some toleration of dangerous opinions is justified as a *quid pro quo*; then other toleration is justified because it makes the first transaction feasible.

Ought we to say, simply: *no* exceptions? It seems as if an exception that works even-handedly, and not to the permanent disadvantage of any opinion, ought to be safe. If we regulate only the manner of expression and not the content, why should anybody think that he has nothing to reciprocate because his own opinion is beyond toleration? Nobody has an opinion that he can express only by falsely shouting fire in a theatre, or only by defamation, or only by obscenity. Yet we know that even such exceptions as these can be abused. Some clever analogiser will try to erase the line between the innocent even-handed exception and the dangerous discriminatory one. He will claim that denouncing conscription is like shouting fire in a theatre, because both create a clear and present danger. Or he will claim that sharp criticism of the conduct of high officials is defamatory. Or he will claim that common smut is not half so obscene as the disgusting opinions of his opponent. If we put any limit to toleration, it is not enough to make sure that the line as drawn will not undermine the treaty. We also need some assurance that the line will stay in place where it was drawn, and not shift under pressure.

No exceptions are altogether safe; maybe some are safe enough. That is a question only to be answered by experience, and experience seems to show that some exceptions – the few we have now – are safe enough. They have not yet undermined the treaty, despite all the efforts of mischievous analogisers, and there is no obvious reason why they should become more dangerous in future. We needn't fear them much, and perhaps we can even welcome such benefits as they bring. But to try out some new and different exceptions would be foolhardy.

A simple, nearly exceptionless, well-established treaty of toleration could in time become not just a constraint of conduct, but a climate of thought. If, in the end, you will always decide that the balance of

14 The second half is quoted from the instructions for a Seagull outboard motor.

cost and benefit comes out in favour of complying with the treaty, why should you ever stop to think about the harm done by tolerating a dangerous error? Eventually you will be tolerant by habit, proudly, cheerfully, and without thought of the costs. You will proceed as if the neutralist tally were the whole story about the costs and benefits of suppression. You will bracket whatever you may think about the harm done by others' opinions. You might still think, in some compartment of your mind, that certain opinions are false and harmful. If the treaty of toleration has become second nature, you might be hard put to explain why these opinions are not dangerous enough to be worth suppressing. But you will never think of the danger as any reason to suppress.

This habit of bracketing might be not just a consequence of a treaty but part of its very content. Not so if the treaty is a formal one, to be sure; that had better regulate action, not thought, so that it can be exact and verifiable enough to permit confident agreement. But insofar as the treaty is an informal understanding, uncodified, growing up gradually, it may prescribe not only tolerant conduct but also habits of thought conducive to toleration. In particular, it may prescribe bracketing. If your compartmentalised habits of thoughts are to some extent within your control – not indeed at every moment, but at those moments when you don't bother to think things through as thoroughly as you might – then you may compartmentalise for a utilitarian reason. You may see, dimly, that when you bracket your fear of others' dangerous opinions, you participate in a custom that serves utility by your lights because it protects opinions you deem beneficial, and that would not long persist if the bracketing that conduces to toleration were not mostly reciprocated.

If a treaty of toleration tends to turn us into Milquetoasts and Millians, that is not wholly a bad thing. It is too bad if we become compartmentalised in our thinking, repressing at some times what we believe at other times about the harm opinions can do. But if we forget the costs of toleration, that makes toleration more robust. And if toleration is beneficial on balance, the more robust the better.

185

13. CONCLUSION

What is toleration good for? A proper utilitarian answer need not omit the neutralist tally. After all, it does carry some weight in favour of toleration. But the principal part of the answer cannot be neutral. The main benefit of toleration is that it protects so-and-so particular opinions, true and beneficial, which would be in danger of suppression were it not for the institutions of toleration. When reciprocal toleration protects such-and-such other opinions, false and harmful, that is a cost to be regretted, and not to be denied. When a utilitarian favours toleration, of course, it is because he reckons that the benefits outweigh the costs.

If you think it would serve utility to 'withdraw tolerance' from such-and-such dangerous opinions, you'd better think through *all* the consequences. Your effort might be an ineffective gesture; in which case, whatever you might accomplish, you will not do away with the danger. Or it might be not so ineffective. To the extent that you succeed in withdrawing toleration from your enemy, to that extent you deprive him of his incentive to tolerate you. If toleration is withdrawn in *all* directions, are you sure the opinions that enhance utility will be better off? When we no longer renounce the *argumentum ad baculum*, are you sure it will be you that carries the biggest stick?

15

Academic appointments: Why ignore the advantage of being right?

Universities exist for the sake of the advancement of knowledge: its transmission by teaching, its expansion by research. Most of those who make academic decisions on behalf of universities will take the advancement of knowledge as their predominant, ultimate aim.

Of course, some people in universities have different aims in mind. They may think the advancement of knowledge is meaningless, or square, or worthless, or unattainable, or just outweighed by some more urgent aim – the cultivation of entertaining new ideas regardless of truth, perhaps, or the civilizing of the future rulers, or the recruiting of a mighty army to smash the state. But let us imagine an especially lucky university, where nearly everyone pursues the ultimate aim of advancing knowledge and where the few dissenters pursue aims so diverse as to cancel one another out.

As a philosopher, I shall tell a story about the philosophy department of this lucky university. But the story applies more broadly. Not perhaps to the department of frenchified literary theory, where skepticism runs rampant and the pursuit of truth is reckoned passé. Not perhaps to the mathematics department, where they are in

First published in *Ormond Papers* (Ormond College, University of Melbourne, 1989). Reprinted with kind permission from Temple University Press.

This paper is based on a lecture given at Ormond College, Melbourne, in July 1988. I thank the audience on that occasion and also Paul Benacerraf, Steven M. Cahn, Philip Kitcher, T. M. Scanlon, and others, for valuable comments.

confident agreement about what's true and how to tell, and they disagree only about what's fruitful and interesting. But in most departments, as in philosophy, (1) the advancement of knowledge is the agreed aim; but (2) there are prolonged disputes over what's true. Wherever both conditions are met, whether it's a matter of the extinction of dinosaurs or of superstrings or of legal realism, my story may be told.

One big academic decision is the decision whom to appoint to the faculty. In the lucky university we are imagining, this decision will be made by those who are already on the faculty in the discipline in question. When there is a vacancy in the department of philosophy, for instance, the members of that department will decide by vote who shall be offered the appointment. In making this decision, they will all be guided (or they will nearly all be predominantly guided) by the aim of advancing knowledge. They will make the offer to the candidate whose appointment would best serve that aim.

(Let me assume hard times: a buyers' market so bad that the disappointed candidates are unlikely to have an academic career elsewhere. Otherwise I might have to assume that the members of the appointing department aim not at the advancement of knowledge per se, but rather at the advancement of knowledge only insofar as it goes on at their own university.)

Note well that in discussing academic appointments, I am not discussing academic freedom. Nobody's academic freedom is violated if the job he wanted goes to someone else, provided he had no prior claim and provided the decision is made on proper grounds.

II

There are many disputed questions in philosophy – as in most disciplines – and each member of the appointing department will hold some opinions about which philosophical doctrines are true and which are false. The candidates for appointment likewise will hold, and will be known to hold, various opinions. Each member of the department can judge, by his own lights, to what extent any given candidate holds true doctrines, and to what extent he is in error.

Holding true doctrines, and not being in error, would seem *prima facie* to be an important qualification for a job of contributing to the advancement of knowledge by teaching and research. *Knowledge* means, in part, being right. It is redundant to talk of knowing the truth, it is a contradiction in terms to talk of knowing what isn't so. (Such talk cries out for scare-quotes: he "knows" it, that is he *thinks* he knows it.) What is not true cannot be known. Advancement of error cannot be advancement of knowledge.

Unless a teacher conceals his opinions altogether, or presents them in an especially unconvincing fashion (both faults in their own right), his students will to some extent come to share his opinions. But to the extent that the teacher imparts false doctrines, what the students gain cannot be knowledge. To the extent that a researcher is guided by false doctrines, he is liable to arrive at new and different false doctrines, since he will choose them partly to cohere with the doctrines he held before. To that extent, the fruits of his research cannot be new knowledge. So error makes one worse at doing the job of advancing knowledge. Being right is a big advantage.

So when the appointing department assesses the qualifications of the candidates, to choose the one who can contribute best to the advancement of knowledge, it would seem that they ought to give a great deal of weight to the doctrines the candidates hold true and hold false. They ought, *ceteris paribus*, to prefer the candidates who hold true rather than false doctrines. Of course this will be a difficult thing to do collectively, if the members of the department disagree with one another. But, as always, each should do the best he can by his own lights, voting in the way that best serves the advancement of knowledge according to his own opinions.

So, by and large and *ceteris paribus*, we would expect the materialists in the philosophy department to vote for the materialist candidate, the dualists to vote for the dualist, and so forth. Likewise elsewhere: we would expect the transformational grammarians to vote for the transformationalist, the Marxist historians to vote for the Marxist, the biologists who think that all evolution is adaptive to vote for the adaptationist. . . . I say this not out of cynicism. Rather, this seems to be how they *ought* to vote, and unabashedly, if they are sincere in their opinions and serious about doing the best they can, each by his own lights, to serve the advancement of knowledge. We can well understand how countervailing considerations might sometimes be judged to outweigh the advantage of being right, but it would be very strange if the advantage of being right were left out of the balance altogether.

Yet what do we see? I put it to you that an appointing department will typically behave as if the truth or falsehood of the candidate's doctrines are weightless, not a legitimate consideration at all. No speaker will ever argue that a candidate should rank high because he has the advantage of being right on many important questions, or low because he is sunk in all manner of error. No speaker will argue thus, not even if he thinks the great majority of his colleagues will agree with him about what is true and false on the matter in question. Most likely, there will be no mention of whether the candidate's doctrines are true or false. If there is mention, the speaker will make clear by hook or crook that what he says is a mere comment, not an argument for or against the candidate. (The signal might be a joking tone: don't say "false," say "goofy." Or it might be a reminder that one's opinion is only one's own, or it might be the placing of the comment within a speech to the opposite effect: "I hate his views myself, but still. . . .") There will be arguments galore that a candidate has academic virtues that conduce to getting things right or vices that conduce to error: "his work is undisciplined," "what he said was shallow and inane," but it will never be said that the virtues or vices have actually led to truth or error. (I wonder why traits conducive to truth and error should be relevant considerations if truth and error themselves are not?) Maybe someone will be accused of being influenced by the fact that he agrees or disagrees with the candidate's views, and all present will presuppose that this ought not to happen. It will seem for all the world, in short, as if the department were convinced that being right or wrong is an illegitimate consideration; but a consideration that tempts them and that they must guard against. It would be less shocking, I think, to hear a case made that some candidate should be preferred on grounds of race or sex, than to hear a case made that the department should appoint the candidate who holds the true philosophy.

(My evidence? Participation in the deliberations of two philosophy departments, in each case over a period long enough to permit a good deal of turnover of colleagues. But also, hundreds of letters written on behalf of candidates by referees hoping to be persuasive, and presumably guided by their expectations about which considerations a department will deem relevant and proper. To be sure, my experience does not come out of the lucky situation in which all concerned are wholeheartedly devoted to the advancement of knowledge. But it comes from something close enough that I think I may be permitted the extrapolation. Accordingly, I shall no longer bother to distinguish actual universities from the hypothetical lucky one.)

Suppose the question whether being right is an advantage came up in a different connection. Suppose we were considering the history of the advancement of knowledge about a certain subject. Then we would find it perfectly in order to explain the success of some researcher by noting that he had been on the right track, that he was right about a lot of things to begin with and therefore found it easy to get more and more things right afterward. And we would also find it easy to explain his head start, in turn, by the fact that he was the student of a teacher who also was right about a lot of things. In this connection, at least, we would have no trouble believing in the advantage of being right.

Or suppose a squad of detectives have investigated a murder, working independently, and different ones began by suspecting different suspects. If, after the fact, we know that Plum dunnit, then once we know that it was Poirot who suspected Plum from the start, we understand very well why Poirot's investigation progressed by leaps and bounds, while his rivals bogged down and got nowhere. Or if some bystander knows from the start who dunnit (as Plum does, for one) then once he finds out that it is Poirot who has the advantage of being right, he will expect Poirot to forge ahead. In fact, anyone who learns that Poirot alone is right about some aspect of the case (even if he does not know just what Poirot is right about) should expect Poirot to gain an advantage thereby in contributing to the advancement of knowledge.

If, instead of a criminal investigation, it were the history of some branch of science or of philosophy, the same should be true. (Unless it is history done from the standpoint of utter skepticism about the subject, in which case it could not claim to be history of the advancement of knowledge.) We know very well, outside the department meeting at any rate, that being right is one important factor that makes for success in advancing knowledge.

III

There are other factors, of course. We can list the costs of blindly going for the candidate who has the advantage of being right, and the possible benefits of preferring the candidate who is in error but has compensating virtues of ingenuity, rigor, originality, open-mindedness, clarity, curiosity, thoroughness, or just difference from the present members of the department. Up to a point, we can make the list *neutral:* equally acceptable to those on both sides of any of the disputed philosophical questions. First comes –

> *Risk of Error.* We might try for the candidate who has the advantage of being right, but we might be wrong ourselves and therefore choose the candidate who has the disadvantage of being wrong.

Yes, we run a risk. But as Mill writes, "If we were never to act on our opinions, because those opinions may be wrong, we should leave all our interests uncared for, and all our duties unperformed. . . . There is no such thing as absolute certainty, but there is assurance sufficient for the purposes of human life. We may, and must, assume our opinion to be true for the guidance of our own conduct."[1]

But is it so, perhaps, that our philosophical opinions are not real opinions? Do we pay them lip service, but always give them credence so close to fifty-fifty that they can play no role in guiding decision? If that were so, and were expected to remain so indefinitely, then it is hard to see how philosophers could be aiming at the advancement of knowledge. For what isn't even believed cannot be known.

But I do think we might be guided by our philosophical opinions, even to the point of betting our lives. Consider our opinions about teletransportation, an imaginary process that works as follows: the

1 John Stuart Mill, *On Liberty* (Indianapolis: Bobbs-Merrill, 1959), pp. 23–24. These words are in the mouth of a hypothetical critic, but Mill does not dispute them.

scanner here will take apart one's brain and body, while recording the exact state of all one's cells. It will then transmit this information by radio. Traveling at the speed of light, the message will reach the replicator. This will then build, out of new matter, a brain and body exactly like the one that was scanned.[2] Some philosophical positions on personal identity imply that one survives teletransportation (unless it malfunctions). Others imply that teletransportation is certain death. Now imagine that a philosopher is caught on the seventeenth story of a burning building. He has some hope, but no certainty, of the ordinary sort of rescue. Then he is offered escape by teletransportation, provided he accepts the invitation right away.[3] At that point, I think his philosophical opinion may very well guide his decision. If he thinks what I do, he will accept teletransportation even if he reckons his chance of ordinary rescue to be quite high. If he thinks what many of my colleagues do, he will decline the offer even if he reckons his chance of ordinary rescue to be quite low. Either way, he stakes his very life on the truth of his philosophy. And yet if this philosopher does survive, only to find himself in a department meeting the next day, he will probably decline to stake the fortunes of the advancement of knowledge on the very same opinion.

However it may be with philosophy, consider the social scientists. A professor of economics, put in charge of the university budget in desperate times, may dare to stake the university's very survival – and *a fortiori* its contribution to the advancement of knowledge – on the truth of his disputed opinions about the causes of inflation. A professor of government who has been appointed to advise on national security may dare to stake the lives or liberty of millions on the truth of his disputed opinions about foreign affairs. If these same professors

2 Derek Parfit, *Reasons and Persons* (Oxford: Oxford University Press, 1984), p. 199. I have amended his description so as not to say that the scanned body is destroyed; for just as it may be held that the person survives teletransportation, so too it may be held that the brain and body survive. The same process, except with the scanning done remotely from the receiving end, is better known as "beaming up."
3 Do not grumble about a farfetched example. The decision problem requires only that the philosopher *thinks* he is offered escape by teletransportation. It is farfetched that teletransportation should be available. It is not farfetched that a philosopher should be bamboozled.

are not too busy to vote in their own departments, and if they must decide which candidates have the advantage of being right and which appointments best serve the advancement of knowledge, shall they then find their opinions too uncertain to play any role in guiding decisions?

When we bear in mind the risk of error, and so are less than certain of our own opinions, we might have reason to promote –

> *Division of Labor.* The researcher who is not running with the crowd may do more to advance knowledge, if he does turn out to be right, just because he is not duplicating others' efforts. Even if we think it probable that he will fail because he lacks the advantage of being right, we can expect a more important success from him in case he does succeed. It may be worth backing the long shot in hopes of winning big.[4]

Consider again that squad of detectives, and suppose you've just taken charge of the investigation. There are several suspects, and at the present stage of the investigation, there's good reason to suspect some more than others. What to do: assign your entire squad to concentrate on the leading suspect? That means giving each detective the maximum chance to benefit from the advantage of being right. But also it probably means diminishing marginal returns: some bits of investigating are apt to get done several times over. Divide your squad equally between the suspects, then, so as to minimize redundant effort? That makes sure that most of their work will go to waste. Compromise, say with five detectives assigned to the leading suspect, two to the runner-up, and one to all the rest? No solution is right a priori. It depends: on whether you're shorthanded, on how far the leading suspect leads the rest, on how good your detectives are at cooperating. . . . There may well be considerations that weigh heavily against the advantage of being right – but not necessarily.

Likewise, *mutatis mutandis*, if you are an only-moderately-convinced materialist choosing between two finalist job candidates. One would be the department's seventh materialist: probably right,

4 See Philip Kitcher, "The Division of Cognitive Labor," *Journal of Philosophy* 87 (1990), 5–22.

you think, but also redundant. The other would be only its second dualist: probably wrong, you think, but possibly right and not redundant. All things considered, the dualist may well be the better bet. But not necessarily – again, it depends.

Continuing our neutral list, we come to –

Change. He who is wrong today may be right tomorrow. If he is open to argument and not too proud to change his mind, his present errors may not persist. And he who is right today may afterward go wrong.

That may happen, sure enough. There are philosophers whose position is in a state of permanent revolution. But it's rare. We would expect to find a strong correlation between positions held now and positions held twenty years later, therefore between having or lacking the advantage of being right now and having or lacking it then.

Different Questions. Someone who has been wrong about the questions he has so far addressed may yet, if he has the virtues conducive to being right, have the advantage of being right about different questions that he will take up later.

There are two cases. One is that he may take up entirely unrelated questions and arrive at true views about them. The other is that he may be right about a host of subsidiary questions in the vicinity of the big question he is wrong about. An antirealist may be right about the flaw in the argument that was meant as the grand bombshell against realism; a champion of epiphenomenal qualia may be right about why one materialist theory of mind works better than another.[5] In general, a philosopher may be importantly right about what the menu of positions looks like, he may know all the advantages and drawbacks and moves and countermoves very well, even though he makes the wrong choice from that menu. Likewise an honest physicist might, on balance, favor the wrong explanation of superconductivity; and yet he might be the very one who best points out which

5 G. H. Merrill, "The Model-Theoretic Argument against Realism," *Philosophy of Science*, 47 (1980), 69–81; and Frank Jackson, "A Note on Physicalism and Heat," *Australasian Journal of Philosophy* 58 (1980), 26–34.

problems his preferred hypothesis does not solve. And whenever the evidence is misleading, as sometimes it is, whoever is right about the balance of the evidence will be wrong about the truth of the matter, and vice versa.

> *Dead Dogma.* The advocate of error will challenge those on the side of truth. He will keep them on their toes, compelling them to think of questions hitherto ignored, and causing them to improve their positions even more in order to answer his arguments.

This may happen or it may not. It depends. Sometimes there is bedrock disagreement, and both sides go their separate ways. Sometimes our only answer to an argument – a fair answer, if unsatisfying – is that since it leads to a false conclusion, it must have some flaw we can't find.

> *The Specimen.* The advocate of error may play a role somewhat like the native informant in the linguistics department, or the snake in formaldehyde in the biology department. Error can be better understood, and better rejected, when it is seen close up. Know your enemy.

Not a respectful attitude toward a prospective colleague! – Still, there's truth to it.

IV

I am not satisfied. Yes, these considerations are cogent. Yes, they carry weight. But they do not, not even all together, carry *enough* weight to do the job. They might sometimes, or even often, outweigh the advantage of being right. But it is not credible that they always and overwhelmingly outweigh the advantage of being right; and that is what they would have to do before they could explain why we treat the advantage of being right as though it were weightless. It remains a mystery why, if someone aims to support the candidate who can contribute most to advancing knowledge, he should not even weigh the holding of true doctrine as one important qualification among others, but rather should dismiss it as an irrelevant or improper consideration.

Indeed, if it's specimens of diverse errors that someone wants, or challengers to dead dogma, or insurance against the risk of his own error, then he should not dismiss being right as irrelevant. Rather he should treat it as, to some extent, a *dis*advantage! This attitude to appointments is not altogether unknown, and not quite as disreputable as trying to pack a department with right-thinking colleagues would be. We hear of "zoo departments" that try to procure one specimen of each main school of thought. (Too bad for the candidate who's so original as to defy classification! And you might think it's a scruffy specimen who'd consent to live in a zoo.) Still, I think the more usual attitude is that the truth of a candidate's position is not a proper consideration one way or the other. Is that because we think the advantage of being right and the advantage of being wrong always cancel exactly? – No; they can't always cancel, because the listed advantages of being wrong will vary greatly depending on the initial composition of the department.

V

Why ignore the advantage of being right? The considerations just listed do not go far enough. But I think there is a better explanation. We ignore the advantage of being right because we comply with a tacit treaty to do so. It is reasonable for all of us to think that this treaty, and therefore our present compliance that sustains it, serves the advancement of knowledge. However we should not all think this for the same neutral reasons.[6]

6 Here I parallel the suggestion I offered in "Mill and Milquetoast," *Australasian Journal of Philosophy* 67 (1989), 152–71 (reprinted in this volume as Chapter 14), concerning a utilitarian defense of toleration. Put society in place of the university; utility in place of advancement of knowledge; toleration of dangerous opinions in place of ignoring the advantage of being right. A Millian neutral list of the benefits of toleration does carry weight. But too little weight, sometimes, for those who most fear the grave disutility of dangerous opinions. If a utilitarian inquisitor thinks that exposure to heresy conduces to eternal damnation, he will find a Millian defense of toleration lightweight to the point of frivolity. But even he might think

First, take a simple two-sided case: the materialists versus the dualists. (Assume, what may be none too realistic, that all concerned think the errors of their opponents matter more than the errors of their misguided allies.) In my own opinion as a materialist, the best thing for the advancement of knowledge would be the universal acceptance of the true philosophy: materialism. Or near-universal, anyway; I can see some good in preserving a small dualist minority as insurance against the risk that we're wrong, or as challengers, or as specimens. Worst would be the universal, or near-universal, acceptance of dualist error. Second best would be a mixture, as at present. A treaty requiring us all to ignore the advantage of being right when we make appointments will raise the probability of that second-best outcome and lower the probability both of the best and of the worst. If the dualists are willing, we can have the treaty if we like. We cannot have what we might like better, which is a rule that only dualists shall ignore the advantage of being right (that is, of being what dualists take to be right). If the treaty is on offer, we can take it or leave it.

It may well seem to us materialists, on balance, that taking it is what serves materialism best, and therefore serves knowledge best. For if we decline the treaty, who knows what may happen in the long run? We cannot predict the fortunes of voting. Majorities in our department, and in the profession of philosophy at large, may shift in unpredictable ways. Even if we are on top here and now, some of us may move away, or change their minds, or decide that the advantage of being right is somehow outweighed in some particular case. And besides, we cannot predict the swing votes of those colleagues who suspend judgment between materialism and dualism.

Likewise, *mutatis mutandis*, according to the dualists' opinions. They too may fear the shifting fortunes of voting. So they may think it better for dualism, hence better for knowledge, to join us in making

that a treaty of toleration serves utility on balance, if he sees it as preventing not only the eradication of heresy but also the possible triumph of heresy. Rather than chance the doubtful fortunes of war, he might think it better, for the cause of salvation and hence for the cause of utility, to give away both the hope of victory and the risk of defeat.

and sustaining the treaty. What they count as the main benefit of a treaty to ignore the advantage of being right is what we count as its main cost: it tends to prevent the triumph of materialism. And what they count as the main cost is what we count as the main benefit. But however much we disagree about which is the cost and which is the benefit, we may yet agree that the benefit exceeds the cost. It is not inevitable that they and we should both think this. (They will not think it if they think the triumph of dualism is just around the corner.) But if both sides do think it, as they reasonably might, that should come as no surprise. And if both sides are found complying with a tacit treaty, that is evidence that (in some inexplicit way) both sides do consider the treaty worthwhile. I suggest that this is exactly what we do find.

In the complex real world, we have not just one disputed question but many, dividing philosophers in crisscrossing ways. Should we therefore expect a big network of crisscrossing little treaties, each one binding the parties to ignore the advantage of being right on a certain specific question? That would be too complicated to be workable. It would be too hard to keep track of which positions are under the protection of which treaty and which are unprotected. Mistakes would be made; and since the treaties are sustained by the expectation of reciprocation, mistakes would tend to unravel the whole network. It would work better to have one big, many-sided treaty to ignore the advantage of being right across the board. True, that would protect schools of thought so weak that others have no need to make a treaty with them.[7] If that is the price we must pay for a workable,

7 Maybe the treaty is limited to "respectable" schools of thought, as opposed to ratbag notions. Is this because a school of thought gains respectability when it gains numbers enough to be a threat, so that bringing it into the treaty is worthwhile protection? I think not. If I am not mistaken, hard-line paraconsistency – the thesis that there are true contradictions – is just now gaining respectability. But not because it has the numbers; the overwhelming majority of philosophers still think it certainly and necessarily false. To gain respectability, all it takes seems to be a handful of coherent and otherwise respectable defenders. Or not quite that, even – rather, defenders who satisfy all standards of coherence save those that are part of the very question at issue (as consistency is at issue when paraconsistency is defended). Graham Priest, author of *In Contradiction* (Dordrecht: Nijhoff, 1987),

199

stable arrangement that prolongs stalemate, and protects true doctrine from the triumph of its opponents, we may find the price well worth paying. Alas, it stops us from doing all we can to keep error out of the university. But in return it helps stop error from keeping out truth.

I stipulated that at the lucky university, advancement of knowledge was the predominant aim. But if the treaty is sustained by a sense of fair play or by respect for customary propriety, are those not quite different aims? Yes, and maybe those different aims are there, but they are extra. The treaty does not require them. It can be sustained solely by its foreseen benefits for the advancement of knowledge. For we cannot gain its benefits once and for all, and then double-cross our partners. As we know all too well, the work of appointments is never done. There will always be a next time.

If we're serious about aiming for the advancement of knowledge, and if we sincerely believe that the advantage of being right matters to the advancement of knowledge, then why ignore it? Because if we, in the service of truth, decided to stop ignoring it, we know that others, in the service of error, also would stop ignoring it. We have exchanged our forbearance for theirs. If you think that a bad bargain, think well who might come out on top if we gave it up. Are you so sure that knowledge would be the winner?

probably could have made hard-line paraconsistency respectable even if he had been a minority of one.

16

Devil's bargains and the real world

The paradox of deterrence, in a nutshell, is as follows. Your best way to dissuade someone from doing harm may be to threaten retaliation if he does. And idle threats may not suffice. To succeed in deterring, you may have to form a genuine, effective conditional intention. You may have to do something that would indeed leave you disposed to retaliate if, despite your efforts, he does that thing which you sought to deter. It seems that forming the intention to retaliate would be the right thing to do if, all things considered, that was the best way to prevent the harm.

Yet it may also be, foreseeably, that should the occasion arise, it would serve no good purpose to retaliate. It would just inflict further, useless harm. Then it seems that retaliating would be the wrong thing to do. Thus it seems, incredibly, that it may be right to form the conditional intention, wrong to fulfill it. That is the paradox.

What to say? We might conclude, as Kenny and others have, that after all it is wrong to form the intention.[1] We might conclude, as Gauthier does, that after all it is right to fulfill the intention.[2] Either

First published in Douglas MacLean, ed., *The Security Gamble: Deterrence in the Nuclear Age* (Totowa, New Jersey: Rowman and Allanheld, 1984). Reprinted with kind permission from Rowman and Littlefield.

1 Anthony Kenny, "Counterforce and Countervalue," in *Nuclear Weapons and Christian Conscience*, edited by Walter Stein (London: The Merlin Press, 1965).
2 David Gauthier, "Deterrence, Maximization, and Rationality," in Douglas Mac-Lean, ed., *The Security Gamble.* My quotations come from the preliminary version of the paper which Gauthier gave at the Maryland conference on "Nuclear

conclusion seems to fly in the face of powerful consequentialist arguments – and the stakes may be as high as you please. Or we might conclude, as Kavka has and as I do, that the truth is indeed remarkable: in such a case it is in truth right to form an intention that it would be wrong to fulfill.[3]

Battle is not squarely joined between Kenny, Gauthier, and Kavka. There are two different paradoxes, depending on what we mean when we speak of right and wrong. We might be speaking of instrumental rationality: of right and wrong ways to serve one's ends, whatever the moral quality of those ends may be. Then the paradox is that, seemingly, it may serve one's ends to form an intention that it would not serve one's ends to fulfill.

Or we might be speaking of morality: of good and evil ways to act or to be, whatever one's actual ends may be. Then the paradox is that, seemingly, it may be a good act to form an intention that it would be an evil act to fulfill; or that a good man might form an intention that it would take a wicked man to fulfill. Gauthier addresses the paradox about rationality; Kenny and Kavka mostly address the paradox about morality.

But it doesn't matter. Suppose that your ends are morally good ones, so that it would be morally right to pursue them in an instrumentally rational way. Suppose also that they are urgent enough that it would be morally wrong to pursue them in an instrumentally irrational way. This may be so – let the stakes be high. Then it doesn't matter whether we speak of right or wrong in an instrumental or in a moral sense. The two senses coincide, the two paradoxes coalesce.

Although I side with Kavka against Gauthier, I admire Gauthier's paper. Most of it is just right. In particular, I applaud the way that he distinguishes paradoxical cases of deterrence from all the other cases there might be. It is not to be thought that just any case of deterrence presents our twofold paradox.

Deterrence: Moral and Political Issues," at which the papers in *The Security Gamble* were first presented. Not all of these quotations appear in his final version.

3 Gregory S. Kavka, "Some Paradoxes of Deterrence," *Journal of Philosophy* 75 (1978): 285–302; see also Kavka, "Nuclear Deterrence: Some Moral Perplexities," in Douglas MacLean, ed., *The Security Gamble*.

It might be wrong for independent reasons to form the deterrent intention. For it might be too risky; it might be unlikely to succeed; it might carry other costs, e.g., in damaging the relationship between the parties. Or there might be better means of dissuasion available. It might be possible to deter without forming a conditional intention to retaliate: by pretending to have the intention, or by making retaliation automatic, or by creating fear not of intended retaliation but of uncontrolled rage, or simply by leaving it uncertain what might happen. It might be better not to use deterrence at all. If it is wrong to form the deterrent intention, for any of these reasons or any other, then our paradox does not arise.

Alternatively it might be right for independent reasons to fulfill the deterrent intention. Retaliation might not be retaliation pure and simple. It might serve some genuine end. Or it might at least seem to stand some chance of doing so. Or it might be foreseeable that retaliation would at least seem useful at the time. (Any of these things might be so by prearrangement, as when one stakes one's reputation in order to enhance the credibility of one's threat.) If it is right to fulfill the deterrent intention, for any of these reasons or any other, then again our paradox does not arise.

So much for agreement. I disagree with only one small part of Gauthier's paper. But it is the vital part, as he has said. (And vital for his views about many things besides deterrence.) What I reject is his "moving from the rationality of intention to the rationality of action, rather than vice versa." I move *neither* way. I insist on considering the two questions of rationality, or of morality, separately – each on its own merits.

In Section 5 of Gauthier's paper, several objectors come on stage one after another. The preliminary objector recommends the method of pretending to intend. He is misguided. By definition, the paradoxical case is one in which that method won't succeed. You don't make a paradox go away by talking about an unparadoxical case instead.

The first and third objectors both say that it is rational to form the deterrent intention only if it would maximize utility to retaliate, should the occasion arise. (The third objector says more besides, but he has already said too much to be true.) They are wrong: we have seen exactly how it might happen that it is rational to form the intention although it would not maximize utility to retaliate.

I am the second objector, the one who says that "it may be rational to adopt an intention even though it would be, and one knows that it would be, irrational to act on it"; I claim that it may be "rational to commit oneself to irrational behavior" (and also that it may be good to commit oneself to evil behavior). Gauthier claims that my position is no different from his own. Not so; I deny what he firmly asserts, that there may be actions which "in themselves and apart from the context of deterrence would be irrational, but which in that context result from rational intentions and so are rational." (Likewise I deny that there are actions which in themselves and apart from the context of deterrence would be evil, but which result from intentions it was good to adopt and so are good.)

When he is done saying that my view is the same as his own, Gauthier goes on to call it inconsistent. "If our objector accepts deterrent policies, then he cannot consistently reject the actions they require." Why not? I accept the policies as right, I reject the actions they (conditionally) require as wrong. My opposed judgments are consistent because I make them about different things. To form an intention today is one thing. To retaliate tomorrow is something else. If we have a genuine case of paradoxical deterrence, the first is right and the second is wrong.

Gauthier fears we are talking at cross-purposes, and so explains his meaning: "To assess an action as irrational is, in my view, to claim that it should not be . . . performed." Right; I *do* speak his language. What I claim about cases of paradoxical deterrence is that the action of forming the intention to retaliate should be performed, and that the action of retaliating should not be. The sad thing is that the action that should be performed might cause the one that shouldn't, if deterrence fails.

And that was all that Gauthier said against the second objector.[4] I rest my case.

---

4 There is something else to be said on Gauthier's side, however, as follows. What is it to "implant an intention" in yourself? It's not enough just to mutter "I shall . . ."

It seems too quick. Perhaps we have asked the wrong question, and bypassed the heart of the paradox. (Henceforth, I shall have in mind mostly the paradox about morality.) We were asked to judge *actions*. And we were free to pass two opposed judgments because we found two different actions to judge. But there is only one *person* to perform the two actions. What shall we say if asked to judge not the two actions but the one person?

What if the nuclear deterrence practiced by the United States on behalf of all of us is paradoxical deterrence? Suppose it is. Then what are we to think of the men in the missile fields, in the cockpits, in the submarines? What are we to think of the Commander-in-Chief? These men, we suppose, have formed a conditional intention to do their part in retaliating if the country comes under attack. In forming that intention, they did the right thing: *ex hypothesi*, they did just what they had to do to protect their country in the best way possible. They are great patriots, and benefactors of us all. And now that they have formed the intention, they are ready to commit massacres whose like has never been seen. They are ready to inflict terrible devastation when they have no country left to defend, when what they do will accomplish nothing at all except vengeance. *Ex hypothesi*, that is what they even now (conditionally) intend to do. They are evil beyond imagining, fiends in human shape.

They are vengeful. Not because they formed the intention to

in the right tone of voice! An intention seems to be some sort of compound of belief and desire concerning your own future actions. To implant an intention, you would have to implant something that would motivate you to fulfill it. But then this something would be a desire that would make it instrumentally rational to fulfill the intention. So if it were instrumentally rational to implant the intention, and if you *did* implant it, then it would be instrumentally rational to fulfill it. (Of course, this argument concerns only the paradox about rationality, not the paradox about morality.) I reply thus. If you implant the intention by implanting a desire that fails to cohere rationally with the rest of your desires, then fulfilling the intention is instrumentally rational only in a minimal sense: it does fulfill a desire you have, but it cannot be said to serve your system of desires taken as a whole. For related discussion of the difficulty of implanting an intention that would not cohere with your other desires, see Gregory S. Kavka, "The Toxin Puzzle," *Analysis* 43 (1983): 33–36.

retaliate; they had a better reason to form the intention, viz., that thereby they protected the country. But after they form it, then they have it; and to have such an intention as they now have – an intention to retaliate uselessly and dreadfully – is to be vengeful.

I myself would not despise them just for being vengeful, though I think many moralists would. For I think their vengefulness is part of a package deal. It is inseparable from their love of their country and their solidarity with their countrymen. Conceptually inseparable, I am inclined to think – could a man really be said to love his country if he were not at all disposed to make its enemies his own? Could he really be said to make them his enemies if he were not at all disposed to harm them? I doubt it. Be that as it may, surely the vengefulness and the solidarity are at least psychologically inseparable for people anything like ourselves. It seems artificial to try to take the package apart, despise part of it, and treasure the rest. And it seems repellent to despise the whole package. I cannot find it in my heart to reproach a fierce Afghan patriot who seeks to avenge his countrymen – I would sooner reproach the moralist who does reproach the Afghan – and I see no call to apply different standards to my own countrymen. True, the vengeful fall short of being utilitarian saints. They are not motivated entirely by impersonal benevolence. But, as philosophers increasingly perceive, the utilitarian saint himself is a repellent figure.[5] If it is the business of moral philosophy to sing his praises, moral philosophy only makes itself repellent. We should be less alienated from the things that real people really treasure. And these include the loyalties and affections from which vengefulness is inseparable.

(The Christians have a special objection to vengefulness. They say that vengeance is the Lord's; a vengeful man pridefully usurps the prerogative of his Superior. We atheists need not concern ourselves with that.)

But whatever may be said in (faint) praise of vengefulness falls far short of exonerating our retaliators, if indeed they would deliver massive nuclear retaliation to accomplish nothing but vengeance. Whatever might be said in favor of some vengefulness, we cannot

---

5 See Susan Wolf, "Moral Saints," *Journal of Philosophy* 79 (1982): 419–39.

condone theirs. For it is almost entirely off target. Only a small share of our vengeance would fall only on the enemy who had chosen to attack us, and on his loyal followers (if he has any). For the most part, it would fall on his powerless and disaffected slaves. By and large, these slaves obey him out of fear – like ourselves, they are subject to *his* deterrence – and do not accept him as acting on their behalf. However much can be said in favor of vengeance against our enemy, the slaves are not our enemy. They are our enemy's victims. And this goes for the slaves in Moscow as it does for the slaves in Warsaw and Prague.

(It would be otherwise if the Soviet Union were a popular democracy, as we are, full of citizens who by and large give allegiance to the regime and accept some responsibility – whether or not they are *causally* responsible – for its actions. Vengeance against such a population, whatever else could be said against it, would at least be on target. (Mostly. But of course there are still the infants.) That suggests a distressing conclusion. It *is* otherwise in the reverse direction. Must we conclude that those Soviet officers who stand ready to retaliate against us are in a better moral position, at least in this one way, than their American counterparts? As an American, I hope that isn't so. And I think it isn't, for reasons that will emerge before I finish.)

We are back to our question: what shall we think of one man who has done right and now stands ready to do wrong, who both does his best to protect his country and is prepared to massacre countless slaves, who is benefactor and fiend in one?

Well – I've just told you what to think. He is a man who does right and would do wrong. He is a strange mixture of good and evil. *That* is what to think of him. Isn't that enough? Why do we need a simple, unified, summary judgment?

If there were a last judgment, it would then be necessary to send the whole morally mixed man to Heaven or to Hell. *Then* there would be real need for one unified verdict. I would be very well content to leave the problem of the unified verdict to those who believe in a last judgment. And they would do well to leave it to the Judge.

(I am reminded of a problem put to me years ago by Philippa Foot: The Case of the Conscientious Nazi (or: Does Erring Conscience Excuse?).[6] The Nazi follows his conscience rigorously, resisting all temptation to do otherwise, and what his conscience tells him is to kill the Jews. What a steadfast sense of duty! What a vile notion of where his duty lies! Then what are we to think of him overall? I decline to think *anything* of him overall. I am prepared to recognize and admire and praise his genuine virtues, even when I meet them in the worst of company. (To some extent – his are not my favorite virtues.) I am no less prepared to detest his wicked and dangerous moral errors. But *is he a good man*? I leave this question to the Last Judge. Apart from Him, who needs it?)

Thus the paradox of deterrence in which persons are judged goes the way of the paradox in which actions are judged. Though we have only one person, that person has many moral aspects. We can still have the opposing judgments that seem called for, because we can still make them about different things.

It is even simpler if forming the intention to retaliate is what Kavka has called "self-corruption." That is: if we start with men who are good through and through, and they see that wickedly vengeful men are needed if their country is to be protected in the best way possible, and they volunteer for the tragic sacrifice of virtue, and they make themselves genuinely evil. Then the difference is one of time: first they are good, afterward evil. The question how they are, not at any time in particular, is another piece of nonsense for the Last Judge. But self-corruption is artificial. The more likely thing – if *any* tale of paradoxical deterrence can be called likely – is a deliberate slacking off in self-improvement, with good and evil mingled all along. Then we need simultaneous aspects, rather than successive temporal parts, as the different things to be judged differently. And we need separable aspects, not parts of a close-knit package deal. But if the evil in

6 A related question, whether to say that a murderer who boldly faces danger in order to commit his vicious crime has acted courageously, comes in for discussion in Philippa Foot, "Virtues and Vices," in her *Virtues and Vices and Other Essays in Moral Philosophy* (Berkeley and Los Angeles: University of California Press, 1978).

question is not just vengefulness, but wantonly off-target vengeful-ness, then I think we have separability enough.

I find it interesting to compare our paradox of deterrence with an-other paradoxical case: the Devil's bargain. It is a puzzle for Chris-tians. They think that salvation of souls is of supreme importance, infinitely more valuable than life or pleasure or earthly love or knowl-edge or any others among the goods we usually cherish. Right; let's adapt a stock example to their new currency. The Devil offers you a bargain; you may give him your soul, and in return he will see to it that seven others are saved. Those seven would not otherwise have stood a very good chance. Here you have an opportunity to serve the very best purpose of all. Will you take it? What should we think of you if you do?

What a noble deed! You will have made the supreme sacrifice that others may live. You will have made the *really* supreme sacrifice – not just given up your earthly life. And you will have bought the seven a gift ever so much more precious than mere life itself. You will be a hero beyond compare.

You will be a damned soul. You will be a genuine damned soul, just like the others around you in the fire. Don't think you will suffer torture with a pure heart – the Devil will not be cheated. You will be despicable in the ways that any other damned soul is. You will be a hater of God. And that, so the Christians say, is the very worst thing that it is possible to be.[7] It seems, incredibly, that if you accept the Devil's bargain you will be each of two opposite things, won-drous hero and damned soul.

What to say? We might conclude that after all you will not be such a splendid hero, perhaps because an embargo against trading with the Devil takes precedence over the service of even the highest ends, or perhaps because you were meant to look after your own

7 Not I; I only take it as a hypothesis of the case. My own opinion is rather that of Mill and McTaggart: see John Stuart Mill, *An Examination of Sir William Hamilton's Philosophy* (London: Longmans, Green, Reader, & Dyer, 1865), chap. VII; and J. M. E. McTaggart, *Some Dogmas of Religion* (London: Edward Arnold & Co., 1906), secs. 174–77.

salvation rather than salvation generally. Or we might conclude that after all you will not really be a damned soul. *Ex hypothesi* you will be something exactly like one in intrinsic character, but perhaps damnation is a historical rather than an intrinsic property and your state will not be damnation when reached in the way that you reached it. Small comfort! Or we might conclude that, strange to say, you really will be both. In succession: first heroic, then damned.

Which conclusion should a Christian draw? None of them, I think. Instead, the Christian should insist that the case is completely bogus.[8] He should draw no conclusion about what you would be if *per impossible* the Devil offered his bargain and you accepted it. It is preposterous to suppose that it is in the Devil's power to give or to deny salvation, to buy or sell souls. God offers salvation to all men, who accept or decline it of their own free will. The most the Devil can do is tempt us to damn ourselves.

I think the most important thing to say about the parallel case of paradoxical nuclear deterrence is exactly the same: the case is completely bogus. The paradox of deterrence is good fun for philosophers. But I think it has nothing to do with the nuclear deterrence that our country practices. It is good that Gauthier and Kavka have insisted that not just any case of deterrence is paradoxical, and good that they have declined to say that our nuclear deterrence is a paradoxical case. But such disclaimers do not go far enough. I am sorry to complain to the Center for Philosophy and Public Policy about their program for this conference, but I think this particular bit of philosophy contributes nothing but mischief to the discussion of public affairs. There is much that philosophers can indeed contribute to our understanding of issues about nuclear deterrence: for instance,

8 At this point I have consulted some who are more expert than I about Christian thought; I am grateful to Robert M. Adams, Mark Johnston, and Ewart Lewis. Adams notes a complication. The case of an *honest* Devil's bargain is bogus, but the case of a fraudulent one is not. Then the thing for a Christian to say resembles our first conclusion. The man who accepts the fraudulent bargain is reprehensible. He was gullible; what's worse, he lacked faith, because he was ready to suspect God of allowing the Devil to buy and sell souls.

to the topics of decision under extreme uncertainty, of incommensurable values, of complicity and innocence of civilians. But I wish we could leave the paradox of deterrence out of it. I am afraid that because paradoxical deterrence is philosophically fascinating, it will be much discussed; and because it is much discussed, it will be mistaken for reality. We don't need a bad reason to be discontented with our predicament and with our country's policies. After all, we have plenty of good reasons. And we don't need a picture of nuclear deterrence that implicitly slanders many decent patriots in the American armed forces and in the White House.

In his contribution to this volume, McGeorge Bundy has a lot to say about our vast ignorance of what would happen in a nuclear war and afterward.[9] It is a vivid awareness of this ignorance, on all sides, that is our great safeguard against nuclear adventures when the time seems as opportune as it ever will be. All that is right. And I add that the ignorance would diminish very little if the war had actually begun.

That is why our nuclear deterrence is not paradoxical. It might indeed be true, if deterrence failed, that our retaliation would serve no good purpose, would accomplish nothing but dreadful and off-target vengeance. It might also be false. What is preposterous, no less preposterous than it would be to think the Devil could grant salvation, is to imagine that anyone could *know* that there was nothing left but vengeance. It is perfectly all right if our retaliators do not intend to inflict useless and off-target vengeance. For the choice whether to deliver that vengeance is not a choice they could ever knowingly face. Whatever happened, the real choice before them would be a harder one.

Imagine the situation of the Commander-in-Chief (de jure or de facto), if deterrence had failed and there had been a large nuclear attack. How much would he know? He would know that there had been many nuclear explosions. He would probably know roughly where some of them had been. He would know something about how much was gone; less, about how much was left. It would be

9 McGeorge Bundy, "Existential Deterrence and Its Consequences," in Douglas MacLean, ed., *The Security Gamble.*

hard for him to know the yield of the explosions, their exact location with respect to vulnerable populations and weapons, which were groundbursts and which airbursts. Perhaps he would know what sort of attack the enemy *could* deliver; but he should not take it for granted that they had done their worst. He should put no faith in scenarios of "wargasm" that flourish mainly because they make for a good read. Neither should he be taken in by circular reasoning to the effect that nuclear war would have to be fought in the most mad and fiendish way possible, because those who fought it would be mad fiends, as is shown by the mad and fiendish way they would fight. Neither should he put his faith in the opposite scenarios of "surgical war." He might indeed have his a priori scenarios for nuclear war – even as you and I do – but he ought to put little trust in any of them.

Even if, *per impossible*, he knew exactly what attack had been delivered, he would still not know how much would be left when its effects had run their course. He would probably not know which way the winds were blowing, or where there had been fog. And he would not know whether to believe all the prophecies that indirect effects – economic disruption, disabling despair, anarchy, plague – would prove more lethal than the blast and fire and fallout. He might have his opinions on the question – even as you and I do – but he ought to know that such opinions are sheer speculation. In short, he would be far from knowing whether or not he had a country left to protect.

He would be far from knowing what would best protect his country, if it still exists. Maybe surrender would be best. But maybe it would be best to destroy the enemy's unfired strategic nuclear weapons – *some* would be unfired, who knows how many. Maybe an attempt at tit-for-tat retaliation would offer the best hope of stopping the war before all was lost. Maybe it would be useful to destroy the weapons and the resources that could give the enemy command over the affairs of the postwar world. A nuclear counterattack would not be *known* to be useless. It might indeed be useless; or it might serve a good purpose. It might even be the only way to save the country. The duty of the Commander-in-Chief is to protect his country, in war no less than in peace. He would have to consider whether some sort of counterattack might be the best way to disarm the enemy, to stop the war, or to give the country some chance of surviving the years ahead. It might well be so. But there could be no certainty that a counterattack would accomplish these things. And it would be risky: it might elicit a further attack that could have been avoided. And it would massacre vast numbers of the enemy's slaves, who are our fellow-victims; there would be no telling how many. And it would devastate a great part of the earth. And if our country were doomed already, the counterattack and its dreadful harm would be all in vain. The decision whether to launch a counterattack, or what sort of counterattack to launch, would be a hard one indeed. It would be a terrible decision under extreme uncertainty, with extremely high stakes and incommensurable values. I say that it might well be right to launch the counterattack: instrumentally rational and morally right, all things considered. As right, that is, as any choice could be in so desperate and tragic a predicament.[10]

Likewise for the men in the missile fields, in the cockpits, and in

10 I do not mean that it is "objectively" right to launch a counterattack: that is, that doing so would in fact produce the best consequences. Maybe so, but I don't know it. In fact, it is my main point that such things cannot be known. Rather, I mean that it might well be "subjectively" right: that it might well be the best gamble, taking account of the full range of uncertainty about what had already happened and about what actions would produce what outcomes. To understand the distinction, imagine that an epidemic is raging and you have inadvertently locked the entire supply of antitoxin in a safe and lost the combination. The subjectively right thing to do might well be to hunt up a skilled safecracker, even if finding him would take a week you can ill afford. That would be objectively wrong. The objectively right thing to do would be to dial 44-0223-65979 straightway, for that is the unknown combination that would in fact open the safe. The objective wrongness of going off to find a safecracker is no reason – or it is merely an "objective reason" – not to do it. Throughout this paper, I have been speaking always of subjective, never of objective, rightness. But take care: subjective rightness is only one department of reason and morality. What you do may be the best gamble, given your beliefs; it may in that sense be rational and right; but it may in a broader (but still subjective) sense be irrational and wrong, if the beliefs on which your actions are premised are themselves irrational given your evidence.

the submarines. They too would know what vital purposes a counterattack might serve, if all was not yet lost; and they too would know the harms and risks that it would bring. They would know even less than the Commander-in-Chief about the attack that had taken place. But they would know that their orders come from someone whose aims are much the same as theirs, who is probably somewhat better informed than they are, and whose orders afford their only hope of coordinated action. I say that it would be right for them to obey orders to fire: instrumentally rational and morally right, all things considered. As right, that is, as any choice could be in so desperate and tragic a predicament.

(Also, they have sworn obedience, at least if the Commander-in-Chief from whom they have their orders is so de jure. I do not at all mean to set aside reasons of honor as morally weightless, but I do think that they fade into insignificance when the stakes get high enough. Consequentialism is all wrong as everyday ethics, right as a limiting case. So I rest my argument on the consequential reasons why it would be right to obey.)

Suppose that our retaliators intend to launch a counterattack if and only if it would be right to do so; and that they intend to launch only the right sort of counterattack. Then what they conditionally intend to do if deterrence fails is no more than what it would be right for them to do. Then our nuclear deterrence is not paradoxical. Nor can they be reproached for intending to retaliate, if they intend to do no more than would be right. They are right so to intend, and they would be right to fulfill their intentions. I think that this is the actual case: that our retaliators rightly intend to do no more than would be right. I certainly hope that this is so.

But suppose it is not so. Suppose instead that our retaliators intend to launch a counterattack whether or not it would be right, or that they intend to launch more of a counterattack than could possibly be right. They would be wicked in so intending, even if they became wicked or remained wicked for admirable reasons, and even if there was much good mixed in with their wickedness. They would also be a danger to mankind, and we ought to remove them from their posts at once. But our nuclear deterrence *still* would not be paradoxical.

For on this supposition, I say that it was wrong for them ever to form such intentions. They would have been mistaken when they thought it beneficial to implant wicked intentions in themselves. There is no paradox if they have wrongly formed an intention that it would be wrong to fulfill.

Their intentions would be wrong to form not because they would be wrong to fulfill, but because they present a needless danger. Here I rely on a premise of fact: that no such intentions are needed to provide deterrence. The intention to launch a counterattack only if, and only to the extent that, it is right provides deterrence galore. We don't need "assured destruction." The sort of counterattack that might serve a good purpose would be a dreadful retaliation as well. If that is our only threat, maybe we threaten less-than-assured less-than-destruction, but our threat remains fearsome. Take an extreme case: suppose we attacked nothing but the enemy's unfired strategic nuclear weapons (plus a lot of empty holes, unless we had better information than seems likely) and suppose we attacked those in the very most "surgical" way. We would still destroy much more than the weapons, for the enemy has by no means cooperated in the separation of targets. And would he not fear to lose the weapons, even if he stood to lose nothing else? He would probably think he had need of them, no less after he had provoked our anger than before.

Anyway, we can threaten worse retaliation than we really intend. For he cannot know just what we do intend, and he cannot know that we would not do worse when angered than we intend beforehand. Again I join Bundy in praise of uncertainty, and in insisting that the owners of an arsenal like ours just do not have any problem in looking scary.

Thirty-five years ago, our nuclear threat was puny by present standards. Yet we thought it a convincing deterrent, and I dare say we were right. In those days, we deterred Stalin himself. Are his successors bolder desperadoes than he? To be sure, the *balance* of threats has changed since then; and advocates of a larger arsenal do claim that an uneven balance is what deters, rather than the size of our threat; but why should that be so?

No; our enemies are cowards. Their cautious adventures scare *us* —

215

because we too are cowards, well and truly deterred, and a good thing too – but they really do not act like people whom it is difficult to deter.

Kavka and Kenny have suggested that although the deterrent threat to launch a counterattack if, and to the extent that, it was right is not itself paradoxical, yet paradoxical deterrence must lurk in the background.[11] Whatever we might do on the lower rungs of the ladder of nuclear escalation, doesn't it remain true that we intend to respond to an all-out countervalue salvo with a like salvo of our own? And wouldn't that be useless off-target vengeance? And isn't it this ultimate threat that affords our only slim hope of staying on the lower rungs?

I don't think so. I agree that an all-out retaliatory salvo could be nothing but vengeance. It could not possibly be right. But I hope and believe that we intend no such thing. If we did receive an all-out salvo, we could not recognize it as such. Our counterattack might in fact be nothing but useless and off-target vengeance on behalf of the doomed, but we would nevertheless launch it in the hope that it would serve a purpose, and we might well be right to do so.

And if I am wrong, and we do intend to deliver a useless all-out salvo if worst comes to worst, then there is still no paradox. It is wrong to form or retain such an intention, unless that intention is needed for deterrence. I say that our deterrence, even if it is deterrence of escalation during nuclear war, needs no such intention. In the very worst case as in other cases, the counterattack thought to serve a good purpose would be retaliation enough, and the threat of it would afford deterrence enough.

I said that I hope and believe we do not intend to respond to even the worst nuclear attack by launching an all-out salvo, a counterattack that would be good for nothing but off-target vengeance. – But do we not have plans for just such salvos? – We do: our war plan calls them "massive attack options."[12] But do not infer our intentions from our plans. I suppose that our planmakers are told that it is not

11 Kavka, in discussion; Kenny, "Counterforce and Countervalue."
12 Desmond Ball, "U.S. Strategic Forces: How Would They Be Used?" *International Security* 7 (1983): 31–60.

for them to set national policy, and that it is better to have too many options than too few; and obligingly they churn out all sorts of plans. These include some very frightening plans that it would be wrong to carry out, no matter what had happened. It is no waste of effort if they produce plans that no one ever intends to follow. For one thing, the making of many plans contributes to our own understanding of nuclear warfare.[13] Further, the plans themselves are part of our deterrent – after all, they do not come bearing the label "will not be followed no matter what." They are no secret, except in their details. If a scholar in Canberra can write about our massive attack options in the unclassified article I cited, surely the enemy is no less well informed. And if you and I find these plans frightening, even doubting as we should that anyone intends to carry them out, surely the enemy finds them no less frightening.

I find myself in unwelcome company. I seem to be agreeing with the views of the war-fighters. I say, as they do, that nuclear retaliation might serve a useful purpose, might accomplish something better than vengeance. I say, as they do, that the right retaliation would be a counterattack meant to accomplish something useful. I say, as they do, that such retaliation is the only sort we ought to intend. I say, as they do, that if it is our policy to deliver useless vengeance, then our policy is immoral and our retaliators are wicked.

It is true that I have taken a leaf from the war-fighters' book. But it is a loose-leaf book, and I insist that I have left most of it behind. Their position is founded on confidence: confidence in certain remarkably optimistic scenarios for nuclear war. Mine is founded rather on skepticism: even-handed skepticism, directed against optimistic and pessimistic scenarios alike. They say that victory is possible.[14] (Provided, of course, that their views about strategy and procurement gain acceptance.) I would not go so far as to speak of "victory," but I do take an

---

13 And thereby makes a welcome contribution to our self-deterrence; as witness the tale of McNamara's unsettling briefing at SAC headquarters, told in Gregg Herken, "The Nuclear Gnostics," in Douglas MacLean, ed., *The Security Gamble*.

14 Colin S. Gray and Keith Payne, "Victory Is Possible," *Foreign Policy* 39 (1980): 14–27.

interest in outcomes that would be noticeably better than total destruction. I would not go so far as to say that such outcomes are "possible" (except in the philosophers' sense, in which it is also possible that pigs have wings); but I do say that we cannot have much confidence that they are not possible, wherefore it might well be right to try for them even by means of a nuclear counterattack.

It's not that they go in for optimism generally, whereas I am a general skeptic. They are optimistic about success in nuclear war, something of which we have next to no experience; they are skeptical about success in deterrence, something of which we have a great deal of experience. With me it's the other way around.

They say that deterrence is difficult, so that one main reason to intend only useful retaliation is that otherwise our threats will be incredible and the enemy will not be deterred. I say that deterrence is easy, given an arsenal like ours and an enemy like ours. Credibility is not a worry. At least, not if we limit the scope of our nuclear deterrence; and probably not even if we extend it beyond (what I would take to be) prudent limits. My reason for intending only useful retaliation has nothing to do with credibility. My reason is that if deterrence failed, it would be better not to do a lot of useless harm.

Bundy has suggested that debates about how to fight a nuclear war are not what they seem to be; really, they are debates about criteria for the procurement of weapons.[15] Often so, I'm sure; but not in my case. I have been talking about how we ought to intend to use whatever weapons we might have. What I have said is consistent with a wide range of positions on questions of procurement. Not with all conceivable positions – it is possible to favor weapons that are no good for anything except useless vengeance, it is possible to favor skimping on command and control – but with all that stand any serious chance of adoption by an American government, and with more besides. It is otherwise with the war-fighters. Their position is indeed part of a case for procurement. They have higher hopes and more confidence than I about what a counterattack could accomplish, if only the weapons were right. Therefore it is more important to them than it is to me that the weapons should be right.

15 Bundy, "Existential Deterrence."

17

Buy like a MADman, use like a NUT

When theoreticians think about nuclear deterrence, often they focus
on a nasty choice between two rival package deals. The two have
gone by various names over the years, but let me take the paired
epithets: MAD (Mutual Assured Destruction) versus NUTS (Nuclear
Use Theorists). Each package is a bundle of policies: centrally, policies
for the procurement of strategic nuclear forces and conditional intentions about how to use those forces in case of war. I think we can
break up the packages and keep only part of each. What we get may
be in some sense MAD and in some sense NUTS – for the terms are
elastic – but I hope it is the better half of both.

In a debate between MAD and NUTS, each side may say that the
other's policies involve a twofold risk: a grave moral risk of committing massacres and a grave prudential risk of inviting and undergoing
massacres. If they say so, they are right. The contest between these
two repugnant alternatives gives nuclear deterrence itself a bad name.
How does the very idea of nuclear deterrence turn into the nasty
choice between MAD and NUTS? Does it have to happen? Is there
no way around it?

First published in this form in *QQ* **6**, No. 2 (1986), 5–8. This paper is an abridgement
by Claudia Mills of David Lewis, "Finite Counterforce", in Henry Shue, ed., *Nuclear
Deterrence and Moral Restraint* (Cambridge, Cambridge University Press, 1989), ©
Cambridge University Press 1989. Reprinted with kind permission from Claudia
Mills and the Institute for Philosophy and Public Policy, and with the permission of
Cambridge University Press.

To trace the reasoning that drives us MAD, start with a simple conception of nuclear deterrence. We deter the enemy from doing X by threatening that if he does, then we will punish him by doing Y. But the enemy might notice that if he does X, we will then have no good reason to do Y. What's more, he may be able to give us a reason not to: he may threaten that if we do Y, then he will punish us by doing Z. Of course we may threaten that if he does Z then we will . . . but he might doubt that as well. In short we have a credibility problem: our deterrence is apt to fail because our threats are not believed.

How to solve it? One way is to make the threatened retaliation very, very severe. Then even if the enemy thinks we would have excellent reason not to retaliate, still he would not dare to call our bluff. If he evaluates risks as he should, multiplying the magnitude of the harm by the probability, we can make up in the first factor for what is lacking in the second. We can threaten a vast nuclear massacre, on an altogether different scale from the ordinary horrors of war. Destruction on this dreadful scale needn't be credible to deter. Although it could serve no good purpose to fulfill the threat, the risk that we might do so in blind anger suffices.

The MADman thinks it obvious that deterrence requires a solution to the credibility problem, and obvious that the only solution is to find a threat so dreadful that it needn't be credible; and he expects the enemy not to overlook the obvious. Therefore he thinks that for the enemy, as for us, an assured capacity to destroy cities will be seen as the *sine qua non* of nuclear deterrence. Further, he thinks it would take no great effort for the enemy to counteract any steps we might take to protect our cities. Therefore he thinks such steps would be, at best, costly and futile. We buy the means to reduce the enemy's strategic forces by counterforce warfare; the enemy buys enough more missiles to assure himself that enough of them will survive. We buy expensive defenses, the enemy buys enough more missiles to assure himself that enough of them will get through. We spend money, he spends money. Afterward there are many more nuclear weapons in the world, and each of them is one more place where an accident could happen. In case of war, not only does the world get fallout and smoke from the destroyed cities, but also it gets fallout (and smoke and dust) from preliminary counterforce attacks and intercepted warheads. And still our cities are subject to vast and intolerable destruction. What have we gained?

The MADman boasts that his goals for deterrence are "finite." If each side can count on having enough surviving weapons to meet the standard of assured destruction, that is all that either side has reason to want. Neither side has an incentive to expand or improve his forces, for all that would hapen is that the balance would be reestablished at increased cost, increased risk, and increased danger to the rest of the world.

Thus the MADman's policy for procurement of nuclear weapons is as moderate and benign as can be, short of renouncing nuclear deterrence altogether. But his policy for conduct of nuclear war is quite the opposite. What is the Commander-in-Chief supposed to do if deterrence fails? He is not supposed to do anything to protect the country entrusted to his care; he cannot, since it was thought futile to provide the means for limiting damage. Rather he is supposed to fulfill the threat to destroy cities – a vast massacre, serving no good purpose whatever. There is nothing else he can do. Thus MADness carries a grave moral risk. According to MADness, anything that can be seen to raise the chance of retaliation is all to the good. But it is all to the bad if deterrence fails: for what is raised is the chance of the most wicked act that it is possible for anyone in our time to perform.

NUTS: THE CREDIBLE WARNING

To trace the reasoning that drives us NUTS, we start as before. The NUT agrees with the MADman that it is essential to solve the credibility problem, but he favors a different solution. His plan is to find some sort of nuclear attack that would not only be a retaliation, but also would serve some vital purpose. Our threat would be credible because we would have, and we would be seen to have, a compelling reason to fulfill it. The retaliation we could have compelling reason to deliver is counterforce warfare. It is worthwhile to

221

destroy the enemy's forces, especially his strategic nuclear weapons. This reduces the risk to ourselves and our allies if war continues.

Thus we solve the credibility problem, and thereby we make it possible to succeed in nuclear deterrence – so says the NUT. But note a consequence of his argument: it has to be ambitious counterforce. If we want a highly credible warning that we would resort to counterforce warfare, there has to be little doubt that we expect its gains to be worth its risks.

But the drawbacks of an excellent counterforce capacity are these. First, and worst, an excellent counterforce capacity demands preemption. If our excellent counterforce capacity has been attacked, it may still be some sort of counterforce capacity, but it will no longer be excellent. The highly credible warning is, alas, not a warning of retaliation, but of preemption. Further, it gives the enemy his own incentive to preempt. His forces are under the gun: use them or lose them. Whatever use he may have in mind had better be done before it is too late.

This pressure to preempt is probably the gravest risk that the NUT embraces in his quest for credibility. But it is not the only one. Besides short-term instability in times of crisis, there is a second, long-term instability. The MADman could boast that his goals for deterrence are finite. Not so for the NUT. If we need enough capacity for counterforce warfare that we can credibly warn of our strong incentive to undertake it, then what we need is an increasing function of what the enemy has. In fact, we need superiority. For reasons the MADman has already given, a risk of arms racing is indeed a grave risk, both moral and prudential.

The third grave risk, this one primarily a moral risk, concerns the collateral damage from ambitious counterforce warfare. Given the proximity of missile fields to Moscow, for example, it makes little difference whether we target the population of Moscow per se, and so the NUT runs a grave moral risk of committing vast massacres, just as the MADman does. Not an equally grave risk: the MADman's attack is useless, whereas the NUT's is meant to destroy weapons that menace us. Further, the NUT's attack kills many fewer people. Too many people live downwind from the enemy's missiles, but not as many as live in the enemy's cities. Yet though the numbers that measure the NUT's moral risk are much better than those that measure the MADman's, even the better numbers are far from good.

The MADman proposes to run grave moral and prudential risks so that a none-too-credible threat can be made very dreadful. The NUT proposes instead to run grave risks so that a somewhat less dreadful threat can be made very credible. His risks are different – most importantly, lesser massacres but more chance of inadvertent war – but no less grave overall.

EXISTENTIAL DETERRENCE

But what else can we do? How could the enemy be very powerfully deterred by a none-too-credible threat of a none-too-dreadful outcome?

This is how. Compare two ways a burglar might be deterred from trying his luck at the house of a man who keeps a tiger. The burglar might think: "I could do *this*, and then the tiger would do *that*, and then I could do *so-and-so*, and then the tiger would do *such-and-such*, and then. . . ." If all such plans turn out too low in their expected payoff, then he will be deterred. But if he is a somewhat sensible burglar, his thoughts will take a different turn. "*You don't tangle with tigers*. Especially when you've never tried it before. Not even if someone (someone you don't trust) claims that these tigers have somehow been tamed. Not even if you carry what the salesman claimed was a sure-fire tiger stopper. You just never know what might happen."

The hypothesis of existential deterrence is that it is through thoughts like these that our nuclear arsenal deters our somewhat sensible enemy. Existentialism says that the credibility problem more or less solves itself. Given an enemy who, like ourselves, is risk averse, pessimistic, skeptical, and conservative, deterrence is easy. To deter such an enemy, it is our military capacities that matter, not our intentions or incentives or declarations. If we have the weapons, the worst case is that somehow – and never mind why – we use them in whatever way he likes least. Of course he is not at all sure that the worst case will come about. But he mistrusts arguments to the contrary, being skeptical; and he magnifies the probability of the worst case, being pessimistic; and he weighs it in deliberation out of proportion to the probability he gives it, being averse to risk. In short: he will be deterred by the *existence* of weapons that are *capable* of inflicting great destruction. And we are the same way.

If existentialism is true, then the package deals of MAD and NUTS fall apart. We can borrow ideas from the MADman and the NUT and have the best of both. But we can leave behind the parts of their reasoning that require us to run grave risks in order to solve the credibility problem.

BUY LIKE A *MAD*MAN, USE LIKE A *NUT*

The MADman's policy for procurement of weapons was as moderate and benign as can be. The forces he requires are comparatively small and cheap. He creates no temptation to preempt. His standards of adequacy are finite, in the sense that both sides at once can meet them. We could be well content – if it were not for his abominable policy about what to do in case of war. But if existentialism is true, we can buy like a MADman if we like, but that implies nothing about what we ought to do in case of war, or what we ought to intend beforehand. We needn't strive to give some credibility to our dreadful threat to destroy the enemy's cities. We needn't threaten it at all. We have weapons and war plans which give us the assured capacity to do it, and their very existence is deterrent enough.

So far, so good; but a big question remains. What if we buy the MADman's finite deterrent, but it lets us down? What if deterrence fails after all, and in a big way? In that case, I say, we ought to use like a NUT. We ought to engage in counterforce warfare with what remains of our forces, hoping thereby to limit further damage to us and to our allies. We should not retaliate by destroying cities; on the contrary, we should compromise the efficacy of our attacks so as to reduce collateral death and destruction. We should proceed as if we valued the lives of the enemy's civilians and soldiers – simply because we *should* value those lives – but less than we value the lives of those on whose behalf we are fighting.

If we use like a NUT, but with nothing more than what remains of a MADman's forces, then our aims in counterforce warfare cannot be too ambitious. We cannot hope to reduce the enemy's remaining forces to the point where he no longer has the capacity to do dreadful damage to whatever remains of our population and our resources for recovery. But the numbers count; they are not infinite, and not incomparable. If tens of millions are already dead, doubtless that is quite enough to exhaust our stock of adjectives and saturate our capacity to feel horror. But that is no reason why it is not worthwhile to save the lives of tens of millions more.

Limitation of further damage is worthwhile. Counterforce warfare, even of a modest sort, is a way to limit further damage. Therefore using our remaining nuclear weapons for counterforce warfare is the right thing to do. It is, of course, a better thing to do than destroying the enemy's cities. That alternative is easy to beat. But also, I say, it is a better choice than doing nothing, and waiting to see what sort of follow-on attack we suffer from the enemy's remaining forces.

It may be objected that it seems senseless to build forces designed for one mission when all the while we intend to use them only for another. If we buy like a MADman, we buy a force that is just right for retaliating against cities; but if the time comes to use like a NUT, we will wish the forces had been made more suitable for their only truly intended use: modest, second-strike counterforce warfare with avoidance of collateral damage.

Now it is the NUT's turn to have his package deal broken up. His policy about what to do in case of war – counterforce warfare meant to limit damage – is comparatively moderate and benign, at any rate compared to the MADman's. We could be well content – if it were not for his dangerous policy for procurement of weapons. Because he wants damage limitation not only for its own sake but for the sake of credibility, he requires weapons capable of meeting ambitious goals. Then the very same strength that supports the credible warning makes dangerous incentives to preemption in the short term and arms racing in the long term. Our solution is to buy suitable weapons, but limit their numbers.

Even a MADman's finite deterrent gives some significant capacity for counterforce. But all agree that the MADman's forces create little temptation to preemption or arms racing. They are not yet above the danger line. Then let them set a benchmark: let us have forces suited for counterforce warfare, but let us have only enough of them to match the counterforce capacity of the MADman's finite deterrent. In that case, they should be no more destabilizing.

For finite counterforce, whatever enhances second-strike capacity without enhancing first-strike capacity is all to the good. Excellent post-attack command and control, for example, would be extremely advantageous. But it would not increase first-strike counterforce capacity in the least – because peacetime command and control is already excellent. Likewise, any improvement which holds capacity fixed while reducing collateral death and destruction is all to the good. If we aim our warheads more accurately and reduce their explosive yield (a trend that is already well under way), we can hold capacity fixed while we reduce the fallout, both local and global. And improved accuracy can mean that we need fewer warheads altogether.

If we trade numbers for accuracy, this reduces our capacity to destroy cities. Of course we do not have reason to want to destroy cities, but we do want the enemy to be deterred by the thought that somehow we might anyway. If the capacity is what deters, dare we reduce the capacity? I suggest that we can reduce it a lot without making existential deterrence any less robust. Any second-strike force that could accomplish something worthwhile in counterforce warfare, even with lower yields than we use today, would a fortiori be capable of enormous destruction.

CONCLUSION

As theoreticians, we want an understanding of nuclear deterrence that is neither MAD nor NUTS. We don't want to be committed to wickedness, and we don't want to fuss over credibility. We don't want deterrence through damage limitation – we want damage limitation for its own sake, and deterrence can look after itself. We don't want to think that damage limitation is worthless unless it is wonderful. We don't want to put adjectives in place of numbers, shirking the responsibility to save tens of millions of lives just because the outcome is dreadful either way.

18

The punishment that leaves something to chance

I

We are accustomed to punish criminal attempts much more severely if they succeed than if they fail. We are also accustomed to wonder why. It is hard to find any rationale for our leniency toward the unsuccessful. Leniency toward aborted attempts, or mere preparation, might be easier to understand. (And whether easy or hard, it is not my present topic.) But what sense can we make of leniency toward a completed attempt – one that puts a victim at risk of harm, and fails only by luck to do actual harm?

Dee takes a shot at his enemy, and so does Dum. They both want to kill; they both try, and we may suppose they try equally hard. Both act out of malice, without any shred of justification or excuse. Both give us reason to fear that they might be ready to kill in the

First published in *Proceedings of the Russellian Society* (University of Sydney) **12** (1987), 81–97; and in *Philosophy and Public Affairs* **18** (1989): 53–67.

Lewis, David, THE PUNISHMENT THAT LEAVES SOMETHING TO CHANCE. Copyright © 1989 by Princeton University Press. Reprinted by permission of Princeton University Press, and with kind permission from the Russellian Society.

This article arose out of discussion of a lecture by Judith Thomson about the guilt of successful and unsuccessful attempters. I am grateful for comments by John Broome, Stephanie Lewis, T. M. Scanlon, Thomas Schelling, and Jonathan Suzman; by the editors of *Philosophy and Public Affairs*; and by audiences at Monash University, the Australian National University, and the Russellian Society (Sydney).

future. The only difference is that Dee hits and Dum misses. So Dee has killed, he is guilty of murder, and we put him to death.[1] Dum has not killed, he is guilty only of attempted murder, and he gets a short prison sentence.

Why? Dee and Dum were equally wicked in their desires. They were equally uninhibited in pursuing their wicked desires. Insofar as the wicked deserve to be punished, they deserve it equally. Their conduct was equally dangerous: they inflicted equal risks of death on their respective victims. Insofar as those who act dangerously deserve to be punished, again they deserve it equally. Maybe Dee's act was worse than Dum's act, just because of Dee's success; but it is not the act that suffers punishment, it is the agent. Likewise, if we want to express our abhorrence of wickedness or of dangerous conduct, either exemplar of what we abhor is fit to star in the drama of crime and punishment. Further, Dee and Dum have equally engaged in conduct we want to prevent by deterrence. For we prevent successful attempts by preventing attempts generally. We cannot deter success separately from deterring attempts, since attempters make no separate choice about whether to succeed. Further, Dee and Dum have equally shown us that we might all be safer if we defended ourselves against them; and one function of punishment (at any rate if it is death, imprisonment, or transportation) is to get dangerous criminals off the streets before they do more harm. So how does their different luck in hitting or missing make any difference to considerations of desert, expression, deterrence, or defense? How can it be just, on any credible theory of just punishment, to punish them differently?

Here is one rationale for our peculiar practice. If the gods see innocent blood shed, they will be angry; if they are angry, none of us will be safe until they are propitiated; and to propitiate the gods, we must shed guilty blood. Whereas if by luck no innocent blood is shed, the gods will not be angered just by the sight of unsuccessful wickedness, so there will be no need of propitiation. – This rationale

1 I do not wish to enter the debate about whether the traditional death penalty is ever justified. If you think not, substitute throughout whatever you think is the correct maximum penalty; my argument will go through almost without change.

would make sense, if its premises were true. And if we put "the public" or "the victim's kin" for "the gods" throughout it still makes sense; and that way, maybe the premises are true, at least sometimes and to some extent. But this rationale does nothing at all to defend our practice *as just*. If our practice is unjust, then the ways of the gods (or the public, or the kin) are unjust, although if the powers that be want to see injustice done, it might be prudent to ignore justice and do their bidding.

A purely conservative rationale is open to the same complaint. Maybe it is a good idea to stay with the practice we have learned how to operate, lest a reform cause unexpected problems. Maybe it is good for people to see the law go on working as they are accustomed to expect it to. Maybe a reform would convey unintended and disruptive messages: as it might be, that we have decided to take murder less seriously than we used to. These considerations may be excellent reasons why it is prudent to leave well enough alone, and condone whatever injustice there may be in our present practice. They do nothing at all to defend our practice as just.

Another rationale concerns the deterrence of second attempts. If at first you don't succeed, and if success would bring no extra punishment, then you have nothing left to lose if you try, try again. "If exactly the same penalty is prescribed for successes as for attempts, there will be every reason to make sure that one is successful."[2] It cannot hurt to have some deterrence left after deterrence has failed. Maybe the experience of having tried once will make the criminal more deterrable than he was at first. – But why is this any reason for punishing successful attempts more severely? It might as well just be a reason for punishing two attempts more severely than one, which we could do regardless of success. If each separate attempt is punished, and if one share of punishment is not so bad that a second share would be no worse, then we have some deterrence against second attempts.

Another rationale sees punishment purely as a deterrent, and assumes that we will have deterrence enough if we make sure that

2 John Kleinig, *Punishment and Desert* (The Hague: Martinus Nijhoff, 1973), p. 132. Kleinig does not take this to afford an adequate justification.

crime never pays. If so, there is no justification for any more penal harm than it takes to offset the gains from a crime. Then a failed attempt needs no punishment: there are no gains to be offset, so even if unpunished it still doesn't pay. – I reply that in the first place, this system of minimum deterrence seems likely to dissuade only the most calculating of criminals. In the second place, punishment is not just a deterrent. I myself might not insist on retribution per se, but certainly the expressive and defensive functions of punishment are not to be lightly forsaken.

Another rationale invokes the idea of "moral luck."[3] Strange to say, it can happen by luck alone that one person ends up more wicked than another. Perhaps that is why the successful attempter, by luck alone, ends up deserving more severe punishment? – I reply, first, that to some extent this suggestion merely names our problem. We ask how Dee can deserve more severe punishment just because his shot hits the mark. Call that "moral luck" if you will; then we have been asking all along how this sort of moral luck is possible. But, second, it may be misleading to speak of the moral luck of the attempter, since it may tend to conflate this case with something quite different. The most intelligible cases of moral luck are those in which the lucky and the unlucky alike are disposed to become wicked if tempted, and only the unlucky are tempted. But then, however alike they may have been originally, the lucky and the unlucky do end up different in how they are and in how they act. Not so for the luck of hitting or missing. It makes no difference to how the lucky and the unlucky are, and no difference to how they act.[4]

---

3 See Thomas Nagel, "Moral Luck," *Proceedings of the Aristotelian Society*, supp. vol. 50 (1976): 141, repr. in Nagel, *Mortal Questions* (Cambridge: Cambridge University Press, 1979), p. 29. Nagel distinguishes, as he should, between the "moral luck" of the attempter and the different sort of moral luck that makes some genuine difference to how one is and how one acts.

4 The luck of hitting and missing does make a difference to how their actions of shooting may be described: Dee's is a killing, Dum's is not. Dee's causes harm and thereby invades the victim's rights in a way that Dum's does not. (Dee invades the victim's right not to be harmed, as well as his right not to be endangered; Dum invades only the latter right.) But this is no difference in how they act, since the

Finally, another rationale invokes the difference between whole-hearted and halfhearted attempts.[5] Both are bad, but wholehearted attempts are worse. A wholehearted attempt involves more careful planning, more precautions against failure, more effort, more persistence, and perhaps repeated tries. *Ceteris paribus*, a wholehearted attempt evinces more wickedness – stronger wicked desires, or less inhibition about pursuing them. *Ceteris paribus*, a wholehearted attempt is more dangerous. It is more likely to succeed; it subjects the victim, knowingly and wrongfully, to a greater risk. Therefore it is more urgently in need of prevention by deterrence. *Ceteris paribus*, the perpetrator of a wholehearted attempt is more of a proven danger to us all, so it is more urgent to get him off the streets. So from every standpoint – desert, expression, deterrence, defense – it makes good sense to punish attempts more severely when they are wholehearted. Now, since wholehearted attempts are more likely to succeed, success is some evidence that the attempt was wholehearted. Punishing success, then, is a rough and ready way of punishing wholeheartedness.

I grant that it is just to punish wholehearted attempts more severely – or better, since "heartedness" admits of degrees, to proportion the punishment to the heartedness of the attempt. And I grant that in so doing we may take the probability of success – in other words, the risk inflicted on the victim – as our measure of heartedness. That means not proportioning the punishment simply to the offender's wickedness, because two equally wicked attempters may not be equally likely to succeed. One may be more dangerous than the other because he has the advantage in skill or resources or information or

description of an action in terms of what it causes is an extrinsic description. The actions themselves, events that are finished when the agent has done his part, do not differ in any intrinsic way.

You might protest that a killing is not over when the killer has done his part; it is a more prolonged event that ends with the death of the victim; so there is, after all, an intrinsic difference between Dee's action of killing and Dum's action of shooting and missing. – No; an action of killing is different from the prolonged event of someone's getting killed, even though "the killing" can denote either one.

5 See Lawrence C. Becker, "Criminal Attempt and the Theory of the Law of Crimes," *Philosophy & Public Affairs* 3, no. 3 (Spring 1974): 288. Becker does not take this to afford an adequate justification.

opportunity. Then if we proportion punishment to heartedness measured by risk, we may punish one attempter more severely not because he was more wicked, but because his conduct was more dangerous. From a purely retributive standpoint, wickedness might seem the more appropriate measure; but from the expressive standpoint, we may prefer to dramatize our abhorrence not of wickedness per se but of dangerous wickedness; and from the standpoint of deterrence or defense, clearly it is dangerous conduct that matters.

So far, so good; but I protest that it is unjust to punish success as a rough and ready way of punishing wholeheartedness. It's just too rough and ready. Success is some evidence of wholeheartedness, sure enough. But it is very unreliable evidence: the wholehearted attempt may very well be thwarted, the half- or quarterhearted attempt may succeed. And we can have other evidence that bears as much or more on whether the attempt was wholehearted. If what we really want is to punish wholeheartedness, we have no business heeding only one unreliable fragment of the total evidence, and then treating that fragment as if it were conclusive. Suppose we had reason – *good* reason – to think that on average the old tend to be more wholehearted than the young in their criminal attempts. Suppose even that we could infer wholeheartedness from age somewhat more reliably than we can infer it from success. Then if we punished attempters more severely in proportion to their age, that would be another rough and ready way of punishing wholeheartedness. *Ex hypothesi*, it would be less rough and ready than what we do in punishing success. It would still fall far short of our standards of justice.

II

In what follows, I shall propose a new rationale. *I do not say that it works.* I do say that the new rationale works better than the old ones. It makes at least a prima facie case that our peculiar practice is just, and I do not see any decisive rebuttal. All the same, I think that the prima facie case is probably not good enough, and probably there is no adequate justification for punishing attempts more severely when they succeed.

Our present practice amounts to a disguised form of *penal lottery* – a punishment that leaves something to chance. Seen thus, it *does* in some sense punish all attempts alike, regardless of success. It is no less just, and no more just, than an undisguised penal lottery would be. Probably any penal lottery is seriously unjust, but it is none too easy to explain why.

By a penal lottery, I mean a system of punishment in which the convicted criminal is subjected to a risk of punitive harm. If he wins the lottery, he escapes the harm. If he loses, he does not. A pure penal lottery is one in which the winners suffer no harm at all; an impure penal lottery is one in which winners and losers alike suffer some harm, but the losers suffer more harm. It is a mixture: part of the punishment is certain harm, part is the penal lottery.

An overt penal lottery is one in which the punishment is announced explicitly as a risk – there might be ways of dramatizing the fact, such as a drawing of straws on the steps of the gallows. A covert penal lottery is one in which the punishment is not announced as a risk, but it is common knowledge that it brings risk with it. (A covert lottery must presumably be impure.)

A historical example of an overt penal lottery is the decimation of a regiment as punishment for mutiny. Each soldier is punished for his part in the mutiny by a one-in-ten risk of being put to death. It is a fairly pure penal lottery, but not entirely pure: the terror of waiting to see who must die is part of the punishment, and this part falls with certainty on all the mutineers alike.

Covert and impure penal lotteries are commonplace in our own time. If one drawback of prison is that it is a place where one is exposed to capricious violence, or to a serious risk of catching AIDS,[6] then a prison sentence is in part a penal lottery. If the gulag is noted for its abysmal standards of occupational health and safety, then a sentence of forced labor is in part a penal lottery.

6 See A. Hough and D. M. Schwartz, "AIDS and Prisons," in *Meeting the Challenge: Papers of the First National Conference on AIDS*, ed. Adam Carr (Canberra: Australian Government Publishing Service, 1986), pp. 171–80.

What do we think, and what should we think, of penal lotteries? Specifically, what should we think of a penal lottery, with death for the losers, as the punishment for all attempts at murder, regardless of success? Successful or not, the essence of the crime is to subject the victim, knowingly and wrongfully, to a serious risk of death. The proposed punishment is to be subjected to a like risk of death.

We need a standard of comparison. Our present system of leniency toward the unsuccessful is too problematic to make a good standard, so let us instead compare the penal lottery with a hypothetical reformed system. How does the lottery compare with a system that punishes all attempts regardless of success, by the certain harm of a moderate prison term? A moderate term, because if we punished successful and unsuccessful attempts alike, we would presumably set the punishment somewhere between our present severe punishment of the one and our lenient punishment of the other. (Let the prison be a safe one, so that in the comparison case we have no trace of a penal lottery.) Both for the lottery and for the comparison case, I shall assume that we punish regardless of success. In the one case, success per se makes no difference to the odds; in the other case, no difference to the time in prison. This is not to say that every convicted criminal gets the very same sentence. Other factors might still make a difference. In particular, heartedness (measured by the risk inflicted) could make a difference, and success could make a difference to the extent that it is part of our evidence about heartedness.

Now, how do the two alternatives compare?

The penal lottery may have some practical advantages. It gets the case over and done with quickly. It is not a crime school. A prison costs a lot more than a gallows plus a supply of long and short straws.[7]

(Likewise a prison with adequate protection against random brutality by guards and fellow inmates costs more than a prison without. So it seems that we have already been attracted by the economy of a system that has at least some covert admixture of lottery.)

---

7 This point would disappear if something less cheap and quick than death were the penalty for losers of the lottery.

Like a prison term (or fines, or flogging) and unlike the death penalty *simpliciter*, the penal lottery can be graduated as finely as we like. When we take the crime to be worse, we provide fewer long straws to go with the fatal short straws. In particular, that is how we can provide a more severe punishment for the more wholehearted attempt that subjected the victim to a greater risk.

From the standpoint of dramatizing our abhorrence of wicked and dangerous conduct, a penal lottery seems at least as good as a prison sentence. Making the punishment fit the crime, Mikado-fashion, is *poetic* justice. The point we want to dramatize, both to the criminal and to the public, is that what we think of the crime is just like what the criminal thinks of his punishment. If it's a risk for a risk, how can anybody miss the point?

From the standpoint of deterrence, there is no doubt that we are sometimes well deterred by the prospect of risk.[8] It happens every time we wait to cross the street. It is an empirical question how effective a deterrent the penal lottery might be. Compared with the alternative punishment of a certain harm, such as a moderate prison term, the lottery might give us more deterrence for a given amount of penal harm, or it might give us less. Whether it gives us more or less might depend a lot on the details of how the two systems operate. If the lottery gave us more, that would make it preferable from the standpoint of deterrence.

(We often hear about evidence that certainty is more deterring than severity. But to the extent that this evidence pertains only to the uncertainty of getting caught, getting convicted, and serving the full sentence, it is scarcely relevant. The criminal might think of escaping punishment as a game of skill – his skill, or perhaps his lawyers's. For all we know, a risk of losing a game of chance might be much more deterring than an equal risk of losing a game of skill.)

From the standpoint of defense, the penal lottery gets some dan-

---

8 See Thomas C. Schelling, "The Threat That Leaves Something to Chance," in his book *The Strategy of Conflict* (Cambridge: Harvard University Press, 1960). Schelling does not discuss penal lotteries as such, but much of his discussion carries over. What does not carry over, or not much, is his discussion of chancy threats as a way to gain credibility when one has strong reason not to fulfill one's threat.

gerous criminals off the streets forever, while others go free at once. Moderate prison terms would let all go free after a longer time, some of them perhaps reformed and some of them hardened and embittered. It is another empirical question which alternative is the more effective system of defense. Again, the answer may depend greatly on the details of the two systems, and on much else that we cannot easily find out.[9]

IV

So far we have abundant uncertainties, but no clear-cut case against the penal lottery. If anything, the balance may be tipping in its favor. So let us turn finally to the standpoint of desert. Here it is a bit hard to know what to make of the penal lottery. If the court has done its job correctly, then all who are sentenced to face the same lottery, with the same odds, are equally guilty of equally grave crimes. They deserve equal treatment. Do they get it? – Yes and no.

Yes. We treat them alike because we subject them all to the very same penal lottery, with the very same odds. And when the lots are drawn, we treat them alike again, because we follow the same predetermined contingency plan – death for losers, freedom for winners – for all of them alike.

No. Some of them are put to death, some are set free, and what could be more unequal than that?

Yes. Their fates are unequal, of course. But that is not our doing. They are treated unequally by Fortune, not by us.

No. But it is we who hand them over to the inequity of Fortune. We are Fortune's accomplices.

Yes. Everyone is exposed to the inequity of Fortune, in ever so many ways. However nice it may be to undo some of these inequities, we

---

9 This question would have to be reconsidered if something other than death were the maximum penalty, and so the penalty for losers of the lottery. It would remain an empirical question, and probably a difficult one, which is the more effective system of defense.

do not ordinarily think of this as part of what is required for equal treatment.

No. It's one thing not to go out of our way to undo the inequities of Fortune; it's another thing to go out of our way to increase them.

Yes. We do that too, and think it not at all contrary to equal treatment. When we hire astronauts, or soldiers or sailors or firemen or police, we knowingly subject these people to more of the inequities of Fortune than are found in ordinary life.

No. But the astronauts are volunteers . . .

Yes . . . and so are the criminals, when they commit the crimes for which they know they must face the lottery. The soldiers, however, sometimes are not.

No. Start over. We agreed that the winners and losers deserve equal punishment. That is because they are equally guilty. Then they deserve to suffer equally. But they do not.

Yes. They do not suffer equally; but if they deserve to, that is not our affair. We seldom think that equal punishment means making sure of equal suffering. Does the cheerful man get a longer prison sentence than the equally guilty morose man, to make sure of equal suffering? If one convict gets lung cancer in prison, do we see to it that the rest who are equally guilty suffer equally? When we punish equally, what we equalize is not the suffering itself. What we equalize is our contribution to expected suffering.

No. This all seems like grim sophistry. Surely, equal treatment has to mean more than just treating people so that *some* common description of what we are doing will apply to them all alike.

Yes. True. But we have made up our minds already, in other connections, that lotteries count as equal treatment, or near enough. When we have an indivisible benefit or burden to hand out (or even one that is divisible at a significant cost) we are very well content to resort to a lottery. We are satisfied that all who have equal chances are

237

getting equal treatment – and not in some queer philosophers' sense, but in the sense that matters to justice.

It seems to me that "Yes" is winning this argument, but that truth and justice are still somehow on the side of "No." The next move, dear readers, is up to you. I shall leave it unsettled whether a penal lottery would be just. I shall move on to my second task, which is to show that our present practice amounts to a covert penal lottery. If the penal lottery is just, so is our present practice. If not, not.

V

To show that they do not matter, I shall introduce the differences between an overt penal lottery and our present practice one at a time, by running through a sequence of cases. I claim that at no step is there any significant difference of justice between one case and the next. Such differences as there are will be practical advantages only, and will come out much in favor of our present practice.

Case 1 is the overt penal lottery as we have imagined it already, with one added stipulation, as follows. We will proportion the punishment to the heartedness of the attempt, as measured by the risk of death[10] the criminal knowingly and wrongfully inflicted on the victim. We will do this by sentencing the criminal to a risk equal to the one he inflicted on the victim. If the criminal subjected his victim to an 80 percent risk of death, he shall draw his straw from a bundle of eight short and two long; whereas if he halfheartedly subjected the victim to a mere 40 percent risk, he shall draw from four short and six long; and in this way his punishment shall fit his crime. Therefore the court's task is not limited to ascertaining whether the defendant

10 I note a complication once and for all, but I shall ignore it in what follows. The relevant risk is not really the victim's risk of death, but rather the risk of being killed – that is, of dying a death which is caused, perhaps probabilistically, and in the appropriate insensitive fashion, by the criminal's act. Likewise for the criminal's risk in the penal lottery. (On probabilistic and insensitive causation, see my *Philosophical Papers*, vol. II [New York: Oxford University Press, 1986], pp. 175–88.)

did knowingly and wrongfully subject the victim to a risk of death; also the court must ascertain how much of a risk it was.

Case 2 is like Case 1, except that we skip the dramatic ceremony on the steps of the gallows and draw straws ahead of time. In fact, we have the drawing even before the trial. It is not the defendant himself who draws, but the Public Drawer. The Drawer is sworn to secrecy; he reveals the outcome only when and if the defendant has been found guilty and sentenced to the lottery. If the defendant is acquitted and the drawing turns out to have been idle, no harm done. Since it is not known ahead of time whether the sentence will be eight and two, four and six, or what, the Drawer must make not one but many drawings ahead of time. He reveals the one, if any, that turns out to be called for.

Case 3 is like Case 2, except without the secrecy. The Drawer announces at once whether the defendant will win or lose in case he is found guilty and sentenced. (Or rather, whether he will win or lose if he is sentenced to eight and two, whether he will win or lose if he is sentenced to four and six, and so on.) This means that the suspense in the courtroom is higher on some occasions than others. But that need not matter, provided that the court can stick conscientiously to the task of ascertaining whether the defendant did knowingly and wrongfully subject the victim to risk, and if so how much risk. It is by declaring that a criminal deserves the lottery that the court expresses society's abhorrence of the crime. So the court's task is still worth doing, even when it is a foregone conclusion that the defendant will win the lottery if sentenced (as might happen if he had won all the alternative draws). But the trial may seem idle, and the expression of abhorrence may fall flat, when it is known all along that, come what may, the defendant will never face the lottery and lose.

Case 4 is like Case 3, except that we make the penal lottery less pure. Losers of the penal lottery get death, as before; winners get a short prison sentence. Therefore it is certain that every criminal who is sentenced to the lottery will suffer at least some penal harm. Thus we make sure that the trial and the sentence will be taken seriously even when it is a foregone conclusion that the defendant, if sentenced, will win the lottery.

Case 1 also was significantly impure. If the draw is held at the last minute, on the very steps of the gallows, then every criminal who is sentenced to face the lottery must spend a period of time – days? weeks? years? – in fear and trembling, and imprisoned, waiting to learn whether he will win or lose. This period of terror is a certain harm that falls on winners and losers alike. Case 2 very nearly eliminates the impurity, since there is no reason why the Drawer should not reveal the outcome very soon after the criminal is sentenced. Case 3 eliminates it entirely. (In every case, a defendant must spend a period in fear as he waits to learn whether he will be convicted. But this harm cannot count as penal, because it falls equally on the guilty and the innocent, on those who will be convicted and those who will be acquitted.) Case 4 restores impurity, to whatever extent we see fit, but in a different form.

Case 5 is like Case 4, except that the straws are replaced by a different chance device for determining the outcome of the lottery. The Public Drawer conducts an exact reenactment of the crime. If the victim in the reenactment dies, then the criminal loses the lottery. If it is a good reenactment, the risk to the original victim equals the risk to the new victim in the reenactment, which in turn equals the risk that the criminal will lose the lottery; and so, as desired, we punish a risk by an equal risk.

If the outcome of the lottery is to be settled before the trial, as in Cases 2, 3, and 4, then it will be necessary for the Drawer to conduct not just one but several reenactments. He will entertain all reasonable alternative hypotheses about exactly how the crime might have happened – exactly what the defendant might have done by way of knowingly and wrongfully inflicting risk on the victim. He will conduct one reenactment for each hypothesis. The court's task changes. If the court finds the defendant guilty of knowingly and wrongfully inflicting a risk of death, it is no longer required also to measure the amount of risk. Nobody need ever figure out whether it was 80 percent, 40 percent, or what. Instead, the court is required to ascertain which hypothesis about exactly how the crime happened is correct. Thereby the court chooses which of all the hypothetical reenactments is the one that determines whether the criminal wins or loses his lottery. If the court finds that the criminal took careful aim, then the chosen reenactment will be one in which the criminal's stand-in also took careful aim, whereas if the court finds that the criminal halfheartedly fired in the victim's general direction, the chosen reenactment will be one in which the stand-in did likewise. So the criminal will be more likely to lose his lottery in the first case than in the second.

The drawbacks of a lottery by reenactment are plain to see. Soon we shall find the remedy. But first, let us look at the advantages of a lottery by reenactment over a lottery by drawing straws. We have already noted that with straws, the court had to measure how much risk the criminal inflicted, whereas with reenactments, the court has only to ascertain exactly how the crime happened. Both tasks look well-nigh impossible. But the second must be easier, because the first task consists of the second plus more besides. The only way for the court to measure the risk would be to ascertain just what happened, and then find out just how much risk results from such happenings.

Another advantage of reenactments over straws appears when we try to be more careful about what we mean by "amount of risk." Is it (1) an "objective chance"? Or is it (2) a reasonable degree of belief for a hypothetical observer who knows the situation in as much minute details as feasible instruments could permit? Or is it (3) a reasonable degree of belief for someone who knows just as much about the details of the situation as the criminal did? Or is it (4) the criminal's actual degree of belief, however unreasonable that might have been? It would be nice not to have to decide. But if we want to match the criminal's risk in a lottery by straws to the victim's risk, then we must decide. Not so for a lottery by reenactment. If the reenactment is perfect, we automatically match the amount of risk in all four senses. Even if the reenactment is imperfect, at least we can assure ourselves of match in senses (3) and (4). It may or may not be feasible to get assured match in senses (1) and (2), depending on the details of what happened. (If it turns out that the criminal left a bomb hooked up to a quantum randomizer, it will be comparatively easy. If he committed his crime in a more commonplace way, it will be much harder.) But whenever it is hard to get assured match in senses (1) and (2), it will be harder still to measure the risk and get assured match in a lottery by straws. So however the crime happened, and

241

whatever sense of match we want, we do at least as well by reenactment as by straws, and sometimes we do better.

Case 6 is like Case 5, except that enactment replaces *r*eenactment. We use the original crime, so to speak, as its own perfect reenactment. If the criminal is sentenced to face the lottery, then if his victim dies, he loses his lottery and he dies too, whereas if the victim lives, the criminal wins, and he gets only the short prison sentence. It does not matter when the lottery takes place, provided only that it is not settled so soon that the criminal may know its outcome before he decides whether to commit his crime.

The advantages are many: we need no Drawer to do the work; we need not find volunteers to be the stand-in victims in all the hypothetical reenactments; the "reenactment" is automatically perfect, matching the risk in all four senses; we spare the court the difficult task of ascertaining exactly how the crime happened. If we want to give a risk for a risk, and if we want to match risks in any but a very approximate and uncertain fashion, the lottery by enactment is not only the easy way, it is the only remotely feasible way.

The drawback is confusion. When a criminal is sentenced to face the lottery by straws, nobody will think him more guilty or more wicked just because his straw is short. And when a criminal is sentenced to face the lottery by reenactment, nobody will think him more guilty just because the stand-in victim dies.[11] But if he is sentenced to the lottery by enactment, then one and the same event plays a double role: if his victim dies, that death is at once the main harm done by his crime and also the way of losing his lottery. If we are not careful, we are apt to misunderstand. We may think that the successful attempter suffers a worse fate because he is more guilty when he does a worse harm, rather than because he loses his lottery. But it is not so: his success is irrelevant to his guilt, his wickedness, his desert, and his sentence to face the lottery – exactly as the short-

11 If it were known that the victim's risk was fifty-fifty, or if we did not care about matching risks, we could just as well reverse the lottery by enactment: the criminal loses if the victim lives, wins if the victim dies. Certainly nobody will think the criminal is more guilty if the victim *lives*.

ness of his straw would have been, had he been sentenced to the lottery by straws.

VI

I submit that our present practice is exactly Case 6: punishment for attempts regardless of success, a penal lottery by enactment, impurity to help us take the affair seriously even when the lottery is won, and the inevitable confusion. We may not understand our practice as a penal lottery – confused as we are, we have trouble understanding it at all – but, so understood, it does make a good deal of sense. It is another question whether it is really just. Most likely it isn't, but I don't understand why not.

19

Scriven on human unpredictability

WITH JANE S. RICHARDSON

In his paper "An Essential Unpredictability in Human Behavior,"[1] Michael Scriven offers an argument intended to show that it is impossible in principle to predict what a person (or indeed a suitable robot) will do in a certain possible kind of situation. Moreover, this unpredictability is independent of any indeterminism in physics, of any limitations on the predictor's knowledge of data and laws, and of any limitations on the reliability or amount of calculation the predictor can do. Scriven's argument is a purported proof that if a person in the designated situation is predicted, even by a predictor who does as well as is in principle possible, the prediction will turn out false.

We shall show that Scriven's argument depends on a hidden premise which we have no reason to accept. Without the hidden premise, Scriven cannot demonstrate any failure of prediction which we cannot explain away as due to limitations, in principle remediable, on the amount of calculation available to a given predictor. We conclude that Scriven's argument does not establish an essential unpredictability

First published in *Philosophical Studies* **17** (1966), 69–74. Reprinted with kind permission from Jane S. Richardson.

1 In *Scientific Psychology: Principles* and *Approaches*, edited by Benjamin B. Wolman and Ernest Nagel (New York: Basic Books, 1964), pp. 411–25. Scriven has summarized his argument elsewhere: part of "The Frontiers of Psychology: Psychoanalysis and Parapsychology," in *Frontiers of Science and Philosophy*, edited by Robert G. Colodny (Pittsburgh: University of Pittsburgh Press, 1963), pp. 120–27; and part of "The Limits of Physical Explanation," in *Philosophy of Science: The Delaware Seminar*, II, edited by Bernard Baumrin (New York: Wiley, 1963), pp. 126–30.

in human behavior in any interesting sense. Rather it is a *reductio* establishing the falsehood of Scriven's hidden premise.

SCRIVEN'S ARGUMENT

Let us imagine somebody who is trying to predict the outcome of a free[2] choice by somebody else who is dominantly motivated to avoid being validly predicted. (The *dramatis personae* are called, respectively, the *predictor* and the *avoider*.) Perhaps the avoider has been put in a position where he stands to lose if the predictor knows in advance what he will choose; or perhaps he is just averse to being predicted. Either way, if the avoider learns in time what he is predicted to do, he will do something else, so the prediction will turn out false. If, for instance, the predictor announces the prediction to the avoider, the avoider chooses contrary to the prediction. But the avoider may be able to find out the prediction without being told it by the predictor. If the avoider has enough knowledge of data and laws and can do enough calculation with high reliability, he can duplicate the predictor's calculation to find out what result it gave. In this case also he will do something else (being *ex hypothesi* free and motivated to do so), so the prediction will turn out false.[3]

Therefore Scriven maintains that if the avoider has a free choice, and if he is dominantly motivated to avoid being validly predicted, and if he uses the stratagem of duplicating and violating predictions, and if he has enough knowledge of data and laws, and if he can do predictive calculations reliably, and if he can do enough calculation

---

2 Free, that is, in some ordinary sense which is neutral as to predictability. To stipulate "contra-causal" freedom would obviously beg the question.

3 The contra-predictive stratagem of duplicating and violating the prediction is entirely independent of another contra-predictive stratagem discussed by Scriven, the "mixed strategy" of game theory: the avoider can decide to let his choice be governed by the least predictable system available, say a quantum randomizer. The stratagem of duplicating and violating the prediction is supposed to render the avoider unpredictable regardless of any other source of unpredictability (such as indeterminism in quantum physics). Use of mixed strategy can make the avoider as unpredictable as anything else, but no more; so it does not suffice to support Scriven's main thesis.

(within whatever are the prevailing constraints imposed by limited computing speed, limited memory capacity, deadlines, and eventual discouragement, fatigue, or death), then it is in principle impossible to predict his choice. No matter how perfect is the predictor's knowledge of data and laws, no matter how reliably the predictor can calculate, no matter how much calculation the predictor can do, no matter how the predictor has tried to compensate for the fact that the avoider is working to duplicate and violate his prediction,[4] still if the predictor somehow reaches a prediction, the avoider will duplicate and violate it and it will turn out false.

THE COMPATIBILITY PREMISE

The predictor's failure is significant only if the predictor can do his task as well as it is in principle possible to do it. Otherwise Scriven's demonstration that the predictor fails does not establish that the avoider's choice is unpredictable in principle; it just shows that this predictor hasn't got what it takes to predict this avoider. The predictor must therefore have perfect knowledge of data and laws, must be able to do predictive calculation with perfect reliability, and must be able to do enough calculation. Scriven does not, unfortunately, state this set of conditions; but they are indispensable to his argument.

The avoider must have as much knowledge of data and laws as the predictor, must also be able to do predictive calculation with perfect reliability, and must also be able to do enough calculation. Scriven does explicitly stipulate this set of conditions.[5] Without them he could not prove to us that the avoider succeeds in duplicating the

---

4 A frequent first response to Scriven's argument is as follows: the predictor should make a prediction and then reverse it to get the correct prediction. But that response betrays a failure to appreciate the generality of Scriven's argument. No matter what twists and turns the predictor goes through on his way – let him reverse himself, let him reverse himself again, let him reverse himself any number of times, let him reflect on his sequence of reversals and transcend it – if a final prediction is ever forthcoming, it is that *final* prediction which is duplicated and violated.

5 "An Essential Unpredictability in Human Behavior," p. 415.

predictor's calculation, and so could not prove that any resulting prediction turns out false. Since Scriven is trying to prove only an existence theorem – that there exists *some* possible situation in which choice is in principle unpredictable – he is entitled to endow the avoider with whatever possible abilities the argument may require.

Since Scriven is apparently not fully aware that his argument uses the first set of conditions as well as the second, it never occurs to him that it may be impossible for any predictor and avoider to meet both sets at once. They may both have perfect knowledge and calculate with perfect reliability; but it is not necessarily possible even in principle for them both to be able to do enough calculation. For the amount of calculation required to let the predictor finish his prediction depends on the amount of calculation done by the avoider, and the amount required to let the avoider finish duplicating the predictor's calculation depends on the amount done by the predictor. Scriven takes for granted that the two requirement-functions are *compatible*: i.e., that there is some pair of amounts of calculation available to the predictor and the avoider such that each has enough to finish, given the amount the other has.

The compatibility of the two requirement-functions is an implicit premise of Scriven's argument, although there is no indication that Scriven is aware of using it. For without it the argument cannot be made to work: unless the predictor can do enough calculation his failure is insignificant; unless the avoider can do enough the failure cannot be shown to occur at all; only by the Compatibility Premise can both insufficiencies be ruled out at once.

We can find no reason whatsoever to accept the Compatibility Premise. The very fact that it yields Scriven's thesis of essential unpredictability looks to us like a convincing reason to reject it.

Figures 1 and 2 represent cases in which the Compatibility Premise is, respectively, true and false. The vertical and horizontal coordinates of any point represent a pair of amounts of calculation available to the predictor and the avoider. Under the Compatibility Premise (Figure 1) there is an area (the upper right) in which both the predictor and the avoider can finish their calculations. Under our rejection of the Compatibility Premise (Figure 2) there are no such points; everywhere one or both fail to finish.[6] If the predictor finishes and the avoider does not, the avoider has no chance to learn the prediction and do something contrary to it, so the predictor succeeds. If the predictor does not finish, he has no valid prediction and is reduced to blind guessing, so the avoider succeeds. (If the predictor does not finish and the avoider does not duplicate his guess, then it's guess against guess. The predictor may succeed at guessing after he has failed at predicting.)

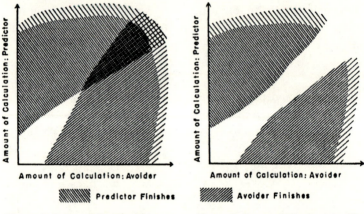

Figure 1. Compatibility Premise true   Figure 2. Compatibility Premise false

The Compatibility Premise is easily hidden by ambiguity in ordinary language. It is true that against any given avoider the predictor can in principle do enough calculation to finish; it follows (unless the Compatibility Premise is true) that any possible avoider is in principle predictable. It is likewise true that against any given predictor the avoider can in principle do enough to finish; it follows (barring a lucky guess by the predictor which the avoider does not duplicate) that any predictor is in principle avoidable.[7] But to say that *both* can

---

6 Cf. Lewis F. Richardson's analysis, in *Arms and Insecurity* (Pittsburgh: Boxwood, 1960), of interdependent national requirements for armament. The truth of the Compatibility Premise corresponds to the existence of pairs of armament-levels which are stable because mutually satisfactory.

7 We accept Scriven's line of argument without the Compatibility Premise so far as it shows only that for any possible predictor there is some possible avoider such

in principle do enough to finish is ambiguous. It may be read as the conjunction of the two innocent statements above; or it may be read as the Compatibility Premise, i.e., as stating that against *each other* both can do enough to finish. We must see that we do not accept the Compatibility Premise inadvertently by slipping from the first reading to the second.

A VARIANT OF SCRIVEN'S ARGUMENT

So far we have supposed that Scriven must stipulate just how much calculation the predictor and avoider can do. Now suppose Scriven stipulates instead that the avoider is unlimited: he can do any amount of calculation he needs, postponing his choice until he has finished.[8] He will never have to make his choice until after he has either duplicated the prediction or found out that the predictor cannot finish. This unlimited avoider would indeed be unpredictable in principle, independently of the Compatibility Premise. For even if the Compatibility Premise is false, in which case the predictor fails only because he cannot do enough calculation, yet under the new stipulation the cause of the predictor's failure is no longer remediable in principle since *no* (finite) amount of calculation would be enough against an unlimited avoider. The unlimited avoider can impose a variable requirement for calculation on the predictor confronting him, which depends on and always exceeds the predictor's own capability.

But if Scriven chooses to posit an unlimited avoider in order to rescue his argument from depending on the Compatibility Premise, he only substitutes one unacceptable premise for another. We grant that an avoider may in principle have any limit, no matter how high; but we do not grant that he may in principle have no limit at all. For we can show that, unless the Compatibility Premise is true after all,

---

that prediction is impossible. But Scriven clearly wants the stronger conclusion that there is some possible avoider such that for any possible predictor prediction is impossible; and to reach that conclusion he must use the Compatibility Premise.

8 Scriven's statement (p. 415) that the avoider is subject to a deadline would, if adhered to, allow an unlimited avoider only if he were unlimited in speed rather than in time.

an unlimited avoider must not only be able to do any amount of calculation but also must be able to do endless calculation. (Consider that if the avoider can be unlimited, so can the predictor. If both are unlimited neither stops until finished. If one finishes and stops the other can eventually also finish. If both finish the Compatibility Premise is true after all. So neither ever stops.) But we certainly do not grant that endless calculation is possible even in principle.

We conclude that neither version of Scriven's argument succeeds in establishing his thesis of an essential unpredictability in human behavior.

Index

academic employment, 3–4, 188–200
acquaintance, imaginative, 77–82
Adam and Eve, 115
Adams, Marilyn, 101n, 125
Adams, Robert M., 101n, 106, 110n, 114n, 210n
Altham, J. E. J., 44n
analyticity, 85–88, 92–93
Anscombe, G. E. M., 59, 67
anti-Humeanism about motivation, 2, 42–67
argumentum ad baculum, 186
Arló Costa, H., 61n, 67
arms racing, 222, 225
Armstrong, D. M., 58n, 67, 90n, 118n, 151n, 159n
Atonement, 3, 130–132
attempts, punishment of, 227–243
Augustine, 120–121

Ball, Desmond, 216n, 217
Ballmer, Thomas, 20n
Becker, Lawrence C., 231n
belief, change of, 47–63, 69–70n
Benacerraf, Paul, 37n, 187n
Bennett, Jonathan, 101n, 136–137n
Bentham, Jeremy, 161, 166
besires, 44n, 69–70n
Bigelow, John, 118

Bishop, John, 101n, 109, 111–112, 121, 128n
Blackburn, Simon, 42n, 93
Boer, Steven, 107n
Brennan, Geoffrey, 159n
Bromberger, Sylvain, 106n
Broome, John, 227n
Bundy, McGeorge, 211, 215, 218
Burgess, John P., 42n
Butterfield, Jeremy, 74n

Cahn, Steven M., 187n
Campbell, John, 80n
Campbell, Keith, 159n
Campsall, Richard of, 125, 126
Castañeda, Hector-Neri, 74n
Chellas, Brian F., 17n, 19, 22–23, 33, 110n
Chisholm, Roderick, 74n
choice functions, *see* value structures
Christ, 130–132
Churchlands, P. and P., 91
collateral destruction, 224, 225, 226
Collins, John, 42n, 45n, 61n, 66n, 67, 69–70n
command and control, 218, 226
commands, 20–33
common knowledge, 143–144
commonsense morality, 153, 155, 157
compatibilism, 109–112

251

Compatibility Premise, 244–250
compensatory punishment, 130, 133
conditional deontic logics, 15–19
conditional preference, 140–143
conditionals and probability, 50–51
consequentialism as a limiting case,
    214
convention, 3, 136–144
copulation, 143–144
Cornides, Thomas, 33
counterforce attacks, 212–213, 215,
    217–218, 221–222, 224–226
credibility of deterrence, 203, 218,
    220–226, 235n
Cresswell, M. J., 150n

damnation, 103, 103–104n, 132, 167,
    168, 170, 197n, 209–210
debts, 129, 132, 134–135
decision theory, 37–41, 45–67, 148
defence versus theodicy, 104–106
de Molina, Luis, 114
deontic logic, 1, 2, 5–9, 34–36, 99–
    100
depravity, 115–120
de se attitudes, 55, 73–76, 82
desire as belief, 2, 42–67, 69–70n
desire by necessity, 59, 60, 64–66, 89–
    93
desires to desire, 70–73
deterrence
    credibility of, 203, 218, 220–226,
        235n
    existential, 215, 217, 218, 223–224,
        226
    nuclear, 4, 172, 201–226
    paradoxical, 200–211, 214–215,
        216
    by punishments, 129, 228, 229–
        230, 231–232, 235
Devil, 101, 103, 108n, 115, 168, 174,
    209–210, 211
dilemmas, 95–100
dispositions to value, 68–94

egoism, 75–76
empathetic understanding, 59, 77–82
equal treatment, 236–238
error theory of value, 90–94
essence, 122–123
existential deterrence, 215, 217, 218,
    223–224, 226
evil, problem of, 2–3, 101–127

Field, Hartry, 92n
fines, 133–135
finite deterrence, 221, 224–226
finkish dispositions, 72n, 118n
folk moral science, 58–59, 90–91
Føllesdal, Dagfinn, 5, 18, 19
Foot, Philippa, 207–208
foreknowledge and freedom, 125–127
Forrest, Peter, 104n
Frankfurt, Harry, 70n
Frederic, slave of duty, 45–53
free will, 2–3, 102–127, 245

Gauthier, David, 201–204, 210
Geach, Peter, 74n, 103–104n
Germany, deception of, 156–157
Gibbard, Allan, 37–38, 41
God, 101–127, 132, 150, 156, 161–
    162, 168, 172, 177, 178, 206,
    207–208, 209–210, 228–229
Goodman, Nelson, 59, 67, 150
grammar, 149–151
Gray, Colin S., 217–218

Hájek, Alan, 128n
halfhearted attempts, 231–232, 238,
    240–241
Hansson, Bengt, 5, 18, 19
Harper, William, 37–38, 41
Hawthorne, John, 3, 147–151
Heal, Jane, 37n
heresy, 168–171, 175–178, 180, 181,
    197–198n
Herken, Gregg, 217n
Hilpinen, Risto, 5, 18, 19

Hinckfuss, Ian, 92n, 93n
Holkot, Robert, 125
honesty, 95–100
Horgan, Terence, 127n
Hough, A., 233n
Humeanism about motivation, 2, 42–67
Hume, David, 55–58, 67
Hunt, Ian, 72n

ignorance about war, 177–178, 211–215, 216–217
imaginative acquaintance, 77–82
imperatives, 20–33
incompatibilism, 103, 109–127
indirect rankings, *see* value structures
infallibility, assumption of, 170–171
Inquisitor, 167–171, 175–179, 181, 197–198n
intentions, 201–206, 208, 214–217, 223, 225

Jackson, Frank, 42n, 58, 67, 85n, 91n, 195
Jamieson, Dale, 3, 136–144
Jeffrey, Richard C., 37, 41, 46n, 62n, 70n
Jetzon tires, 171, 174
Johnston, Mark, 210n

Kavka, Gregory S., 202, 204–205n, 208, 210, 216
Kelly, Ned (Edward), 2, 95–100
Kenny, Anthony, 114n, 201–202, 216
Kitcher, Philip, 159n, 187n, 194n
Kleinig, John, 229
Kripke, Saul, 150–151
Kripkenstein, 150–151
Krygier, Martin, 159n

Langtry, Bruce, 128n
laws of nature, 58, 101, 102, 110, 111, 246

'Leibniz's Lapse', 116n
Lemmon, E. J., 17n, 19
Leslie, John, 111n
Levi, Isaac, 61n, 67
Lewis, Ewart, 210n
Lewis, Stephanie, 159n, 227n
liberalism, 3, 159–200
logics, conditional deontic, 15–19
lotteries, penal, 233–243
luck, moral, 230

Mackie, J. L., 90, 93
MAD (Mutual Assured Destruction), 219–226
Mahoney, Michael, 159n
Malabar, 142
Marcuse, Herbert, 171, 181
Martin, C. B., 72n, 118n
Martin, Robert, 20n
McCloskey, H. J., 159n, 167
McLaughlin, Megan, 128n
McMichael, Alan, 2, 34–36
McNamara, Robert, 217n
McTaggart, J. M. E., 209n
meaning and use, 145–151
Mellor, D. H., 42n
Merrill, G. H., 195
middle knowledge, 103n, 114–127
Mikado, 235
Mill, John Stuart, 3, 161–176, 185, 192, 197–198n, 209n
Mills, Claudia, 219–226
Milquetoast, Caspar, 174–175, 179, 185
Molinism, 103, 114–127
Moore, G. E., 2, 57, 59, 71, 75
moral functionalism, 58–59, 90–91
moral luck, 230
Morris, Henry M., 173–174

Nagel, Thomas, 159n, 175n, 230n
Nayar, 142
nestings, *see* value structures

neutralism, rule of, 161–164, 169, 170, 175, 179–180, 185, 192, 197
Newcomb's problem, 2, 3, 37–41, 45–46, 56, 125–127
Normore, Calvin, 37n, 101n, 125n
nuclear deterrence, 4, 172, 201–226
NUTS (Nuclear Use Theorists), 221–226

obligation, 1, 2, 5–19, 34–36, 98–100
Oddie, Graham, 62n, 67
Oldenquist, Andrew, 76n
organ snatching, 156–157

paraconsistency, 199–200n
paradoxical deterrence, 200–211, 214–215, 216
Parfit, Derek, 193n
Pargetter, Robert, 80n
Payne, Keith, 217–218
penal lotteries, 233–243
penal substitution, 3, 128–135
performatives, 21–33
permission, 1–2. 5–19, 20–33, 34–36
Perry, John, 74n
Pettit, Philip, 42n, 44n, 58, 67, 91n
Pigden, Charles, 88
Plantinga, Alvin, 101n, 104–108, 110–111, 114–116, 120n, 125, 127n
prediction, 4, 39–41, 126–127, 244–250
preemptive attack, 222, 224, 225
Price, Huw, 63–64, 67
Priest, Graham, 199–200n
primitive societies, 142
procurement of weapons, 217–218, 219, 221–222, 224–226
punishment, 4, 128–135, 227–243

Quine, W, V., 86, 167
Quinn, Philip, 131
Quinton, A. N., 128n

Railton, Peter, 58, 67
rankings, see value structures
rationality, 37–41, 42–67, 147–149, 202–204
realism about values, 69, 88–94
relativity of values, 69, 82–85, 89
Rescher, Nicholas, 5n
Richardson, Jane S., 4, 244–250
Richardson, Lewis F., 248n
risk, 227, 228, 231–243

Scanlon, T. M., 159n, 187n, 227n
Schelling, Thomas, 227n, 235n
Schiffer, Stephen, 145–146, 151n
Schlesinger, George, 104n
Schwartz, D. M., 233n
Scriven, Michael, 4, 244–250
separation, 155–158
Shaw, George Bernard, 169n
Siegel, Susanna, 101n, 116n
significant freedom, 106–109
simplicity of treaties, 183–186, 199–200
sin, 35–36, 130–132
Skubik, D. W., 159n
Slote, Michael, 76n, 79n, 110n
Smith, Michael, 42n, 43–44n
Soviet Union, 4, 165, 172, 174–175, 207, 222, 233
Stalin, 107–108, 215
Stalnaker, Robert, 20n, 29–30, 37n
Stenius, Erik, 23, 33
Sterelny, Kim, 159n
strangers, assistance to, 3, 152–158
Stump, Eleonore, 131n
Suarez, Francisco, 114
subjectivity of values, 68, 105n
Suzman, Jonathan, 227n
Swinburne, Richard, 103n, 132
Sylvan, Richard, 95n

teletransportation, 192–193
Ten, C. L., 170n
theodicy, 2–3, 101–127

theoretical terms, 58–59
Thomson, Judith, 227n
time travel, 126–127
toleration, 3, 159–200
Tooley, Michael, 72n
treaties, 3–4, 175–186, 197–200
truth, advantages of, 187–200
truthfulness and trust, conventions of, 145–149
truthmakers, 118

U-maximizing, 37–41
unconscious mental states, 136, 138–139, 142–143
Unger, Peter, 3, 152–158
UNICEF, 152–154, 158
universities, 187–188, 191, 200
utilitarianism, 34–36, 153, 161–186, 197–198n, 206

values, 68–94, 103, 157
value structures, 8–15
van Fraassen, Bas, 5, 18–19
van Inwagen, Peter, 101n, 110n
Velleman, David, 77–78n
vengeance, 205–207, 208, 211, 217, 218, 221
V-maximizing, 37–41, 46–47
von Wright, G. H., 5n

war, 3, 156–157, 169, 176–179, 181, 198n, 201–236
Webster, H. T., 174n
wholehearted attempts, 231–232, 238, 240–241
Wittgenstein, Ludwig, 150–151
Wolf, Susan, 206n

Zeno, 151

DATE DUE

Printed in the United States
40840LVS00002B/123